No Rocking Chair for Me

Esther Leeming Tuttle celebrates in August, 2003.

No Rocking Chair for Me

Me

*

**Memoirs of a vibrant woman still seeking
adventure in her 90s**

Esther Leeming Tuttle
with Rebecca E. Greer

iUniverse, Inc.
New York Lincoln Shanghai

No Rocking Chair for Me
Memoirs of a vibrant woman still seeking adventure in her 90s

iUniverse, Inc.

For information address:
iUniverse, Inc.
2021 Pine Lake Road, Suite 100
Lincoln, NE 68512
www.iuniverse.com

ISBN: 0-595-30454-0

Printed in the United States of America

This book is dedicated to the memory of
Franklin Benjamin Tuttle,
my darling husband for 47 years.

—Esther Leeming Tuttle

"The great thing about getting older is that you don't lose all the other ages you've been."

—from *Wrinkle in Time* by Madeleine L'Engle

Contents

Acknowledgments

So many people have provided help and support to this project that it is difficult to name them all, but I would like to give special thanks to the following:

- My cousin Ann Goldsmith, one of the first to encourage me to write down these stories, for her ongoing interest and assistance.

- Estelle Girard for her cheerful and tireless efforts to transcribe my initial tape recordings onto paper.

- My granddaughter Elizabeth Tuttle Carroll for her invaluable help in sorting out the photographs and transferring them to computer files.

- My grandniece Sarah Webster for her cover suggestions.

- Photographers Michael Goldman, John Hart and Jennifer Weisbrod for permission to use their photographs in Chapter 14, and Paul Eckhoff for the frontispiece photograph.

- My grandson Tom Tuttle, my granddaughter Honor Debye-Saxinger and my friend Betty Scholtz for their continuing encouragement.

- My sons, daughters-in-law and grandchildren for their interest, patience and support from the start.

- Rebecca Greer, a great editor, for helping me to turn my stories, adventures and philosophy of life into a book.

1

Who, Me? Write a Book?

It was a beautiful summer day as I sat on the terrace in front of my little farm house in Kinderhook, New York on July 1, 2001. A gentle breeze was riffling the water of the pond and stirring the leaves of the giant maple that has guarded that farm house for more than 200 years.

My children, grandchildren and great-grandchildren were all very busy preparing for a gala celebration of my 90th birthday. Inside a huge white tent on my lawn, the caterers were setting up tables. The boys were busy hauling in young trees to decorate the tent, while the "gals"—my daughters-in-law, granddaughters and two great-granddaughters—were arranging wild flowers in baskets to decorate the tables. The day lilies and black-eyed Susans, which always greet me on my birthday, seemed more glorious than usual.

As we worked, we chatted about the many summers we had all enjoyed on the farm. It always seemed to draw us back, no matter where we'd worked or traveled in the world. Each memory we shared reminded us of others. My own memories were bittersweet, as I couldn't help thinking of the wonderful times I'd enjoyed with loved ones no longer with us—especially my dear husband, Ben, our only daughter, Missy, and Ben's mother, who'd been such an important part of all our lives.

My sadness lifted quickly, though, as a marvelous party got into full swing. It wasn't until most of the guests had gone home and the celebration was winding down that the subject of favorite memories came up again.

"Granny, now that you're ninety," said my granddaughter, Elizabeth, "why don't you make a written record of everything you've done in your life? You've told us so many interesting stories over the years! I'd like to pass them on to my own children, but I'm afraid I won't remember many of the details. It would be such a help to us if you'd write them down."

"That's a great idea," someone else agreed. "Just be sure to tell about the time when you performed on Broadway with Humphrey Bogart."

"And don't forget to write about your friend, Thomas Wolfe, who wrote one of my favorite books," said another.

My grandson, Tommy, had a different idea. "I think you should write a how-to book," he said. "I know women half your age who aren't having nearly as much fun as you are. Some act as if their lives are over when they reach sixty or sixty-five. Yet, you're still going strong at ninety. How do you manage to stay so healthy and active—to live on your own, work as an actress and still do volunteer work at your age?"

Before I could reply, one of the little ones spoke up. "I've wondered about that, too. None of my friends turns on TV and sees his granny in a commercial. I don't know anyone who goes to New York City and watches a giant picture of his granny sailing by on the back of the bus, either."

After listening to them talk—and thinking it over—I decided to try recording some of my reminiscences. As I began dictating favorite stories for the pleasure of my grandchildren and their children, I started wondering if some of my unusual experiences—and the many celebrated people I've been privileged to know—might interest others outside our family.

I didn't feel qualified to write the kind of how-to book that Tommy suggested, but I gradually began to realize that I do know quite a lot about living a long time—and thoroughly enjoying it, despite the tragedies I've experienced along the way. Perhaps I can inspire others by writing about what I've discovered from living an active life for more than 90 years.

Being healthy makes it easier to stay active, of course, but I don't believe that good health comes solely from having good genes, as some people claim. Neither of my parents lived to age 50. It's not a matter of luck, either. I really work at staying healthy.

Of all the things I've learned over the years, the most important may be the value of staying physically active. I've exercised faithfully almost every day for 90 years. Although I reluctantly gave up riding my horse at the age of 89, I still swim, take a two-mile walk before breakfast and do thirty minutes of yoga and stretching exercises every day. I do these things because I enjoy them—and because I really like the way a healthy body feels. I believe this exercise is largely responsible for my high energy, too.

Like many older women, I was devastated when my husband died in 1987. We'd been happily married for more than 47 years, so I felt the loss keenly. But at 76, I wasn't about to give up and retire to a rocking chair. My children and grandchildren have busy lives of their own, so I was equally determined to avoid becoming dependent on them.

Instead, I decided to fill the hole created by my husband's death with rewarding activities, both new and old. My parents had always encouraged us to share our talents with others, so I've been active in volunteer work most of my life. When my three children were young, I was involved primarily with groups that benefited children—such as their schools, UNICEF and the Girl Scouts. I now believe those activities helped me to be a better mother and a more interesting companion for my husband.

As the years went by, my focus shifted. One of my most satisfying activities for more than fifty years has been my work at the Brooklyn Botanic Garden. I began helping with plant sales and worked my way up to Chairman of the Board of Trustees—a challenging position I held for seven years. Although I retired from the Board in 2002, I still love the Garden and the unselfish spirit of the devoted people working there. My own work at the Garden has been invaluable to me, adding beauty, self confidence and many wonderful friends to my life.

My most serious life-long interest, however, has been the theater. I gave up professional acting when I married, but I've been active—both onstage and off—with amateur theatrical groups for more than 50 years. I continue to perform whenever a suitable role comes along. In May 2002, for example, I appeared in a dramatic club production of *The English Teachers*. Learning my lines was harder than it used to be, but it was also more gratifying for me to succeed at an age when memory loss is so common.

Performing has always given me great pleasure, but I've gradually realized that it has given me a lot more, too. All that memorizing has stimulated my brain and helped to keep it active. My theatrical experience also led to my newest career as a professional "granny" model. Since 1990, I've appeared in more than 100 print ads and television commercials—and in a variety of small roles on TV as well.

Modeling hasn't made me rich, but it has introduced me to many fascinating people. It has also added a great deal of fun to my life and provided many new stories to tell my grandchildren. One of their favorites involves the time I appeared on the Conan O'Brian show on NBC (February 12, 1998). Dressed in a flowered dress, a fancy garden hat and red leather boxing gloves, I boxed with a gorilla in an attempt to coax a laugh out of Andy Richter, who was Conan's sidekick at the time. At first, I appear to be winning the match, but then the gorilla steals my hat and that changes everything. It's hard not to laugh when we play the videotape of that sketch.

My favorite modeling job, however, was one I almost skipped because it was called "The Stripper." It wasn't what I thought at first, but it did require me to shed a few clothes. I played an old lady coming home from church, wearing a hat, gloves, purse, shawl and long skirt. My line was, *"When I want to thrill the guys down at the bridge club, I tell them I'm going to take it off, take it all off. Nobody's going to put me out to pasture."* As I spoke, I pulled off my hat, gloves, shawl and bag, and tossed them aside. Then, as I went off camera, the rest of my clothes dropped, one by one, into a big chair. In the final frames, I'm wearing shorts, preparing to climb into a Jeep Cherokee (the sponsor) and "take off" to the wild country.

I had a marvelous time making "The Stripper." Although I was 88 at the time, I was treated like a movie star from the moment the limousine picked me up at my apartment. The client flew me out to Detroit for the shooting, put me up in a deluxe hotel and gave me a generous dining allowance. Such luxuries are a treat at any age, but are appreciated even more at 88. I was a little embarrassed to cash the residuals (payment for repeat showings of the commercial), however, because "The Stripper" was written on each check. One bank clerk almost sneered as she looked from my face to the check and back again before she handed me the money.

One of the ironies of modeling in my 80s and 90s is that I never had the face or the figure to model when I was young. But now that I have white hair and wrinkles, it seems to work. Perhaps it shows that you never really know what you can do until you try. I continue to view life as a grand adventure, so I'm willing to try almost anything. If those modeling jobs stop coming, I'll just find something else to keep me busy. I've been invited to talk to a number of garden clubs and women's groups recently, so maybe I'll launch a new career as a public speaker.

In the meantime, it's fun to look back on the highlights of a long and happy life. It hasn't always turned out the way I planned, but it has been interesting. I've made my share of mistakes, but I've tried to learn something valuable from each one, and then move on. That's probably one reason why I'm still around to talk (and laugh) about my mishaps.

I've enjoyed many exciting experiences in my work and travels, but underpinning it all has been a warm home life with a loving husband, three wonderful children and the fine people they married. They've given me 11 grandchildren and 12 great-grandchildren so far, making me feel like a very rich lady—rich in friendship and in love.

Once this collection of memories and reflections began to take shape as a book, I considered calling it *Footprints*, after a passage that I have always liked from Henry Wadsworth Longfellow's *Psalm of Life*:

> *We can make our lives sublime,*
> *And, departing, leave behind us,*
> *Footprints on the sands of time;*
> *Footprints, that perhaps another,*
> *Sailing o'er life's solemn main,*
> *A forlorn and shipwrecked brother,*
> *Seeing, shall take heart again.*

2

Childhood: Privilege and Loss

I've heard experts say that the first few years of a child's life are the most important in forming character. I believe that's true because my early childhood was filled with all the warmth, love and excitement any child could want. It was truly an idyllic life while it lasted. Although the good days were cut short by tragedy, I remember them well and can see how much they influenced the rest of my life.

I was the youngest of four children, born on July 1, 1911 to upper-middle-class parents. My older sister, Honor, was almost 10 at the time. My brother, Howard, was three and a half, while Elizabeth (called Lee) was just 16 months old. We were a very close family, particularly the three youngest.

Lee and I were so close in age that we rode in a double carriage.

I was named Esther after my mother, so it was probably inevitable that I'd have a nickname to make it easier for everyone. Howard started calling me "Wifey" because he'd noticed that people often came in couples and he wanted to be paired off, too. Soon, the whole family was calling me "Wifey." Lee, who was just learning to talk, had a lisp so she pronounced it "Faify." Somehow Faify became "Faity" and the name stuck. To this day, everyone calls me Faity, except the people I know professionally in my work as an actress and model.

In the early 1900's, before this country had an income tax, upper-middle-class Americans lived very well. During the school year, our family lived in a large house at 277 Henry Street in Brooklyn Heights, New York. It was a traditional, five-story brownstone in the middle of a tree-lined block of similar houses. The kitchen and my father's studio/workroom were on the ground floor, slightly below street level. The drawing room, dining room and breakfast room were on the first floor. A dumb waiter connected the two floors, so that our Irish cook, Margaret, could send up food to be served by Douglas, the English butler. My parents' bedroom and Honor's room were on the second floor, with dressing rooms and baths in between and a small sewing room at the end of the hall. A large nursery was on the fourth floor, with the top floor reserved for the servants.

Both of my parents had English ancestors who settled in Brooklyn. My mother's family, the Howards, came from England in 1730. (My father's family arrived later, having settled first in Canada.) My mother, Esther Howard, was born on January 18, 1877. She was brought up in affluent circumstances at 183 Willow Street, a brick house that's now a landmark building in Brooklyn Heights. She and her only sister, Ruth, attended Brooklyn Heights Seminary. Mother was a beautiful, artistically talented woman with a delightful sense of humor and great style. She had a variety of interests, but found special joy in the performing arts.

My father, Woodruff Leeming, was born July 14, 1870, in Quincy, Illinois. He was the third of five talented children who spent their early years in Canada where their father owned and ran a successful importing business. The children were all educated in private schools and prestigious New England colleges. After receiving degrees from MIT and *L'Ecole des Beaux Artes* in France, Daddy became a successful architect. He was a talented, charming man who happened to be a wonderful dancer and a skillful ice skater, horseman and sailor.

(I mention these things because they affected my own interests and hobbies. Like my father, I've enjoyed dancing and horseback riding most of my life. My mother's love of the theater, on the other hand, undoubtedly influenced my career choice. The pleasure of hearing my mother's infectious laugh probably encouraged me to develop my talent for comedy, too.)

My father designed many buildings during his architectural career, but one has special meaning to me because I pass it regularly. Designed as a retail store for Coty Cosmetics in 1907, it's now the Henry Bendel store at 712 Fifth Avenue in New York City. I still get a thrill from seeing the lovely art glass windows that Daddy asked his friend, René Lalique, to design more than 90 years ago. The exquisite window wall rises from the second to the fourth floor. The frosted relief of entwined vines and poppies is a delight from both sides—and made to last. The building received landmark status in 1985. I was invited to the ceremony when the building reopened as Bendels.

Shortly after my mother and father were married in 1899, my mother's parents, Clara and Edward (Ned) Howard, bought a 50-acre farm on Oenoke Avenue, about two miles north of the village of New Canaan, Connecticut. In 1901, Daddy redesigned and enlarged the old Dutch farm house to make it more suitable for three generations of a growing family. Once completed, that became our summer home.

Sadly, my grandmother didn't have much time to enjoy the home she'd helped to create. She died of breast cancer in 1904. Gramp had a miniature portrait of Grandma Darling (as Honor called her) painted by Alice Searle, a famous artist of the time. He put it into a solid gold frame and kept it under his pillow until the day he died. I still have that miniature and it's clear that Grandma was quite beautiful. In fact, Henry Ward Beecher, the famous abolitionist preacher, is supposed to have said, "The Lord might have made a more beautiful woman than Mrs. Howard, but he never did."

Gramp bought the farm because he loved animals, especially horses. Grandma had a deep fear of horses and didn't want animals drawing flies near the house, so the old barns were demolished and a new one, with a caretaker's cottage on one end, was built about half a mile down the hill. It had an entrance on what later became Country Club Road. The new barn housed horses, cows, chickens, pigs, cats and dogs, which made it a real paradise for us children. We loved to collect eggs, help the farmer milk cows and turn the crank of the separator that skimmed the cream from the milk.

Near the main house, we had a formal garden and a rose garden surrounded by a hedge, an apple orchard and a well-tended bowling green that we also used for croquet. Further down the hill were a vegetable garden, other fruit trees and berry bushes. I remember picking peaches, strawberries, raspberries and grapes, then helping my mother and the other women of the household make jars of jelly, jam and preserves. When the house was redesigned, large verandahs were added on the south and east to catch the summer breezes, as air conditioning did not exist yet. We could look out across the valley to Long Island Sound. On a clear day, we could even see Long Island, ten miles away.

Howarden, as the farm was known, was an ideal place for children to grow up. Howard, Lee and I shared a big nursery with an open fireplace. Our Irish nurse, Bella, slept there with us until I was about six. By then Howard had moved into a room of his own. (Honor always had her own room because she was so much older than the rest of us.) The commodious house had six bedrooms and three bathrooms on the second floor, plus a guest room and a bath on the main floor. The servants had their own rooms and bath on the third floor.

Margaret reigned supreme in the kitchen, which always seemed to smell of cookies baking. I remember that kitchen as a warm and jolly place which we children loved to visit. Someone was always singing, usually Irish songs, because Bella helped out in the kitchen when we grew older.

Douglas often shed his white jacket for a navy blue one, donned a peaked cap and chauffeured us around in an enormous Locomobile. He also churned ice cream every Sunday morning in a little shed under the side porch. We all liked to help with the ice cream, hoping we'd get to lick the dasher. We truly loved all of these people and spent a good deal of time with them.

The smallest person at my second birthday party, I watched Lee blow a bubble as our neighbors, Sammy (left) and David Knox watched.

Gramp continued to spend summers with us at Howarden until his death in 1918. He commuted into New York City where he had a successful advertising agency, E.T. Howard and Co. He placed ads in numerous magazines, which he brought home with him. (We had so many magazines at Howarden that one young neighbor, Hobart Weeks, used to walk to our house just to read them. Hobie later became an editor of *The New Yorker*.)

When Gramp returned home in the evening, he often came up to the nursery with an enticing roll of individually-wrapped Peters chocolates that he'd toss to us. Mostly, though, I remember him sitting on our unscreened porch reading, with his fly swatter nearby. He loved having us gather around to listen to his stories, some of which I didn't fully appreciate until I heard other relatives repeat them years later.

Gramp told us, for example, that his favorite sea shells had been collected in the Canary Islands during his trip around the world in 1867 when he was 23. He started out with a group of about 70 people from the Plymouth Church in Brooklyn. They were traveling to the Holy Land on a steamer called *Quaker City*. Most of the group was over 50, but Gramp became friendly with a young reporter who was sending travel diaries back to a San Francisco newspaper. That reporter was Samuel Clemens, who later wrote *The Adventures of Tom Sawyer* and other popular books under the name Mark Twain. *Innocents Abroad*, Twain's first book published in 1869 was based on that trip to the Holy Land (which became Israel many years later).

We especially liked hearing Gramp describe the first time he invited his new friend to dinner after they returned home. "I had to warn my parents," he said, "so they wouldn't be shocked by Sam's salty language." His conservative parents probably were shocked, but Sam's stories about life on the Mississippi and his other adventures as a reporter were so fascinating that they invited him back again. Aunts and cousins who met Mark Twain at one of those dinners enjoyed telling us about them later.

Gramp also liked to explain the history of the beautiful fountain pens, covered with gold filigree, which he'd given to Lee and me. It seems that a man who sold Gramp his daily newspaper pulled him aside one day to show off an object he'd invented. Gramp was so fascinated by the man's invention that he offered to provide financial backing and advertising, in exchange for a share of the company. That man was Lewis E. Waterman, his invention was the first leak-proof fountain pen, and the Waterman Pen Company earned a fortune for both men.

Mr. Waterman used to come to Howarden for lunch with Gramp. I remember him as a balding man who had bushy black eyebrows and one lock of black hair combed across his forehead. Our family loved to tell about the time that Howard, who was about six, looked across the table at Mr. Waterman and asked, "Why do you have three eyebrows?"

Another important member of our Howarden household was Great Aunt Mary Louise (Mamie) Kelsey, the younger sister of Grandma Howard. Aunt Mamie was one of those selfless people who never married, but devoted her life to others. She took care of her widowed mother for many years. Later on, she helped Gramp after Grandma died. In her sunny room at the top of the stairs, she spent many hours embroidering scallops on our underwear or crocheting inserts for our nighties. Aunt Mamie was always willing to drop everything to read us a story or tell us one she'd made up. We adored hearing those stories! She also taught us a great deal—how to embroider and crochet, for example, and how to identify birds and wild flowers. (Later on, she also taught us how to cook and keep house.)

Aunt Mamie did not share her sister's fear of horses. In fact, she was a very good driver who often drove us into the village in a two-wheeled horse cart, pulled by Gramp's favorite mare, Brownie. (In those days, New Canaan had hitching posts on the main street where you could tie up your horse.) We all loved Aunt Mamie dearly. She was a terrific role model because she seemed to derive so much pleasure from helping others.

Our summers at Howarden were full of adventures. Howard, Lee and I loved to roller skate near our house on a steep road that had just been paved. We'd carry our skates up the hill and then we'd skate down very fast. Lee and I fell and skinned our knees so many times that we called it "bloody-sit-down-hill," but that didn't stop us. Sometimes a neighbor would see us trudging up the hill with our skates and offer us a ride to the top.

One day, we accepted a ride with a farmer in an ox cart. As we rode up the hill, he told us about the young oxen he'd trained to pull a small cart. "Would you like to see my baby oxen?" he asked. That was an offer we couldn't resist. When we reached his farm several miles up the road, he demonstrated a fascinating machine he'd made for hoisting up the oxen so they couldn't kick while he put shoes on them. After showing us around, he hitched up the beautiful cart he'd made and let us drive it.

We were having such a lovely time on that farm that we didn't realize we'd been away from home for several hours. Our poor mother was frantic. When she looked for us on the hill, we'd vanished. She'd called all the neighbors and was on the verge of calling the police when we trudged in, all excited about the baby oxen we wanted her to buy for us. We never got the oxen, but we never forgot that day, either.

This lovely life began to unravel when World War I broke out. Daddy was determined to help save France from the Germans. A middle-aged father of four, he nonetheless enlisted and was commissioned a major in the AEF (American Expeditionary Forces). After using his architectural skills to redesign a military camp at Gettysburg, he was sent to Plattsburgh, New York, for training.

Daddy came home for Thanksgiving 1917. I remember going with Douglas to the railroad station in Norwalk to meet him. When the train finally pulled in late, it was filled with khaki-clad troops leaning out the windows, waving. On the drive back to Howarden, we had a blowout. Cars didn't have spare tires in those days, so the old one had to be removed, patched, and put back on, with the only illumination provided by a flashlight. That delayed us another hour, so our gala Thanksgiving feast with Daddy was very late. He left the next morning for New York City, sailing for France on November 28, 1917.

To economize, Mother rented out the house in Brooklyn and we spent the winter at Howarden. It must have been a very difficult time for her, with Daddy away. She had a family to raise and a farm to run—with frozen pipes, coal shortages and other emergencies to deal with. Our Locomobile was too costly to maintain, so it was replaced by a balky Model T Ford that had to be cranked to start. On some icy mornings, the whole family—including Margaret in a flapping apron—was enlisted to help Douglas push the car to the crest of the hill so the motor would catch on the way down. Despite all these hardships, Mother remained cheerful and never lost her sense of humor—an example I've always tried to emulate.

Honor commuted by train to Rosemary Hall School in Greenwich, while Howard, Lee and I walked to the little red brick school about two miles away. We could cut our walk in half by cutting through the Taggart's property, but we chanced that only when the bull was not in the pasture. The road took us past a deserted house that was reputed to be "haunted." We walked by very fast, daring each other to go up and look in the porch windows. The danger was mostly in our heads, but Lee and I were glad to have our big brother along for protection.

Our school, like many others at that time, had one room and one teacher for all eight grades. The class whose turn it was to recite moved into the front row by the teacher's desk, with the rest of us studying on our own. About 20 students, mostly from farm families, attended.

My hat was falling off as I played soldier during World War I with Howard, Lee and Honor.

Lee (right) and I saluted the flag as we led a Memorial Day parade in 1918.

Going to that school, which had no running water, was an education in itself. We learned to pump water from the well and to use the privies out back. (We also received an introduction to sex education from the crude drawings on the outhouse walls.) It was all a grand adventure to us, so we didn't mind the inconveniences. I think it also helped us to understand that happiness doesn't depend on the luxuries we'd become accustomed to.

Miss Ellwood, the teacher, walked two miles from her home every morning. She always arrived in time to get the fire going in the pot-bellied stove before the children showed up. We began each day by singing a patriotic song, accompanied by Miss Ellwood on the pump organ. She was a good teacher who was well liked and respected by her students.

That was the first school Lee and I attended. At six, I was in first grade, and Lee was in second. Although her "delicate health" had kept her out of school the previous year, Lee was very bright and had already learned to read, write and add. Howard was in fourth grade, having spent three years at the more sedate Friends School in Brooklyn. He was a good student and a leader in the rowdy games of kick-the-can and red rover played at recess and after lunch. Unlike the other boys, Howard wore corduroy knickers, so he was dubbed "Whistle Britches" by fellow students.

That winter of 1917–18 was unusually severe, with heavy snow and high drifts. Some days we snuggled under lap robes as we were whisked to school in a small sleigh, with bells ringing. At other times, we couldn't get to school at all. We didn't need much adult attention at home because Howard was always inventing games or building something, with Lee and me as his willing slaves and partners. Using wooden blocks, he constructed elaborate tunnels and bridges for the wind-up trains that took our dolls on death-defying rides all over the nursery.

When Howard came down with chicken pox that winter, he was quarantined in Aunt Mamie's room. (She was in Brooklyn.) The door was kept closed and we were forbidden to go in. But Lee and I mischievously opened the door a crack and threw in modeling clay for Howard to rub over his face and return to us. Soon, we had chicken pox, too, so we all played happily together in the nursery again.

Our first Christmas at the farm was very exciting. The portieres were drawn across the living room doorway, and I remember waiting breathlessly for the magic moment when we could enter. What a glorious sight! Under the huge tree, lighted with real candles from top to bottom, was a heaping pile of toys. Our guests for the Christmas feast included Gramp and Aunt Mamie, but we could hardly wait to go sledding on the hill behind the house with Sammy and David

Knox who lived nearby (and became lifelong friends). It was a joyous winter for the three of us, providing some of our fondest memories.

Summers at Howarden were always glorious, too. Years later, Howard remembered them as "one perfect day after another." He especially enjoyed reminiscing about Billy, the goat he had one summer. He was determined to get that goat to pull a cart, so he and the Knox boys built one out of a large wooden soap box, a set of old wagon wheels and an axle they found at the dump. The first time they harnessed Billy to the cart, though, he took off, terrifying the visiting child who was "treated" to the first ride.

Billy was tethered to a chain near our play house. One day he broke loose just as Bella's kitchen helper was spreading dish towels on the grass to dry. As Mrs. Hammer bent over the towels, her large backside provided an irresistible target for Billy. He lowered his head and sent her flying. It was hard to stop laughing once we realized she wasn't hurt. At the end of the summer, the uncontrollable Billy was renamed William the Conqueror and returned to the farmer who'd sold him to Howard.

When it was time to return to school in the fall of 1918, Daddy was still away and the Brooklyn house was still rented, so we moved into an apartment in New York City. Honor enrolled at Finch Junior College and Howard went to the Stone School on Storm King Mountain, a military boarding school. Lee and I attended a private girls' school, the Lenox, in Manhattan.

The classmate who became my best friend that year was Ethel Colt, daughter of the famous actress Ethel Barrymore. At Ethel's birthday party at the Algonquin Hotel, I met her uncles, John and Lionel, and her great uncle, John Drew. Mother had taken me to see the Barrymores perform on stage and in the movies, so I was thrilled to meet them in person.

My most memorable experience of that year, though, was trying out for the class play. Ethel, a pretty blonde with golden curls, wanted to be the princess. She wept bitterly when she didn't get the part (because someone considered her "too chubby"). I was equally chubby, but I didn't care about a leading role. I just wanted to be on stage, so I played the part of a frog that turned into a door knocker. Ethel and I both went on to become professional actors, so we were able to renew our friendship as adults.

Living with Loss

Two months after classes began that fall, the armistice ending the war was signed on November 11, 1918. My father stayed in France to help with the peace settlement, returning in April 1919. That was a day of great rejoicing for us all. We soon realized, however, that Daddy was not well. Although his work—drawing plans to convert schools and other buildings into hospitals—had kept him off the front lines, it had exposed him to numerous sick people and he'd contracted tuberculosis. Daddy was promoted to Lieutenant Colonel and awarded Silver Palms by the French Academy, but he never knew about the latter. It was signed in Paris on November 20, 1919—the day he died. I was eight years old.

Daddy's death was hard on all of us, but it was especially difficult for Mother. She'd lost her own father—our beloved Gramp—just a year earlier. But she gave us a valuable lesson in the way she handled her grief. She didn't dwell on the past or bemoan what we'd lost. She just began making new plans and focusing on the future.

Mother moved the family back to the comfortable familiarity of Howarden. This time Lee and I attended the New Canaan Community School. Once we were settled, Mother started working with Jess Dall, an architect married to one of our cousins, to convert our Brooklyn house into 14 rental apartments. When the conversion was complete, those apartments provided income needed to cover our expenses. In the fall of 1920, we moved into a six-room apartment at 64 East 86 Street in Manhattan. Lee and I changed schools again, enrolling in The Brearley, a private girls' school where I stayed several years.

One of my favorite memories of that period was a beautiful fall day when I was alone with Mother—a rare treat in itself. We were walking up Fifth Avenue, holding hands and singing Irish songs. After stopping for ice cream, we continued on to 59th Street, where open, horse-drawn carriages were waiting for passengers. "Let's hire one of those to take us home," Mother announced suddenly. After we hopped into a carriage, she sang silly songs and told me funny stories all the way to our apartment on 86th Street. I had so much fun with Mother that I always tried to be like her.

Mother didn't really have time to mourn our father because she was too busy devoting herself to our well-being. She taught us to take good care of our bodies, making sure that we ate well, exercised regularly and saw the best doctors and dentists. She wanted us to be well-rounded, so she sent us to the Mannes School of Music for afternoon classes and to a wonderful dancing school run by Rosetta O'Neal.

She asked Honor, a talented artist, to give Lee and me painting lessons and arranged for us to have private instruction in French. (Our French teacher, Madame Borglum, was the widow of Solon Borglum. His brother, Gutzon, was the sculptor who designed Mount Rushmore.) Mother liked to read aloud and often read to us from classic books written by Robert Louis Stevenson, Walter Scott and Charles Dickens, among others.

We were constantly exposed to all the arts, going to exhibitions, concerts and dance performances. I remember being particularly taken with the dancers Pavlova and Michio Ito. We went to Broadway shows, seeing performances by everyone from the Marx Brothers to the Barrymores, from Will Rogers to Alfred Lunt and Lynn Fontanne. We even went to the opera. My father's brother, Thomas Leeming, was president of the Brooklyn Academy of Music, so we sat in the president's box for opera and concerts.

Our house was often full of people because Mother was active in many causes, such as the effort to secure voting rights for women. She was always helping others, including five of our first cousins whose own mother had died. Mother loved beautiful things and was accustomed to an extravagant life style, but she no longer had the money to do everything she wanted. She was forced to sell the big house at Howarden, plus all the animals and half the land. She and Jess Dall then converted the barn into a new, smaller house we called Leeming Lane. By that time, Bella was our housekeeper and only servant.

After Mother converted the barn at our Connecticut farm into a residence, we called it Leeming Lane (above).

We continued to spend summers and holidays in New Canaan. In 1920, Howard, Lee and I went to camp for two months while Mother took Honor on a "grand tour" of Europe. We each chose different camps, so Lee and I were separated for the first time in our lives. My camp in Maine was set in a forest of magnificent hemlock trees that I turned to for consolation whenever I felt homesick. I've loved and found comfort in trees ever since.

I was a shy child who'd always depended on Lee to make overtures to others. Being on my own at camp helped me to become more independent and taught me how to get along with other kids. I also learned how to swim, play tennis, handle a canoe and ride a horse—skills that became very important to me as I grew up. Ironically, the separation also helped Lee and me to become better friends. We learned to respect our differences and to stop our usual sibling fights after that.

The highlight of the following winter was Honor's debut in February 1921. To Lee and me, our beautiful big sister was a very glamorous figure. We loved to sneak into her room, where we'd rifle through her movie magazines and try on her clothes. Nothing was more fun to us than teetering around in Honor's high-heeled shoes or traipsing through the halls in her elegant Parisian evening gowns.

Honor had many admirers, so her debutante season was an exciting time for us all. I was delighted to be her unofficial secretary, helping to keep track of all her appointments. Lee and I went to the debut party in beautiful organdy dresses that Mother had ordered in Paris. Reluctant to leave the festivities, we hid behind a huge bank of flowers in the rear of the ballroom whenever anyone came looking for us. That ploy enabled us to avoid capture until around two am.

Two weeks later, Honor sailed for Paris to study art. She was accompanied by our cousin, Dorothy Leeming, who became her roommate. Mother planned to take the rest of us to visit them in Paris for the summer, but when the time came she was too ill to make the trip. We went back to our respective camps instead. When we returned home, we were distressed to find that Mother's health had deteriorated. She suffered from diabetes, but we had no idea how serious that was. Insulin injections were not yet available, so doctors had already told Mother she had only six months to live. She managed to stretch that out to two years—two years she spent trying to prepare us for life without our parents. She even sent us to a psychoanalyst after Daddy died.

One of our uncles, Smith Ely Jelliffe, was a prominent psychiatrist, so it was probably his idea for us to see a therapist. Lee and I went once a week. The doctor told us to keep cards by our beds so we could write down our dreams. At the next session, we'd describe the dreams we'd written down. "What's that remind you of?" he'd ask. Lee and I both thought it was fun to have an adult so interested in our thoughts and activities. I sometimes reported that I'd dreamed about having my own pony—something I desperately wanted—but my devious little plot didn't work. Honor and Howard had ponies, but Lee and I never did.

Mother had these portraits taken in preparation for Honor's debut in February 1921. That's me, age 9, on the left.

Once, after Lee and I'd been caught sneaking cigarettes, Dr. Stragnell gave us each a cigarette to smoke while he sat back, smoking his pipe. We both got so sick that neither of us ever smoked again during our childhood. We never sought psychiatric help again, either. (Our school's headmistress told us later that Lee and I were the only students she'd ever had who didn't go crazy in our teens, so that therapy must have done some good.)

In the fall of 1922, Mother sent us to a wonderful girls' boarding school—the Warrenton Country School in Warrenton, Virginia. I think she chose it primarily because it was a French school. She'd always wanted us to speak French, though we don't have a French heritage. The school had only about 60 boarders, so we made friends easily. Much as I loved school, I still felt homesick during my first year, so I looked forward to going home for summer vacation.

Shortly after we reached home in June 1923, though, our darling mother died at age 46. I was almost 12, Lee was 13 and Howard was 16. Honor, 22, had come back from Paris and was working in New York with the stage designer, Norman Belle Geddes. We were all absolutely devastated. In fact, I don't think anything that's happened to me since then has been as hard or hurt as much as losing my mother. It was far worse than losing Daddy, who'd been away from home, either at work or at war, for most of my life.

Mother had been the dominant figure in our childhood. She was a beautiful, generous, loving person—a wonderful mother whom we all adored. My siblings and I tried to help each other grieve, but we all missed Mother terribly. She had taught us not to feel sorry for ourselves, so we tried to remember that. We were fortunate to have the support of many loving relatives and friends of our parents, but it was still very difficult for us.

Looking back, I believe that losing my parents so early probably made it easier for me to cope with other tragedies later in life. I was too young to give it much thought at the time, of course, but I think I developed an intuitive understanding that I could survive anything after that. Even more important, I learned I could be happy again after suffering horrendous losses. It was an important lesson that some people never seem to learn.

In the space of a few years, we lost not only our parents but our carefree life style as well. Mother had continued to be very extravagant while accumulating a stack of medical bills for Daddy's illness and her own. Instead of cash, she left us $36,000 in debts and a lot of worthless stock that an "expert" had advised her to buy. We were blissfully unaware of these problems, however, during our final summer at Leeming Lane with Honor and Bella. We spent many delightful hours with David and Sammy Knox, neighbors slightly older than Lee and me.

The major adventure of that summer began with the boys' decision to build a tree house. David Knox and our brother Howard had it all planned for a huge oak tree, but we needed lumber to build it—and we had to earn the money to buy materials. The Knox boys' parents put Sammy in charge of their berry patch, so he hired the rest of us to get up at 5:30 a.m. to pick strawberries. After loading boxes of berries onto a horse-drawn farm cart, Sammy drove into the village to sell them. When the strawberries were gone, we picked raspberries and blackberries. As soon as we accumulated $10 from selling berries, we all went to the lumber yard to buy our supplies.

We loaded the lumber onto the rickety old farm cart, and then started toward home. Just before we reached the crest of the first hill, though, we heard a huge crash. A back wheel had broken off the cart and our new lumber was sliding down the hill. We unhitched the horse and assayed the damage. The boys thought it could be repaired, so David was dispatched to the village to buy another wheel. (Fortunately, New Canaan still had a wheelwright back then.) By the time David returned, the opposite wheel was cracking, so he had to go back for a second replacement.

As the rest of us sat in the hot sun waiting for David, one of Honor's beaux, Sam Swift, came by in his car. Eager to gain favor with Honor, he offered to take Lee and me for a swim at the Tokenoke Club. It was really mean of us to even consider abandoning the boys, but we couldn't resist an invitation to swim on such a hot day. Howard and the Knox brothers spent the rest of the afternoon getting that old cart and the lumber home, but they finally made it.

The next day, the boys began building the tree house, about 30 feet up. It took several weeks, but they were very resourceful and did a terrific job. The finished project was about six feet square, with a tar paper roof, a window and a door. It even had a piece of canvas we could let down to keep out the rain. The views from the top were unbelievable, so we all used the place as a special club house. The boys put their sleeping bags on the floor and sometimes spent the night there. Lee and I were eager to join them, but we were never allowed to sleep out. Despite that disappointment, we still managed to spend many wonderful hours in our tree house.

The boys soon decided that we needed a way to communicate between the tree house and our play house, about half a mile away. They strung up the necessary wires so we could tap out the Morse code. There was only one problem: none of us knew the Morse code. Always eager to please, I volunteered to ride my bicycle into the village to borrow a copy. The others quickly agreed, so I felt very important as I rode off.

The friendly owner of the electric store listened politely to my request. "I can't let you take the Morse code from the shop," he said, "but you can sit here and copy it if you like." This was long before copy machines, so I wrote down all those dots and dashes by hand. It was tedious work—and I had to pedal my bicycle two miles uphill to get back home—but I didn't mind. As the youngest, I was glad to have an opportunity to make a real contribution to our project. Thanks to my effort, we all learned the Morse code together that summer. That made me feel very proud—and I still derive great pleasure from being useful.

What was truly special about that tree house experience, I now realize, was that it was our project—one completed without any adult involvement. I didn't understand all the implications at the time, but I'm sure it affirmed my view of life as one glorious adventure after another. It also showed us that all kinds of obstacles can be overcome by determination and hard work.

The following winter, Leeming Lane was sold by the bank handling Mother's estate. All the proceeds went to pay off debts—which probably affected me more than I realized at the time. I definitely grew up to be much more frugal and careful with money than Mother ever was.

Aunt Mamie had bought her own small house in New Canaan by then, so we spent the next few summers with her. It was a frustrating—sometimes boring—life for teenagers compared to "the good old days." We didn't have a car and no longer belonged to the private clubs, so we had no place to swim, ride horses or play tennis. Lee and I spent many hours sewing—often making over hand-me-down clothes given to us by Honor's friends.

We spent most of our fall and winter holidays from school at Aunt Mamie's apartment in Brooklyn Heights. She never divulged her age, but I think she was in her late sixties or early seventies when she assumed responsibility for three teenagers. She must have given up many of her own activities to care for us, but all we were aware of was her love and her generosity. As it happened, Aunt Mamie was both frugal and very smart about money, so she helped us to manage our small resources.

Other generous relatives also came to our aid. Aunt Gertrude and Uncle Tom Leeming paid our tuition so Lee and I could stay at boarding school. After so many changes in our lives, we were grateful for that continuity. I loved the Warrenton School and learned a lot there. Some of our classes were taught in French and we were expected to speak the language to each other. Most of us eventually became quite fluent—a skill that has given me great joy ever since. I still read French with pleasure and can converse, according to one French friend, "without an accent."

Our headmistress, Lea Maria Bouligny, was a great educator and a wonderful role model. She not only made sure we had all the basic tools, she also inspired us to continue educating ourselves for the rest of our lives. The joy of learning that I acquired at boarding school has made my life more interesting and has helped to keep my mind agile, too.

Mademoiselle Bouligny helped us to develop a sense of responsibility for ourselves and others. A strict disciplinarian, she expected us to have good posture and behave in "a lady-like manner" at all times. She was, in effect, a substitute parent who reinforced many of the values we'd learned at home. All the teachers at Warrenton emphasized the importance of sound bodies as well as sound minds. No matter how much time we spent playing basketball or other sports, we were required to exercise in the gym for 30 minutes every morning before breakfast. That's a habit I've continued most of my life—one that has undoubtedly helped me live longer.

As private schools go, Warrenton was much lower key than others Mother had considered for us. Since we all wore uniforms, Lee and I never had to worry about having the right clothes. Every student was allowed to have the same amount of spending money each week, so our lack of funds was never the problem it might have been elsewhere.

Snobbishness stemming from family wealth was a fact of life at the private schools I had attended in New York City, but everyone at Warrenton was accepted for who she was and what she could do. We made friends easily and always felt comfortable visiting classmates' homes, even if they lived on grand estates. By the time we graduated, Lee had studied at Warrenton for six years, and I'd been a student for seven years.

We had no money for college, so we returned to New York City to look for work. Aunt Mamie had moved to Greenwich Village—because she thought that was easier for the three of us—so we all moved in with her again.

3

Bitten by the Acting Bug

The only thing I'd ever wanted to do was become an actress. I was stage struck from early childhood. Lee and I used to dress up and put on plays for our parents, the servants and anyone else we could find to provide an audience. Along the way, I discovered that I was a pretty good mimic, especially with accents.

That was important to me because I was the chubbiest and plainest child in our family. My brother, Howard, was a very friendly person who was loved by everyone. My two sisters were not only beautiful, they also had a talent for drawing and painting that I lacked. I couldn't help feeling inferior to them, so I was truly delighted to find something—acting—that I could do better than any of my siblings.

The first time I appeared on a big stage, I was nine years old. A charming play called *Aucassin and Nicolette* was being performed for the benefit of French war orphans, so children from various New York dancing schools were interviewed. The cast had to wear the painted costumes made for the Boston production, so we were also measured. To my dismay, I was too chubby to fit into the costume for the part I wanted, so I decided to go on a diet.

My sister Honor, a student at Smith College at the time, told me about a diet that was the rage on campus. All I ate for a week (despite Bella's protests) was baked potatoes and milk. I managed to lose five pounds, which was enough to get the part. This showed me that it's possible to get what you want if you're willing to make sacrifices and work hard. Although I recited only one line, I learned how to project my voice—a skill that proved very useful to me later.

I played a lady of the court. My daughter was played by Jean Bellows, a child only three or four years younger than I. It was my job to keep Jean quiet back stage. She loved to draw, so all I had to do was give her a pencil and paper. Her drawings were remarkably good, which made me envious. It wasn't until years later, when I saw George Bellows' "Portrait of Jean" in a museum, that I realized Jean's artistic talent was probably inherited from her famous father.

We did five matinees and one evening performance of *Aucassin and Nicolette* at the New Amsterdam Theater on Broadway. I loved every minute of it. All my usual shyness disappeared when I was pretending to be someone else on stage, so I decided that I was meant to be an actress. Unlike most people who choose a career in childhood, I never changed my mind.

Aunt Mamie was strongly opposed to a theatrical career. She was part of a generation that didn't have much respect for theater people. She also believed that women who acted professionally had a terrible life. I loved Aunt Mamie, but I refused to let her objections stop me. My mother had been so interested in the performing arts that I was sure she'd have approved of my career choice.

When I graduated from boarding school and moved to New York City, Lee and Howard were already sharing Aunt Mamie's apartment on West 10th Street. Lee was a very slim, elegant-looking gal, with a graceful walk, so she'd found a job modeling for a retail furrier. She earned $40 a week just for parading around in fur coats when a customer came in. Howard was working as a comparison shopper for Macy's, the large department store.

I was not so fortunate. I thought it would be easy to find a job in the theater, but I was very naïve. I didn't know how to meet theatrical agents or find out who was casting a play. And, of course, I started looking for work in the fall of 1929, just before the stock market crashed, beginning the Great Depression. The popularity of the new "talking pictures" also took audiences away from the theater. Suddenly, big plays with large casts were no longer produced. In fact, some productions cut costs by using recorded voices to replace actors in minor roles.

I was fortunate to be living almost rent-free with Aunt Mamie, but I still needed money for food, clothes and transportation. I was desperate to find work of some kind, so I began studying the want ads. Macy's was advertising for people to work in their book department, so I applied. I loved books and thought it might be fun to sell them.

Despite having no work experience of any kind, I was hired by Macy's to sell humor books during the Christmas season. One of the best sellers of the day was *Caught Short,* a book about the stock market by the actor Eddie Cantor. It sold for only one dollar a copy, so I tried to sell five or ten copies to each customer to use as gifts. To my surprise, I was so successful that Macy's asked me to stay on after Christmas. They also offered me a place in their executive training program. I wasn't interested in a retailing career, but told them I'd be happy to continue selling books until I found work in the theater.

That winter, a friend introduced Lee and me to St. Bartholomew's Church on Park Avenue at 50th Street. St. Barts' Community House had an excellent drama department, with a terrific director, Leonard Young. He began casting us in plays he directed and produced. Leonard cast me as the lead in *Androcles and the Lion*—my first part in New York. I wasn't paid, but playing that role boosted my confidence as an actor. It meant rehearsing every night after working at Macy's all day, but I enjoyed it so much that I appeared in several other plays at St. Barts' that winter.

That experience made me realize that actors use their entire bodies in performing so I decided to study dancing to help me move better. Then, to learn how to project my voice to the back of large theaters, I arranged to have singing lessons two days a week during my lunch hour. When I finished work at Macy's, I'd rush home for a quick bite to eat, then take a subway back up town to rehearse at St. Barts'.

After six months on this crazy schedule, I became ill with something similar to mononucleosis, but that term wasn't used then. The doctor said I was very run down. His remedy: "Eat more red meat and drink acidophilus milk." It was horrible! While trying to regain my health, I spent a weekend in New Canaan with old family friends. Sally Parsons was my age (19), her sister Betty was 21, and their brother Hal was 17 or 18. Mrs. Parsons was taking the entire family to Europe for the summer. Her own departure had to be postponed, so she had an extra ticket on the *S.S.Rotterdam*. "Why don't you spend the summer with us at St. Jean de Luz?" Sally asked. "It's a charming French village on the Atlantic Ocean near the Spanish border."

It sounded wonderful. I'd been yearning for a chance to speak French after studying it for so many years, but I didn't think I could afford to go to Europe. "You won't need much money," Mrs. Parsons insisted. "The round-trip ticket from New York to Rotterdam is only $199—and you'll be able to board inexpensively with us in France." That made it even more appealing, but I decided to consult my doctor first. He assured me that relaxing in the sun and swimming in salt water would help me recover. That was all I needed to hear.

The Parsons were leaving in ten days, so I had to rush to get ready. I managed to scrape together the grand sum of $250—most of it gifts from relatives over the years. Considering that I earned only $25 a week at Macy's, it was probably foolish to quit my job and empty my bank account in the midst of the Depression, but I didn't hesitate. I had a small income (about $65 a month) from my father's life insurance and my share of the rental income from our Brooklyn house, so I figured I could manage. I was too young and eager for new experiences to worry about the future—and I'm glad I didn't.

One of my first cousins, Helena Jelliffe Goldschmidt, was living in Amsterdam with her Dutch husband, Carel. They'd already invited me to visit, so I sent them a cable: *Arriving in Holland on May 15.* They cabled back: *Great! We'll meet you in Rotterdam.* It was all so exciting that I could hardly wait to get going.

Europe on a Shoestring

Betty, Sally, Hal and I had a fantastic time crossing the Atlantic. A students' association had taken over the second class section of the ship. The head of that association organized a series of dances, shuffle board games and other activities for passengers. Most were about our age, so we had good fun together.

Carel Goldschmidt met me in Rotterdam and drove me to Amsterdam in his very snappy car, an Italian Lancia. He and Helena lived near the stadium used for the 1928 Olympics. In the mornings, I took their young son, Dolph, for a long walk around the stadium. When Carel finished work, he usually took me sightseeing. (Helena was quite pregnant at the time and preferred to stay home.) It was late spring and the tulips were still in bloom, so everything was beautiful.

At the end of my two-week visit, Carel drove me to the airport. As it happened, a friend of his was on the same plane—my first commercial flight. It held all of six passengers, three on each side. Carel's friend and I sat opposite each other. We flew so low that I couldn't stop looking out the window at the wonderful pattern of bright colors in the tulip fields.

When we landed at Rotterdam, the young man got off, but I continued on to Paris. I was so excited about flying over Brussels that I kept moving from side to side, looking out the windows. Finally, the pilot opened the cockpit door and said, "Lady, will you please stay put on one side or the other. You're upsetting the whole balance of the plane." That was so embarrassing that I stayed in my seat for the rest of the flight. When we landed at Le Bourget airport in Paris, I was happy to find Betty, Sally and Hal waiting for me.

Luckily, I also had relatives in Paris. Dorothy Leeming, a second cousin who'd spent many school holidays at our home, had fallen in love with a charming Frenchman, Philippe LeCorbeiller, while sharing an apartment with Honor in 1922. Honor had returned home the next year, but Dorothy married Phillipe and stayed in Paris.

My cousins lived in a spacious apartment on the Ile St.-Louis overlooking the River Seine. The Parsons stayed on in Paris for a few days, making sure that I saw their favorite sights, including the stained glass windows in Sainte Chapelle, the cathedral of Notre Dame and the views from a boat sailing along the Seine River in the middle of Paris.

When my three friends went off to meet their mother and three younger siblings in St. Jean de Luz, I stayed on with my cousins for another ten days. They introduced me to an old family friend, a Frenchman named Olivier (Olif) Regnault. He was almost twice my age and had been divorced a couple of times, so I was reluctant to go out with him at first. But I was eager to experience Paris, so I relented. He turned out to be a terrific escort who loved the city, knew it thoroughly and enjoyed sharing it.

Sometimes Olif took me out to dinner at a beautiful (and still famous) restaurant called La Tour d'Argent or to the famous night club Maxims. When money was short, we'd just take long walks around the city, stopping in a little bistro where everyone sang French songs and ate cherries dipped in brandy. One day Olif took me to the horse races at Longchamps, but we lost so much money we had to return home on the Metro instead of by taxi.

Those few days launched a friendship that lasted many years. Although Olif remarried and lived on the island of Majorca, we stayed in touch until he was killed during World War II. That experience showed me that young girls could have close, enduring friendships with men who were not beaux.

After an exciting two weeks in Paris, I took the overnight train to St. Jean de Luz. The Parsons had advised me to rent a pillow at the station. "You can just curl up in a corner of the compartment with a good book," they said. I boarded the train early as they'd suggested, but I was still too late to get a seat by the window. I had to sit between two rather large Frenchmen—one munching pungent sausages, the other trying to practice his English on me. I didn't sleep all night.

In the morning, my seat mates were replaced by a charming Basque priest. He was also going to St. Jean de Luz, so I enjoyed chatting with him. At various stops along the way, I noticed that some passengers jumped off the still-moving train, rushed into the station and returned with breakfast. I was afraid the train would leave without me if I tried that, so I was both hungry and exhausted when I finally reached my destination around 11 am.

The Parsons met my train and took me to the enchanting apartment above an artists' studio that they'd rented for the summer. Next, we walked into the vine-covered courtyard next door to see the place they'd rented for me. It was a cozy little room on the ground floor, with pretty wall paper, so I was delighted.

That evening, the Parsons insisted that I join them at the town square where a lively band was playing. I quickly forgot how tired I was when I saw a large group—including many Basque people from France and the neighboring Spanish province—gathered at outdoor tables. The Basque men, dressed in white shirts and pants, with red sashes and blue berets, did a colorful dance called the "Fandango." The upper part of their bodies stayed absolutely still while the lower part moved rapidly. One man had a wicker tray on his head, filled with little cornucopias of peanuts that he was selling. I was amazed to see him dance with that tray balanced on his head, his legs going like mad in his Basque espadrilles.

An American woman at the next table generously offered us some of the peanuts she'd bought, so we began to chat with her. As the evening wore on, we learned her name: Edna Ferber. A popular writer of that period, she'd already won a Pulitzer Prize for her novel, *So Big.* I'd enjoyed her novel, *Show Boat,* so I was thrilled to meet her. She told us she was working on her next book about the Basque country. (Published later under the title, *Basquerie,* it brought back great memories for me.)

By the time the Parsons escorted me back to my little room that night, I'd had no sleep for about 48 hours. I could hardly wait to crawl into bed. As soon as I pulled the light chain, however, giant cockroaches started crawling all over the walls, rustling the wall paper. My friends quickly offered me a mattress on the floor in their place so I wouldn't have to sleep with the roaches. I accepted gratefully. The next day I found another room, a few blocks away. It was up two flights of stairs, but I figured the cockroaches wouldn't climb that high.

None of us had any money in those days, but we didn't feel poor because we were all in the same situation. Amazing as it seems now, I was able to live in France on my meager $65 a month. It was a real challenge at times, but that was part of the fun. Soon after we arrived, for example, we bought second-hand bicycles for $12 each. We sold them for $8 when we left, so our transportation for the entire summer cost us only $4.

We found a tennis club we were able to join for $5 for the summer. The Parsons were all good tennis players, so we had some great doubles matches. St. Jean de Luz also had a beautiful beach, so we spent $8 to join one of the four beach clubs based in boats anchored off shore. The clubs competed in swimming races, so the man who ran ours—a big Greek with enormous muscles—taught us the back stroke and the racing moves. We had a great time racing against others our age. Whenever we managed to scrape up a few spare coins, we'd go to the Casino, where elegant people went to gamble and dance on an open verandah overlooking the ocean. We didn't do much gambling, but we enjoyed being there.

St. Jean de Luz is very near the Spanish border and Irun Mountain. We spent many delightful hours hiking and biking around the area. One day we rode horses across the mountain stream that marks the border just so we could say we'd been into Spain without visas. It was a carefree life with a lot of outdoor exercise, so I quickly regained my health.

In September, Mrs. Parsons moved her family to Switzerland and put the younger children in Swiss schools instead of returning to New York. I took the train to Paris and spent another week with my cousins, Dorothy and Philippe. My months in France had stimulated a desire to see more of the world, so I accepted an invitation to visit friends of Honor's in England before going home.

A French friend told me I didn't need a visa to go to England, so I got on the boat train without one. When I reached the other side of the English Channel, however, the British customs agent asked, "Where is your visa?"

"I don't have one."

"Well, you can't come into England without a visa," he insisted.

"I have no place else to go," I said. "I'm visiting friends who are meeting me here." He hesitated, so I burst into tears. That proved to be too much for him.

"All right," he said. "I'll let you in this time, but don't try to come into England again without a proper visa." (My friend wasn't entirely wrong; it seems that French citizens did not need visas, but Americans did.) My acting skills probably helped me get by, but I don't think tears would work today. I now check with the appropriate authorities to make sure I have all the right travel documents before leaving home.

Honor's friend Hubert Parker, a young barrister, met me at Dover and drove me to his home in Sussex, near Guilford. His wife Lauren (Larry) was one of Honor's classmates at Parsons School of Art in Paris. Although newly married, the Parkers had a large, lovely home. I was amused by their "butler" who actually worked as a gardener during the day. He changed into a tail coat and stood like a statue behind Hubert's chair at dinner every night. Their cook, a former sauce chef at the Ritz Hotel, prepared delicious meals. Larry and I spent our days riding horses or driving around the countryside. She took me on sightseeing tours of Hampton Court and other interesting places.

One day we drove to Oxford to visit Hubert's nephew, a student there. I'm embarrassed to admit that I was perfectly awful to him and his friends. We were all about the same age, but they seemed much younger and naïve to me. I was reserved and probably a bit haughty, so they started calling me "Duchess." Secretly pleased by the title, I was a little nicer to them after that, so we got along better. Larry and Hubert were wonderful hosts who made sure that I enjoyed my time in England. Hubert later became The Lord Chief Justice of Great Britain. When I returned to London many years later, I loved going to the Old Bailey courthouse to see him presiding in his full bottom wig. To me, it was a lot like going to a costume drama at the theater.

On one of my visits to London, Hubert got me a ticket to the opening of Parliament. As we walked in together, he pointed out all the Lords and Ladies. Watching the royal procession that day, I felt like a real duchess. Later, I was pleased to see photographs of that occasion in the November 1961 issue of *National Geographic*. I was standing in the front row in a red hat, so I was able to find myself in one full-page picture.

In October, I finally boarded the *S.S. Rotterdam* and sailed for New York. It took about ten days to cross, but so many young people were on board that I never felt lonely. I even had my first real romance with Frank Webster, a man who lived on Beacon Hill in Boston. I'd heard about shipboard romances, but I thought this one might last because Frank wrote me such a nice letter when he returned home. He also sent me a large wooden box full of apples from his family's farm in New Hampshire, but the invitations I expected never came.

Only a few months later, I was heartbroken to learn that Frank was engaged. He sent me an invitation to the wedding, but I couldn't bear to go.

Return to Reality—and the Sales Floor

When I arrived back in New York, my money was gone—and the Depression had grown worse—but I had no regrets. I was glad I'd had the courage to seize the opportunity to travel abroad and experience a different way of life. It was a fantastic summer that had a permanent effect on my life. My health improved and so did my ability to speak French. Even more important, the trip showed me new ways to enjoy life with very little money.

I still had to earn a living, though, so I returned to work at Macy's book department. During a price war with Gimbels, their major competitor, Modern Library editions of classic books were selling for as little as 61 cents each. Finally, Macy's decided to compete with Gimbels by giving away one book with every one they sold. It worked, so business was good.

This time I was in charge of "domestic science and medical books," most of which were about cooking or sex. I didn't know much about either subject at the time, so I studied all the promotional material so I could discuss the books with customers. It wasn't my dream job, but I tried to make the most of it.

In my spare time, I appeared in more plays at St. Barts'. I also joined another amateur theater group at the Barbizon Hotel, but professional work in the theater continued to elude me. Most of the aspiring actors I met were going to drama school, but I couldn't afford that. During a party at my uncle's house, however, I had the good fortune to meet Arthur Hopkins, one of the top directors in New York. He'd directed all the Barrymores, including John in the title roles of *Hamlet* and *Richard III*.

I told Arthur Hopkins about my interest in acting, and he kindly invited me to visit him in his office. When I asked for advice, he told me not to go to drama school. "You either have it or you don't," he said. "Just try your darndest to get a small part, then listen carefully and observe what's going on so you can learn from the other actors." He also advised me to study dancing and singing. "You want your body to be supple, and you need good diction and a voice that projects. You don't have to go to drama school for any of that."

I took his advice and signed up for more lessons. Between those and my roles in various amateur plays, I gradually learned about the acting trade. As I got to know my way around the theater, I went to see all kinds of agents in search of work. Most were polite, but didn't pay much attention to me. I remember one pair named Brisko and Goldsmith who practically bowed each time I came into their office. "Come back in two weeks," they'd say. "We might have something then." I'd get my hopes up, but nothing ever came of it.

In the summer of 1933, I sang with my brother Howard in the chorus at The Theater-In-The-Woods, a summer playhouse in Wilton, Connecticut. Only a few miles from Aunt Mamie's place in New Canaan, the theater was run by Greek Evans and his wife, Henrietta Wakefield. Greek had been a famous tenor in Chicago's Lyric Opera Company and Henrietta was a former mezzo-soprano at the Metropolitan Opera in New York. They put on a lot of operettas and usually sang together in their productions.

The chorus was directed by Max Cushing, a delightful man who taught music at Columbia University. He spent summers in Wilton in a beautiful old barn he'd converted into a studio. Max was a warm, genial host, always ready to receive guests. His barn had three stone fireplaces and five pianos, so the chorus often rehearsed there. Musicians of all ages seemed to gather at Max's barn, so it became our favorite place for parties. The most special moments I remember include hearing Morton Gould play the piano and watching Paul Draper do a brilliant tap dance.

I had so much fun singing in that chorus that I returned the following summer. One night, after rehearsing for the musical, *Desert Song*, I brashly announced, "Now I'll dance the part of Azuri, the harem girl." I'd been studying oriental dance—similar to belly dancing—and was eager to show off my new skills. Max and the others seemed surprised, but they liked my dance and insisted I do a repeat performance for the director. I wouldn't have approached Greek on my own, but with the encouragement of my friends, I danced for him the next day—and landed my first speaking part. That's when I realized that it doesn't pay to be a shrinking violet.

*I was thrilled to get the part of Azuri in a summer stock production of **Desert Song**.*

The role of Azuri was my first paying job in the theater. Students who danced or sang in the chorus did not get paid, but Azuri was a leading part so I was finally considered a professional. The value of all those dance lessons that I'd taken over the years became clear when I played that part. It also helped me appreciate the importance of immersing yourself in a role. The whole experience really boosted my self-confidence.

In those days, opportunities for aspiring actors to get professional experience were very limited. We didn't have television, of course, nor did we have the small off-Broadway and off-off Broadway theaters that are now scattered all over New York City. Many talented people worked at summer theaters in resort areas, but those jobs lasted only a few weeks.

When I returned to New York in the fall of 1934 to resume my quest for a stage career, I had a little more to offer producers. I'd been paid for one summer theater job, and had performed lead roles in several other plays at St. Bartholomew's. I still had to earn a living, though, so I got a new job selling toys at Saks Fifth Avenue. It was more fun than selling books. Eager to be more independent, I went apartment hunting with Winifred (Win) Stevenson, an old friend and classmate from New Canaan. We found a place on West 51st Street, just off Fifth Avenue. It was only a five-minute walk from Saks and from the fancy French dress shop where Win worked.

We paid $55 a month for a one-bedroom apartment on the seventh floor of an elevator building. The huge living room had a big fireplace and a skylight window overlooking the spires of St. Patrick's Cathedral. It felt like being in Paris. (When the chef in the French restaurant on the ground level started cooking garlic in butter, I was sure I was in Paris.) One thing we did not have, however, was a kitchen. Our "stove" was a two-burner electric hot plate in the living room, and dishes had to be washed in the bathroom sink, so we didn't do much cooking. We were so thrilled to have our own place in the city, though, that these inconveniences never mattered.

Win had studied at the University of Grenoble in France, so she spoke excellent French. Together, we made friends with the manager of the French restaurant downstairs, a woman we called Madame. She'd give us a large bowl of soup and a hunk of crusty French bread for 50 cents. The complete dinner cost $1.25, which was more than we could afford, so we ate a lot of soup. It was so delicious that we never felt deprived.

During my lunch breaks at Saks, I'd walk a few blocks over to Broadway and look for work in the theater. I'd heard about the casting couch, but no one ever asked me to perform special favors in exchange for a job. I did go to one audition in a man's apartment, though. He asked to see my legs, so I raised my skirt. When he asked me the raise my skirt higher and higher, I just gathered up my things and left. I didn't want to find out what might be next.

4

Broadway at Last

When a director was casting a play, word usually got out. If actors saw a light in Arthur Hopkins' office in the Plymouth Theater on West 45th Street, they'd line up at the bottom of the stairs leading up to it. Whenever I happened to see such a line, I'd join it. Hopkins had directed so many plays that he knew many of the actors and didn't waste time. "No, nothing for you today," he'd say. He finally asked me to read for a part, but another actress got it. The next time Hopkins asked me to step aside, he said, "I think I might have something for you—the part of a Spanish girl in a new play."

"Oh, good," I said. "I've been to Spain and I know Spanish." I didn't tell him I'd spent only three days in Spain—or that my Spanish "tutor" was actually my friend, Hal Parsons. We'd decided to study Spanish together during our summer in France, but the only book we could find was written in French. Two beginners teaching each other Spanish from a French book is not the best way to learn, but we were both eager to speak the language so we kept working at it.

As soon as we thought we'd made some progress, we'd cross the border into Spain, buy tickets for a bull fight, then try to talk to the people around us. We sat in the cheap seats on the sunny side, along with Basque workmen who wore handkerchiefs (knotted on each corner) on their heads. They all carried goatskin wine carafes, called *botas,* which they held up at arm's length as they squirted wine into their open mouths. That was amazing to watch! We didn't learn much useful Spanish, though, because most of the phrases we heard were curses.

It was really daring of me to claim knowledge of Spanish after such limited exposure, but I'd learned that timidity doesn't get you very far. My boldness must have helped because Arthur Hopkins asked me to come back again in two weeks. When I returned, he introduced me to Robert Sherwood, author of a new play called *The Petrified Forest.* It had no Spanish roles, but did include a Mexican girl who worked in the kitchen.

Robert Sherwood was very tall—about six feet seven, it seemed to me. He unfolded his long, lanky body, and said, "How do you do, Miss Leeming? I'm so glad to meet you—and so glad you know Spanish. I know only one Spanish word—*patio*—and I learned that in Southern California. I want you to write the Spanish into the play for me."

That was far more than I'd bargained for, but I've always enjoyed challenges. (I now believe that they help keep the brain active—an important asset at my age.) I rushed over to the Berlitz language school and signed up for a crash course in Spanish. Hopkins had asked me to return to his office in another two weeks, so I had to work quickly. Fortunately, I joined a very small class with a good teacher, so I learned a number of useful Spanish phrases.

I had to continue selling toys at Saks, of course, so I could pay for the lessons. When Hopkins asked me to report to the theater at 11 am for a reading of *The Petrified Forest*, I switched lunch hours with another clerk so I'd be able to make it. Just as I was preparing to sneak out a little early, though, a charming lady came in to buy gifts for her grandchildren. I had to wait on her or I'd lose my job—but she was shopping for six grandchildren and wanted the gifts mailed to six different addresses! We had to write up all the orders by hand, so that was a lot of work.

Keeping one eye on the clock as I helped the customer select toys, I grew increasingly frantic as it reached 11, 11:05, 11:10. When the order was finally finished, I rushed out and took a taxi to the theater. The stage manager met me at the door with a steely glare; I was more than 20 minutes late. He handed me a script, ushered me onto the stage and pointed to a chair. About 20 actors, including Humphrey Bogart, were sitting in a circle. Robert Sherwood was also there, along with Arthur Hopkins, the director. Only the leading man, Leslie Howard, was missing.

I opened my script (called sides) and found only two-word cues preceding my lines. I had no idea how far they'd gone, when my cues came in, or even what the play was about. My part was in English, but I was expected to translate those words into Spanish on the spot. I studied the cue sheet in absolute agony all morning, but we never came to anything I was supposed to say.

At one o'clock we were excused for lunch, with instructions to be back in the theater by two. I rushed to a phone to call my boss at Saks. "I'm terribly sorry, but an emergency has come up," I lied. "I won't be able to return to work until tomorrow morning." Then I grabbed a quick bite to eat before hurrying back to my seat in the theater.

The afternoon was more of the same, with me anxiously studying the cue sheet, waiting for my turn to speak. Finally, I recognized a cue and mumbled something garbled in Spanish. At least no one laughed. It took us until six p.m. to read through the entire play. "You're all excused," Hopkins announced. "Please be back here at eleven tomorrow morning."

When I arrived at Saks the next day, I went in to see the buyer in charge of the toy department. "I've done something terrible," I began.

"Well, you sold more toys than anyone else last Saturday, so it can't be that bad," she said. "What have you done?"

"I've been asked to read for a part in a Broadway play," I blurted out. "I've always dreamed of having a career in the theater, so this could be a great opportunity. They're just trying me out, though, so I might not get the part. I have to attend all the rehearsals for the next week before I find out. If I do not get hired, I'd love to continue working here."

"Oh, dear," she said, "I have a lot of new people coming in for the Christmas season and I was hoping you'd help me train them. Can you give me any time?"

"Well, I don't have to be at the theater until eleven," I replied, "so I could work here until ten forty-five. If that would work for you, I'd love it." She agreed, so I came in every morning to help the new people in the toy department. Afterwards, I'd walk to the theater for the rehearsal, so it was a great arrangement for me. Saks paid me only $5 a week for my part-time work, but I was happy to have it. Actors rehearsed without pay until they received a contract and I was already struggling to pay my bills.

After we rehearsed for three days with a stand-in for Leslie Howard, Robert Sherwood asked, "Where is my leading man? I think I'll send him a cable saying, *All is forgiven. Please come home. Signed, Mother.*" This was several years before Leslie played Ashley Wilkes in the movie, *Gone with the Wind*, but he was already a huge star. He had played the romantic lead in *Barclay Square*, *The Scarlet Pimpernel* and *Outward Bound*, among other shows on Broadway and in London.

Peggy Conklin, the young actress playing the ingénue role, was very curious about this star playing opposite her. "Esther, do you know Leslie Howard?" she asked.

"I've seen him in plays and movies, of course," I said. "And my sister introduced us at a party once. He's absolutely divine." The next day, Leslie finally showed up, wearing horn-rimmed glasses, a snap brim hat and long hair—something only English actors had in those days. He was 41, but seemed much younger to me.

Peggy was not impressed. "I don't think he's so attractive," she said.

"You just wait," I told her.

By then, Peggy had memorized most of her lines. Leslie was still reading his, so he was looking down at the script most of the time. When Peggy (as Gabrielle) asked, *"Wouldn't you like to be loved by me, Alan?"* Leslie suddenly looked up at her and replied, *"Yes, Gabrielle, I would like to be loved by you."* Something about the way he said it caused Peggy to just gasp and run off the stage.

"Oh, Esther; now I know what you're talking about!" She'd been completely bowled over by a bolt of sex appeal he'd thrown at her. It was her first experience with a quality other women had seen for years. Many of the female fans who came to see Leslie's plays and movies were dying to go to bed with him. They'd write him passionate letters, hang around the stage door after each performance and even pull buttons off his coat when he came out.

*Humphrey Bogart helped Leslie Howard shoulder a bag during a performance of **The Petrified Forest** on Broadway in 1935.*

Leslie Howard was a slight man with a rather wistful quality that seemed to make women want to mother him. In *The Petrified Forest*, he played Alan Squier, a poor intellectual, hitch-hiking across the country. Humphrey Bogart played Duke Mantee, the macho role. Apparently, many women loved that tender, vulnerable man that Leslie personified—and he took advantage of it. Although he had a nice wife and two teen-aged children in England, he often had a girlfriend in New York, too. For a while it was the glamorous Indian-born actress, Merle Oberon, who'd played opposite Leslie in *The Scarlet Pimpernel* in England. She often came backstage and waited in his dressing room. We'd see them holding hands between scenes.

Once Peggy got to know Leslie, she didn't really like him, but other women continued to find him attractive. During the second act of the play, I had to scream off-stage because the gangsters were supposed to be bothering me in the kitchen. While I was listening intently for my cue, Leslie would sometimes sneak up and playfully put his arms around me. What electricity! It was great fun to be working with such a marvelous actor.

Leslie hated all those screaming fans at the stage door, so he figured out a way to get from the back of our theater, on 44th Street, into the back of the Plymouth Theater on 45th Street. Sometimes he'd ask me, "Are you walking home tonight?" If I answered, "Yes," he'd say, "Well, let's escape out the back way and walk together." We'd sneak through the stage door of the Plymouth, then walk up to my apartment on 51st Street. Leslie always kept the brim of his hat down as he continued on to his hotel on 55th Street. During one of those walks, I happened to mention my sister Honor. Suddenly a shocked look came over Leslie's face. "You mean Honor Leeming is your sister?" he asked. "I used to be in love with her." Ironically, he'd even offered Honor a part in a play he was directing, but she turned him down. "I'll be happy to design the stage set," she said, "but I'm not an actor."

Leslie was never a beau of mine, but we did become pretty good friends. He even invited me to go horseback riding in Central Park when his daughter was visiting from England. They both loved to ride as much as I did. (Leslie had his own horses in England and in Hollywood.) One night, Leslie and I traveled to Brooklyn together. He was playing in a polo match at one of the armories and I thought it would be fun to watch. He wasn't a very good polo player, but I enjoyed seeing him in such a different role.

As rehearsals for *The Petrified Forest* continued, I began to believe I might get the part—until Gilbert Miller, a rather pompous man who was producing the play with Arthur Hopkins, called me aside.

"Miss Leeming," he said. "Please step out on the fire escape with me." I'd heard stories about Gilbert that made me reluctant to be on a fire escape with him, but I didn't have much choice. After shutting the door, he said, "Please repeat some of your Spanish phrases for me."

"*Que voy a hacer*" I said.

"Ah," he said. "That should be pronounced *hath*-ere, not *has*-ere. Spanish, you see, is my second mother tongue."

I'll never get the part now, I thought. Then I remembered something my Berlitz Spanish teacher—who'd helped me with the script translations—had said. "But you see, Mr. Miller," I protested, "Paula is not Castilian or even Spanish. She's Mexican, and Mexicans don't use that 'th' pronunciation."

He didn't say much after that, but he didn't look pleased. I was heartsick to think I might lose the part because of my Spanish pronunciation when I'd tried so hard to get it right. I'm a pretty good mimic of accents, but very few Mexicans were living in New York back then. I asked my beau to take me to a Mexican restaurant so I could hear the accent, but our waiter spoke no Spanish at all. After burning our insides on Mexican chili, we asked to speak to the manager. He turned out to be a Jewish boy from Brooklyn, who had nothing to do with Mexico. I was forced to improvise the accent after all. I'd already learned the importance of a positive attitude, though, so I focused on the bright side: chances were good that hardly anyone else would know how a real Mexican sounded either!

Although I had very long, dark hair, I didn't really look Mexican. I learned later that Gilbert Miller had wanted to replace me with a real Mexican woman, but Arthur Hopkins refused to let me go. "Esther has real vitality," he explained, "and that's what I want in the part." Since he was the director, he won out—and I finally got my contract. Needless to say, I was thrilled that my persistence had paid off and that I was on my way to appearing on Broadway at last.

*I braided my long, dark hair when I played the role of Paula, the Mexican cook, in **The Petrified Forest**.*

Once I had the part, I assumed I'd go to a costume designer and a makeup artist, but I was mistaken. As a granny model, I sometimes spend an hour with a makeup artist and a hairdresser just to prepare for a small non-speaking part on television, but it was different in the thirties. One day, the director just came up to me and said, "It's time to go over to Eve's and pick out your costume. Ask for Miss Thorne; she's expecting you. Once you've found something suitable for Paula, come back and present yourself."

I picked out a flowered skirt, a blouse with a scarf, canvas espadrille shoes and big gold bangle earrings. I parted my hair in the middle, braided it, tied the braids with red ribbons and looped them up over my ears. I also put on a big white apron, since Paula was a cook, but the spotless apron didn't look right. I opened my dressing room window, ran my hand across the sooty ledge outside, then smeared it on the apron. After washing my hands, I applied dark, greasy makeup on my face before presenting myself to Hopkins. He stood back, looking me up and down. Finally, he said, "You look pretty good, dear. You even look as if you might have fleas." That was meant to be a compliment.

Hopkins was a man of few words, but he was an excellent director. Quiet and unassuming, he gave actors a lot of freedom. I remember making one entrance from the kitchen during a rehearsal. A gangster had a gun in my stomach, so I was yelling hysterically in Spanish. Hopkins came over to me and quietly said, "You're supposed to be really terrified, my dear." The next time we rehearsed that scene, I put as much terror into my scream as I could muster. I must have succeeded, for that was the last time he corrected me. (I was not surprised to discover, years later, that John Barrymore had written about Arthur Hopkins with great reverence in his autobiography.)

As soon as my contract was signed, I went to Saks to turn in my resignation. "Oh, please don't leave us now," the buyer said. "The Christmas season is just getting started. Can't you continue to come in before your rehearsals?"

I really needed that extra $5 a week. Before the play opened, we received only half our regular pay—just $25 a week in my case. I agreed to stay on at Saks until the week before Christmas, when the play went out of town. We performed one night at the Parsons Theater in Hartford, Connecticut, before taking the train to Boston. We opened at Boston's Schubert Theater on Christmas Eve.

This was quite an adventure for me. It was my first Christmas away from my family. I felt sad about that, but I was finally doing what I really wanted—I was working in the theater as a professional. It was the fulfillment of a life-long dream!

Boston was the most enchanting place on Christmas Eve. I remember walking on Beacon Hill where all the elegant old houses had lighted candles in the windows. Many residents seemed to be having a simultaneous open house, as we saw groups of people in festive dress strolling from one brightly-lit home to the next. Everyone appeared to be in high spirits as they greeted each other on the street.

The next day, the entire cast gathered at a hotel on Boston Common for a delicious Christmas dinner. We all stayed in various hotels around the Common during our two week stint in Boston. The three big leads—Leslie Howard, Humphrey Bogart and Peggy Conklin—stayed at the Ritz Carleton. The next echelon stayed at the Copley Plaza. I ended up in a little hotel that smelled of stale cigarettes. We did visit each other, though, so I escaped from my dreary room by going to the Ritz to have tea with Peggy.

Alfred Lunt and Lynne Fontanne, the famous husband/wife acting team, were also in Boston, trying out another play destined for Broadway. They came over to our theater to see Leslie, so I got to meet them—another big thrill for me. They were such a great success during their many appearances on Broadway that New York City now has a Lunt Fontanne Theater named after them.

The Petrified Forest was a wonderful play, with only three women in the cast. Blanche Sweet, a silent movie queen who played a millionaire's wife, was the third. She had a marvelous scene with Humphrey Bogart, whose character had just led an escape from prison. She tells him, "You've had the one supreme satisfaction of knowing that at least you're a real man."

"Yeah, that's true," he responds, "but what has it got me? I've spent most of my time since I grew up in jail, and it looks like I'll spend the rest of my life dead. So what good does it do me to be a real man when you don't get much chance to be crawling into the hay with some dame?"

"I wonder if we could find any hay around here," she says. It was a very daring line for those days—especially coming from a proper banker's wife—but it brought down the house.

We got very good reviews in Boston, but that didn't guarantee the play's success on Broadway. We opened at the Broadhurst Theater in New York on January 7, 1935. Tickets for opening night were very expensive, so I didn't expect anyone I knew to be there. (Later on, I was able to get free "house seats" for relatives and friends, but not on opening night.)

To my surprise, Max Cushing, my music coach from The Theater-in-the-Woods, had a seat in the balcony. Afterwards, he came backstage to see me. "This is your debut," he said. "I want to take you out on the town to celebrate." It was a very generous gesture, as he was not a wealthy man. He was just very proud to see one of his students appearing on Broadway.

My Aunt Gertrude had sent me a lei of my favorite flowers—gardenias—for an opening night present. I put it around my neck, feeling like a horse that had just won the first race at Santa Anita, but Max wasn't daunted at all. He was wearing a tuxedo and insisted on taking me out to several nightclubs. "Max," I said, "I can't go out wearing this lei unless I'm somebody else. I'll be a French woman."

"That's fine with me, Mademoiselle," he said. Fortunately, he was also a French teacher, so we were able to converse convincingly in that language. At each place we went, Max told the head waiter, "Mademoiselle has just made her debut." They must have been impressed, because they gave us great seats on the edge of the dance floor. Max was an excellent dancer so we had a great time dancing, even though he was about 50 and I was only 23. We ended up in Harlem at the Cotton Club and the Savoy Ballroom, popular spots at the time. About 3 a.m., we returned home and bought the morning papers to read the reviews. The play was a big success—the perfect ending to the opening night of my dreams!

I settled down to enjoy a great run in New York. We did eight performances a week—every night but Sunday, plus matinees on Wednesday and Saturday. Although my part was small, playing the role of Paula turned out to be one of the most satisfactory periods of my life. I found it particularly exciting to experience the rapport with different audiences. You feel their energy and anticipation. No two performances are exactly alike because people don't always respond the same way or even laugh at the same lines. In fact, we'd taken our characters so seriously during rehearsals that we were actually shocked by all the laughter when we performed before our first audience in Hartford.

The cast spent so much time together that some of us became good friends. I was closest to Peggy Conklin. She was just a few years older than I, but had already appeared in six or eight Broadway plays. Peggy went on to have a successful career, with leading roles in *Picnic* and other Broadway shows. Our friendship continued for many years, even after we married and had children. I hate to let go of a good friend, so I made an effort to stay in touch—a quality that has served me well as I've grown older.

I also became quite friendly with Humphrey Bogart, whose dressing room was next to mine. His part required a two-day growth of beard, so the only night he dared to shave was Saturday. His second marriage was on the rocks and I think he was lonely. He often wandered into my dressing room, singing and joking as he lathered up for his weekly shave. He worked on his prison pallor by going to El Morocco for a couple of scotches every night.

After one matinee, Humphrey and I went off to a cocktail party together. It wasn't a date; we were just the only cast members who'd been invited. The hostess, a woman I'd known since childhood, was Kay Swift, who wrote "Can't We be Friends?," "Fine and Dandy" and other songs. Her beau at the time was George Gershwin, who often played the piano at her parties. When we returned to the theater for the evening performance, the stage manager greeted me with a big hug. That was his way of checking my breath for the smell of alcohol. "Ah ha!" he said. "I think we'll put the understudy on tonight."

"But I've had only one drink and I'm perfectly capable of playing my role," I assured him. He hesitated, but finally let me go on. It's interesting to note, however, that Mr. Bogart received no such treatment from the stage manager.

Humphrey's sister, Kay Bogart, was a friend of Honor's, and lived near her in Westport, Connecticut. Whenever Humphrey planned to spend a weekend with his sister, he'd invite me to ride up with him. We'd leave the theater about 11:30 on Saturday night and zip along in his Ford Roadster with the top down. He'd drop me at Honor's home, then pick me up on Monday afternoon so we'd get back to the theater in time for our next performance. During those rides, I learned that Humphrey's father was a successful New York doctor and his mother, Maude Humphreys, was a well-known portrait painter. In contrast to the bad-guy roles that later made him famous, Humphrey was really a jolly man who liked to sing and laugh. I also found him to be a perfect gentleman.

The Petrified Forest was doing well at the box office and could have continued for at least a year, but Leslie Howard decided that New York City was too hot in summer. As the star, he had the power to close the show—and did exactly that on July 1. He returned to England to join his family, but he put 21 American actors out of work during the Depression. (Actors don't have such power today.)

After the final curtain, Arthur Hopkins gave a party for all the actors. During the evening, he got up and said, "I've had the pleasure and privilege of producing many plays on Broadway. I've assembled numerous casts, but this is what I'd call 'a perfect cast.' At no time during the play's run did I ever want to change anyone I'd selected for a part."

I was so flattered to be a member of that cast that it felt like cheating to cash my paychecks. I'd enjoyed it all so much that I'd have performed for nothing. I couldn't afford to work without pay, of course, but the pleasure of doing exactly what I wanted was enormous. I was so glad that I'd persisted. In fact, that experience was a great lesson in the value of persistence—a quality that has helped me overcome setbacks and remain optimistic about life.

5

Beyond Broadway: The Harsh Realities

After *The Petrified Forest* closed, Win and I gave up our little apartment and returned to New Canaan for the summer. Sadly, dear old Aunt Mamie had fallen down the stairs and broken her hip while I was rehearsing in New York. The subsequent operations were just too much for her aging body. She died on January 4, 1935. None of us ever knew her age, but she must have been close to 80. She left us her little house, which we continued to use for many years. Honor and Lee were married by then, so Howard and I shared Aunt Mamie's house that summer. (Honor moved back in later, after her divorce—and Howard lived there for a time as a newlywed.)

In the fall, Win and I returned to New York City and found a new apartment on East 72nd Street. It wasn't as nice or as convenient to the theater as our old place, but it was easy for Win to get to her new job with the Margab Linen Company on West 57th Street.

Hollywood made a movie of *The Petrified Forest*, which also starred Leslie Howard. He was allowed to pick the other actors, but he chose only two from the original Broadway cast—Slim Thompson, the black man who played the gangster's driver, and Humphrey Bogart. (Duke Mantee was Bogart's first tough guy—and considered his breakthrough role. It was such a big success that he continued playing tough, macho men the rest of his life. He appeared in more than 75 movies and was nominated for an Academy Award for his role in Casablanca in 1942, but he never acted on Broadway again.) Peggy Conklin's role was played by Bette Davis, who'd just won an Academy Award. She was much better known than Peggy, and Hollywood wanted big names. My role was played by a Mexican actress, whose name I've forgotten.

I was disappointed, of course, but understood why they wanted a real Mexican for the movie. At least I was better known to theater agents after being in a

Broadway hit. Brisko and Goldsmith seemed surprised that I'd played a Mexican woman. "Arthur Hopkins does one cock-eyed piece of casting in every show," Brisko told me. "But you're good!" Like other agents, they began sending me out more, so I was able to get jobs here and there. I worked for the WOR-Radio Mystery Theater for a while, but roles on Broadway were still hard to find.

In January 1936, I was hired by a theater in Bridgeport, Connecticut, run by the Work Projects Administration (WPA), a federal program launched in 1935 to provide meaningful work for the unemployed. Like other WPA workers, I received $99.46 a month—and had to pay my room and board out of that. We performed eight shows a week while rehearsing the next production, so it provided some good experience.

In my most memorable part, I played a shady lady in a melodrama. At the play's climax, I was supposed to tear off my black wig to reveal "a cascade of red hair." I wasn't sure how to handle that since my hair wasn't red, but an older actor offered a solution: "Just go to the hardware store and buy the copper powder they use to mix radiator paint." When I brushed that powder into my dark hair, it created a very effective red glow. There was only one problem: my scalp began to turn green. I had to wash that stuff out every night. Since we didn't have portable hair dryers, I spent hours trying to get my hair dry.

The WPA theater in New York City featured terrific actors, but ours was not in the same league. Some of our performers had worked mostly in Vaudeville or the circus. I wasn't learning much from them, and I wasn't happy about living in a cheap hotel far from my current beau, either. When Burleigh Morton, one of our best actors, was hired to run a summer theater at the Chapel Playhouse in Guilford, Connecticut, I signed on.

That July and August, I performed in *Three Men on a Horse* and *Sailor Beware*. I needed a car to get back and forth, so I bought a wonderful MG midget, a fast little sports car that Honor's second husband, Rod Luttgen, found for me. It cost only $250 second-hand, but I had to tap the small trust fund I'd received from Gramp to pay for it. The previous owners—the Collier Brothers who'd started *Colliers* magazine—had raced it in England.

On the Road

In November 1936, I was hired to repeat my role in *The Petrified Forest*, which had just become available to theater companies. I'd have preferred a new part, but playing Paula was still fun. I joined a road company known as "The Subway Circuit" because all the theaters could be reached via the New York City subway.

The producers bought the sets, costumes and props from a warehouse and hired a cast at the minimum wage allowed by Equity, the actor's union. We played the first week in Jersey City, New Jersey (reached by what's known as the PATH train). We performed next in Jackson Heights, Queens, going on to Brighton Beach, at the far end of Brooklyn.

I commuted from my Manhattan apartment to the various theaters. The subway was safe in those days—even at midnight—but the ride to Brighton Beach was more than an hour each way. Fortunately, I had a copy of a big new book (*Gone With the Wind*) to help pass the time. Sometimes Flora Campbell, who also had a role in *The Petrified Forest*, would ride to Brighton Beach with me in my little MG. That was faster and more pleasant than the subway, but I was wary of making the trip alone. I worried that my temperamental little car would break down. It was made in England, so parts were difficult to find.

In this production, the female lead was played by Elaine Barrie. Her mother, who epitomized the pushy stage mom, was always backstage. Almost every night Elaine received beautiful flowers from John Barrymore. Mama (who's real surname was Jacobs) was encouraging this romance—even though Elaine was in her early twenties and Barrymore, 54, had already been divorced three times. The night we closed, mother and daughter flew to Hollywood. Elaine married John Barrymore the next day.

In the summer of 1937, I played Paula again in summer stock productions of *The Petrified Forest*. In June, we were at the Dennis Playhouse on Cape Cod. Oliver Jennings, my beau at the time, decided to come up from New York City for the weekend. He was able to get a train only as far as Providence, so I agreed to pick him up after the show. I told him I'd probably get to Providence by 12 or 12:30.

I was so eager to see Ollie that I didn't think twice about driving the inky black Cape road in my MG. I'd driven only about 20 miles, though, when I went over a bump and the car died—no motor, no lights, nothing. There I sat, all alone, on a deserted highway late at night. I finally noticed a light in a farm house, so I walked there.

When I rang the bell, a woman poked her head out an upstairs window. "What do you want?" she shouted.

"I'd like to use the telephone," I said.

"What for?"

"My car broke down and I'd like to call a garage."

"No garage is open at this time of night."

"But I have to do something," I protested. "I can't just sit out on the road all night."

"Well, my son just got home," she said, softening. "He's pretty good at mechanics so I'll see if he can give you a hand."

The son turned out to be a very nice man as well as a good mechanic. He fixed a broken cable and got the MG's motor running. He was still trying to figure out how to get the lights back on when another car came along and stopped. A black man got out and asked, "Can I help?"

After we explained the situation, he told us he was a Boston policeman, returning from a vacation on Cape Cod with his wife and children. His family was waiting in the car. "May I see your badge?" the Yankee asked.

"Sure," he said. "You're not the first white man to doubt my word." As he pulled out his badge, he said, "It seems to me that the only way I can help this lady get to Providence is to follow her, with my headlights beamed high enough to go over her little car and light up the road ahead."

"That would be wonderful," I said, "but isn't it out of your way?"

"Madame," he replied, "I'm used to helping people and I'll be very glad to help you." I got back in my car and drove on, with his headlights lighting the way. When we reached a garage in Providence, I offered to pay him for rescuing me. He refused to accept any money. "I did it because I wanted to help, not because I wanted a reward," he insisted. "But it wouldn't hurt if you'd write a note to my precinct captain telling him I did a good deed on the road."

"I'll certainly do that," I said, and I did. It wasn't until I looked at a map, though, that I realized just how far he'd traveled out of his way to help a stranger. Later on, he even wrote to thank me for writing to his precinct captain.

In any event, I finally got to the train station and found Ollie. We spent the night in Providence, and arranged to get the car fixed the next day. But I often think about how much has changed since then. That road to Cape Cod is always full of cars, every hour of the day and night, now. And not many people would be as kind to a stranger as that policeman and the man who fixed my car were.

Looking back, I think the whole experience affirmed my optimistic view of human nature. I've always expected people to be kind—and I'm rarely disappointed. I guess that's why I wasn't surprised to read that studies by Martin Seligman, PhD., and other psychologists indicate that optimists live longer than pessimists. I'm no expert, but most of the long-lived people I've known have been optimists.

That summer I also had a small role in *The Virginian*, a play based on Owen Wister's famous story. It had already been made into a movie, starring Gary Cooper, but our leading man was a young actor named Henry Fonda. After a week of rehearsals, we appeared for one week at the Country Playhouse in Westport, Connecticut. The next week we did the same play at the Lawrence Farms Theater in Mt. Kisco, New York. Henry Fonda went on to become a celebrated movie actor, of course, but he was not well known at the time. (His children, Jane and Peter, and his granddaughter, Bridget Fonda, have also had successful movie careers.)

Playing the villain in that cast was an excellent young actor named Harry Bratsburg. I remember Henry Fonda telling him: "Harry, you're a darn good actor, but you'll never get anywhere with that name. For God's sake change it!" Harry did, in fact, change his last name to Morgan and he never stopped working after that. He was best known for his roles in several long-running television series, playing Bill Gannon in *Dragnet,* and Colonel Potter in *M.A.S.H.* He continued to perform for more than 50 years in numerous plays, films and television shows.

The three of us were good friends that summer. After the final curtain, we'd drive to one of the road houses in the area. The men always wore their jeans, boots and cowboy hats from the show. Fonda often put his thumb under his hat and recited one of the play's most famous lines: "When you call me that, smile." All the patrons seemed to know that line and loved hearing him say it. I had a great time with those two actors—especially Harry, who also played Duke Mantee in *The Petrified Forest.* I don't know where Fonda's wife, Frances Brokaw, was during those three weeks, but their daughter Jane was born a few months later. Perhaps the pregnancy kept her home.

Later, I performed at the "Theater by the Sea," in Matunic, Rhode Island. A resident company of students from Yale Drama School was putting on *The Wind in the Rain.* They'd asked a New York agent to send a character actor to play Mrs. McPhee, the middle-aged Scottish woman who ran a boarding house. (Mildred Natwick, who'd been playing such roles, had been called back to New York for a Broadway play.)

Everyone looked startled when I arrived at the theater in my MG. I was wearing a light summer dress and sandals, with my long hair blowing in the wind. "You're not an older woman," someone said. He was right, of course. I was only a few years older than the students, but I had a contract—and that's what mattered. Still, I think I did a good job of making myself look older and heavier—and of speaking with a Scottish accent.

Douglas Montgomery played the lead. He and I also worked together in a production of *The Petrified Forest* in Maplewood, New Jersey. (He played Leslie

Howard's part.) An older man who'd appeared in several Broadway shows, he was quite charming—and a good friend for a time.

When I returned to New York that fall, I continued to call on agents and go for auditions. Since I'd played a Mexican girl, I received calls mostly for roles as a foreigner. One week I auditioned for two parts: a French girl and a Russian drama teacher. I was hired to play the Russian, Madame Karnoff in *Straw Hat*, a play about a summer theater. Although I still didn't get to speak English, I was delighted to get another part on Broadway. After four weeks' rehearsal, we opened at the New Amsterdam Theater on New Year's Eve, 1937.

Once again, Aunt Gertrude celebrated my opening night with flowers—a magnificent orchid corsage. Ollie picked me up at the theater after the show. We'd been invited to a party near Gramercy Park, but it was New Year's Eve. Times Square was so crowded with people waiting for the ball to drop at midnight that we couldn't get across Broadway. We went around the corner to Sardi's Restaurant, ordered a drink and waited for the crowds to thin out. Sardi's was a hangout for theater people, so the radio was tuned to a station that aired reviews of new plays at midnight.

The critic gave *Straw Hat* a terrible review, but went on to say, "An actress named Esther Leeming did a wonderful job as Madame Karnoff. She has excellent stage presence. I'd like to see her perform in something by Eugene O'Neill so we can see what she can really do." I was never able to get a written copy of that review, but it was very exciting to hear it.

Ollie and I finally managed to get a taxi to the party given by Muriel Draper, mother of the well-known tap dancer, Paul Draper. It was a delightful party, with numerous celebrities performing. I was particularly struck by a rendition of "Ol' Man River," sung by my friend, Taylor Gordon. He'd just returned from a tour of Europe, where he'd sung for the royal families. Taylor's specialty was a type of song known as Negro spirituals. (I suppose they're called African-American spirituals today, but Taylor always referred to himself as a Negro.)

Gilbert Seldes, a popular theater critic, invited about twenty party guests back to his home for breakfast. I was wearing a white satin evening gown, with my orchid corsage and Ollie's silk top hat, so I looked like a Hollywood actress. I did feel rather awkward, though, as I left Gilbert's house in broad daylight, still wearing my evening gown and orchids. (Recently, I happened to meet his daughter, Marian Seldes, who performed in *45 Seconds from Broadway* in 2001. She was amused to learn that I'd had breakfast in her home when she was a little girl, asleep upstairs.)

My joy over the perfect opening night was short-lived. *Straw Hat* got such terrible reviews that it closed after only three performances. That was a huge disappointment. Instead of having a steady job on Broadway, I was looking for work all over again. I had a strong belief in myself and my talents as an actress, but I hated being unemployed so often. And I never got used to dealing with rejection—something that even the most successful actors face.

One day I went to three auditions and was rejected for all three parts. At the first audition, they said I was too tall. At the next, I was too big, "much too womanly, my dear." The third part was a circus performer, and I wasn't big enough for that one. So I was too tall, too fat and too thin, all in one day. I began to feel that I just couldn't win.

Most discouraging of all was being rejected solely on my appearance, without being allowed to read for a part. I was 5'8" tall, with broad shoulders and a big chest, so I was too big for the ingénue roles played by my petite contemporaries. Many leading men were only about 5'8", so they didn't want a tall gal on stage with them. I wasn't particularly good looking, but some leading ladies didn't want me around either. One even insisted I be fired from a role for which I'd just been hired. She seemed to think I'd stand out and overshadow her in some way.

The worst rejection I remember came from Robert Edmund Jones, a successful set designer who was actually trying to be helpful. After meeting at a party, we shared a taxi to Grand Central Station, where I caught the train back to New Canaan. During that taxi ride he told me I was "too much of a lady" to succeed in the theater. "The problem is," he continued, "you don't have any special feature, such as flaming red hair, that anyone will remember. You're a good looking gal, but you're not really beautiful—and that's what producers are looking for." Everything he said was so true that I just burst into tears. It took me a long time to get over that.

That year—1938—was my lowest point in the theater. I was sharing a small apartment with Edna Julian, a friend who was also very poor. I remember being home one day with a bad cold. Edna was practicing an oratorio she'd been hired to sing at a church. Over and over, she sang, *The son of God is dead.* It was all so depressing that I finally snapped and yelled, "Please stop that." We both burst out laughing then, because life was about as low as it could get. We felt certain it had to get better after that.

In retrospect, I think I should have studied more—read more plays and learned more parts on my own. My love for the theater made me determined to be a professional actor, but I was probably too busy living—and earning a living—to give it my full attention. It got to the point where I was delighted to be offered a job as a salesgirl. "Great," I thought, "someone actually wants me enough to pay me." I liked working in department stores because they gave me a 20 percent employee discount on all the clothes and other necessities I bought. The jobs I had were not important, so I never made a real commitment—and didn't feel guilty about quitting whenever I found work in the theater.

At one point, I was so hungry for extra cash that I started a sideline business with Taylor Gordon to produce and market several children's games he'd invented. (His ideas stemmed from having traveled with the circus when he was a young man working as John Ringling's valet.) We both had good contacts so we managed to arrange some excellent publicity, but the venture was not successful. I had no regrets, though, because it was fun to work with Taylor—and it taught me a number of valuable lessons.

I learned that it's virtually impossible to start a manufacturing enterprise without substantial capital, which we lacked. I also discovered that hard work and clever publicity are not enough; you also need an appealing product to sell. Taylor was an enthusiastic man with a beautiful singing voice and other talents, but his games weren't very good. I was happy to return to department stores for my extra money.

My pal, Henry Fonda, visited me backstage at The World's Fair of 1939. He also knew Maxine (right) when they were growing up in Omaha, Nebraska.

*For one of my roles in **Railroads on Parade**, I rode sidesaddle in a long, velvet dress.*

In 1938, I played Paula in yet another production of *The Petrified Forest*. I was getting tired of the role by then, but it was better than not working. This was a low-budget operation, so we traveled by bus to theaters in Princeton, Philadelphia and Baltimore. When the script called for machine gun shots off stage, I helped the stage manager fire a set of pistols in rapid succession to imitate a machine gun. It worked well, but by the time we finished shooting we were practically blinded by all the thick smoke backstage.

My next big professional job was at the 1939 New York World's Fair, which featured a Shakespeare Theater and various other shows. I was hired in March to begin rehearsing for *Railroads on Parade*, a History of Transportation of the 20th Century. It was actually a pageant, with a wonderful score by Kurt Weill performed by a full orchestra. I appeared in four very different scenes. In one, I played Mrs. Abe Lincoln. In another, I rode on a canal boat, then made a quick change to play a nun. My favorite part was riding a horse sidesaddle in a cerise velvet riding habit and top hat, but that got pretty hot in the summer. (The Fair continued through October.)

We did four shows a day, seven days a week, so it was a very busy season. The cast of about 40 actors spent so much time together that many of us became good friends. Several also became famous later on. John Lund, for example, was a leading man in dozens of movies in the 40's and 50's. Betty Garrett sang in Broadway musicals from the 40's up to 2001, when she appeared in a revival of *Follies*. Horton Foote went on to write plays and movie scripts, for which he has won a Pulitzer Prize and several Academy Awards. Michael Kidd became a choreographer for top Broadway musicals, including *My Fair Lady* and *Guys and Dolls* (1950 to 1953). Michael both directed and choreographed *Subways are for Sleeping* (1962) among other Broadway shows.

After I gave up professional theater, I still enjoyed following the careers of all the people I'd known when they were just starting out. Quite a few went on to achieve great success on the stage, in movies and on television. I never wanted to return to professional acting, though, because it really is a difficult life—especially when you spend more time looking for work than performing. I also discovered that my greatest pleasure comes from creating a role—not playing one over and over. I still love to act, but I prefer doing it in a more limited way. Working on TV commercials is fun because they're usually shot in one day, then you move on to something else.

Nonetheless, I'm very glad that I had the courage to follow my dream and become a professional actress. If I'd never attempted a theatrical career, I'd have always wondered what might have been—and I'm sure I'd have felt very disappointed in myself and my life.

I've come to believe that it's very important to be flexible—about your goals as well as many other aspects of life. I've also observed, however, that people who never pursue their own special dreams are seldom able to find true happiness.

6

Travels with Belinda

The one person who probably influenced my life the most during my years as an actress in New York City was Belinda Jelliffe. She was the second wife of my Uncle Ely and the step-mother of my cousin Helena Jelliffe Goldschmidt and her four siblings. Their mother, my father's sister, died of a brain tumor in 1916 when I was a little girl. According to those who knew her, Aunt Helena was a brilliant woman who graduated from Barnard College and spoke seven languages. She'd been a great help to her husband in his work—especially in translating letters and articles from abroad into English.

Uncle Ely (Dr. Smith Ely Jelliffe) was a prominent neurologist and psychiatrist. He had so many degrees and accomplishments that I hardly know where to begin. He taught pharmacology at the New York College of Pharmacy and edited the *Journal of Pharmacology* for four years. Later, he was a professor of mental diseases at Fordham University Medical School and edited *The Psychoanalytic Review*. He co-founded the *Journal of Nervous and Mental Diseases* and edited it for 43 years. After studying in Vienna with Sigmund Freud and Carl Jung, he began practicing Freudian psychoanalysis in New York City, where he had many famous patients.

I once asked Uncle Ely how he became interested in psychiatry. "When I was a young doctor in a Brooklyn hospital," he told me, "I saw many patients suffering severe pain that doctors could not explain. Sometimes they'd operate, find nothing wrong, and just sew the patients up again. This was so horrifying to me that I became determined to find out what was causing all this pain." Mental illness and the mind/body connection were not well understood in those days, so he was a pioneer who is sometimes referred to as "the father of psychosomatic medicine."

When I was about eight, Dr. Jelliffe married Belinda Dobson, a woman 26 years younger than he was. Uncle Ely's children and most of our other relatives were opposed to the marriage. His two sons—Ely and Leeming—interrupted their studies at Princeton and Yale in an effort to stop their father from making "an inappropriate marriage," but he'd made up his mind.

Belinda was one of 10 children of a poor Southern tobacco farmer. She was born in a barn, picked cotton as a child and walked to school barefooted. After years of struggle and hard work, she received nurse's training and moved to New York City. For a while, she lived in Harlem with the mother of a black porter she'd met on the train. "I know people say that Dr. Jelliffe married me because I was his best patient," Belinda used to say. "But that suggests that Ely is crazy, too, and he's obviously quite sane."

Despite her lack of education, Belinda had a brilliant mind and a great sense of humor that appealed to Uncle Ely. She was also good looking, with flaming red hair, flashing green eyes and a great sense of style. My mother was one of the few family members who liked and befriended Belinda. Mother found her very amusing, and so did I—though I understood how her blunt talk and sarcastic manner could offend others.

Uncle Ely Jelliffe and his second wife, Belinda, had this photograph taken
shortly after their marriage in 1919.

Belinda had a tendency to be very critical. "For God's sake, stand up straight and hold your stomach in," she'd say to me. I didn't mind that because I knew she was trying to be helpful—and often succeeded. She usually said exactly what she thought, which shocked some people. One day, for example, she walked up to a New York City policeman and said, "For God's sake, what did your mother feed you as a baby? You're the most gorgeous man I've ever seen." The Irish cop blushed, but I couldn't help laughing. Belinda was soon laughing, too.

At the time of Belinda and Ely's marriage, his daughter, Helena, was 14 and the only child still at home. She didn't like this brash young woman replacing her genteel, well-educated mother. Belinda tried to be a good step-mother, but she didn't know how. She'd never received much mothering herself. I understood why she and Helena resented each other, but I liked both women and became good friends with them.

Belinda had been devoted to my mother and even nursed her for a time. She loved helping young people, so she took me (and various others) under her wing. She even made over some of her beautiful clothes to fit me. My life was greatly enhanced by the many interesting and accomplished people she arranged for me to meet. She introduced me to Arthur Hopkins, the director who gave me my first part on Broadway, and to Robert Edmund Jones, the stage designer.

"My niece is interested in an acting career," she told Jones. "What does she have to do to succeed on the stage? Sleep with the stage manager, then work her way up to the director and the producer?"

"No," he insisted, "that's old hat. She just has to be good." I was relieved by his reply, for I'd found Belinda's question rather disconcerting. That's just the way she was, though, and I accepted it because she had such a good heart. Belinda helped me to become more accepting of people who were different. As the years went by, I was very grateful for that.

It was Belinda who introduced me to the black singer, Taylor Gordon, who became a good friend of mine. She also invited me to a dinner party that she and Uncle Ely gave for Essie and Paul Robeson, the famous black actor who'd just starred in *The Emperor Jones,* by Eugene O'Neill. I was thrilled to meet him and hear about his life in the theater.

Another good friend of Belinda's was Grandma Moses, who began painting at 75, then had her first show in New York when she was 80. One day when I was visiting Belinda at her summer home on Lake George, she said, "Let's go see Grandma Moses." We drove to Cambridge, New York, on the Vermont border, where the artist was still living in a big old farm house.

Grandma, as everyone called her, showed us a recent picture of herself sitting on a Victorian sofa with an actor named Monty Woolley. He'd just finished playing Sheridan Whiteside in *The Man Who Came to Dinner* on Broadway, but according to Grandma Moses, "He wasn't a very nice man."

"What do you mean?" Belinda asked.

"Well, I was telling him a story about my father as a young man. Father had named his mare "Closer," so when he took a young lady out in his buggy, he'd say, 'Get up, Closer, get up, Closer.' As I told this story to Monty, he kept edging nearer to me. He wasn't a very nice man!"

Belinda was drawn to people in the arts and always supported their work. She often bought paintings by contemporary artists, including several by Grandma Moses. She made friends on her own as well as through her husband. Dr. Jelliffe was such a brilliant man that successful people in many fields were drawn to him. In the early days of his marriage to Belinda, their home was like a salon. My mother often told me about fascinating people she met there. One she particularly liked was John Barrymore, the leading actor of the time, who was reputed to be a patient of Uncle Ely's.

As Uncle Ely got older, he lost interest in entertaining and gadding about New York. He preferred to stay home writing reviews of new books for his journals. But the Jelliffes continued to be invited to numerous openings, exhibitions and parties, so Belinda often took me along in his place. I was a good companion for her because I was young, laughed at her antics and let her boss me around. In return, she added great fun to my life.

One of Belinda's most interesting friends was the writer, Thomas Wolfe. I'd liked his first novel, *Look Homeward Angel*, so much that I'd fallen a bit in love with him. I was delighted to meet Tom at one of Belinda's parties. He was an enormous man—about six-feet-seven and 250 pounds, I'd guess. In fact, he sometimes complained about being "a giant in a land of pygmies." Tom was quite shy and stuttered badly, which may explain his shyness. Perhaps his mind was going so fast that his voice couldn't keep up, but I thought the stuttering was part of his charm.

At our first meeting, we began talking about Brooklyn. Tom was living in Brooklyn Heights at the time and I knew that area well. He told me he loved Brooklyn because things happened there that couldn't happen anywhere else in the world. "What kind of things?" I asked.

"Well," he began, "I like to walk the deserted streets after working until two or three in the morning. On one of my early morning prowls, I saw a horse-drawn milk wagon pull up to the curb. As I drew closer, I noticed that the driver had wrapped his arms around the horse's neck, and was crying as if his heart would break. My first instinct was to try to comfort him. But I decided it was something private between the man and his horse, and I shouldn't interfere." A horse lover myself, I was rather touched by that story.

When I got to know Tom better, I learned that he was obsessive about his writing. He'd write page after page in long hand, tear off the sheets and throw them on the floor until there was a huge pile. Belinda was always prodding him to use a typewriter and be more orderly, but he never changed. He also ate and drank to excess—and he didn't change those habits, either.

Belinda liked to write, too, and was constantly writing letters. She grew up around Asheville, North Carolina and knew many of the places that Thomas Wolfe wrote about, so she felt a strong connection with him before they met. She wrote him a letter describing how much she admired his writing. When he didn't reply, she wrote again. Finally, he called her late one night and they had a spirited conversation. When she found out he was calling from a New York City phone booth, she said, "We really must meet."

"Well, I'm having lunch with my editor, Max Perkins, tomorrow. Why don't you join us?"

"I'd love to," she told him. That lunch was the beginning of Belinda's long friendship with both men. One day she left a few stories about her childhood on Max Perkins' desk at Scribner's publishing house. Max was intrigued, so he encouraged her to write more stories. Then he used his considerable talents as an editor to shape them into an autobiographical book Scribner's published under the title, *For Dear Life*.

This project made Thomas Wolfe furious. "I can't believe that you—a woman who never finished high school—got Max Perkins to edit your manuscript," he told her. "I have a masters' degree from Harvard, but I still wrote for years before I was able to get an editor like Max and a company like Scribner's to publish a book of mine. Now they're publishing your book! I can hardly believe it!"

Wolfe had a point. Max Perkins was a legendary editor who worked with a long list of illustrious writers, including Ernest Hemingway and F. Scott Fitzgerald. And, in truth, Belinda's little book was not very good. Still, she was very excited about it and could hardly wait for publication in the fall of 1936. She called me one day from their summer home on Lake George. "I'm a nervous wreck," she began. "I just can't spend the summer sitting here waiting for my book to come out." I said something sympathetic, so she continued. "I've decided to go abroad and visit all those people we've entertained in New York and Lake

George all these years. I don't want to travel by myself, though. Do you have any money?"

"Not much," I admitted. Although I was making less than $100 a month at the WPA theater, I'd always tried to save half of my earnings so I'd have a cushion if I lost my job. Because of that, I was able to tell Belinda that I had at least $200 in my savings account.

"That's enough," she said. "The French Line is offering a special fare—only $199 round trip on the *Normandy*. The ship is brand new, but it vibrated so much on the maiden voyage that no one wants to sail on it. That special fare is for third class, but third class is beautiful on the *Normandy*. We don't need money for hotels because I plan to stay with friends everywhere I go. Why don't you join me?"

"Let me think about it," I said. I've always loved the adventure of travel, and I knew it would be fun to go with Belinda. But I wasn't as footloose as she was. First, I'd have to quit my job at the WPA theater. Although I was tired of living in a cheap hotel, I'd agreed to stay on until my summer theater job began in July.

An even bigger concern was how the trip might affect my serious romance with Andrew Carnegie Whitfield. (He was named after his uncle, the legendary steel magnate and philanthropist.) Andy was a handsome, dashing beau and I was quite taken with him, but I had nagging doubts about where our relationship was going. When I told him about Belinda's invitation, part of me was hoping he'd ask me not to go, but he didn't. The next day I called Belinda and said I'd be delighted to join her.

In the meantime, Belinda had learned that John Dewey, a close friend of Uncle Ely's, was going to visit his daughter in Vienna. He'd planned to travel to Europe on a freighter, but Belinda persuaded him to join us on the *Normandy* instead. I'd already met Dr. Dewey, a professor of philosophy at Columbia University, and thought he was a delightful man.

Thomas Wolfe had heard a lot about John Dewey and was eager to meet him. When Belinda mentioned that he was sailing on the *Normandy* with us, Tom invited the three of us to a going-away party. The only other guests were Uncle Ely, Max Perkins and Max's wife, Louise. The evening began with cocktails at Tom's apartment on First Avenue, between 49th and 50th Streets. When we arrived, Tom asked if I knew how to make cocktails.

"Sure," I said. "Would you like me to be your bartender?"

"Please," he replied. "I only know how to drink out of a bottle. I asked my secretary to arrange everything." His secretary had done a good job. Next to the glasses lined up on the kitchen counter, I found all the ingredients for a popular cocktail called an Old Fashioned—orange slices, Maraschino cherries, sugar lumps, bitters and Bourbon. I was so much younger than all the others that I felt honored to make their drinks.

After passing the cocktails, I began to look around. The first thing I noticed was the beautiful view of the East River from the living room. I knew from reading *Of Time and the River* how much Tom liked rivers. Then I happened to look up and see the words "Happy New Year, Tom" written on the ceiling. I couldn't resist asking about that.

"I had a New Year's Eve party a few months ago," Tom explained. "One of my friends noticed how much soot had accumulated on the ceiling and said, 'Tom, you're so tall, I bet you could write on the ceiling with your fingers.' So I did." We were all amused by that, as Tom was very tall. And most of the buildings in New York were still heated by coal, so soot was a problem everywhere in the city.

It was a wonderful party. Cocktails were followed by a delicious dinner at a French restaurant around the corner. Later, we were all invited to the Perkins' lovely Kips Bay townhouse for an after-dinner drink. It was a warm spring evening, so we sat on a porch overlooking a garden shared by all the brownstones on that block. I spent most of the evening listening with fascination to the spirited conversation.

Not yet 25, I felt immature and ignorant among such brilliant people. I didn't learn their precise ages until later, but I knew all four men were at the top of their professions: Dr. Jelliffe, 70, was a prominent psychiatrist, John Dewey, 77, was a world famous philosopher and educator, Max Perkins, 52, was an important book editor, and Thomas Wolfe, 36, was a best-selling novelist. At 44, Belinda was less accomplished, but she was savvy enough to hold her own in the conversation. I wish I could have recorded their discussion, for I don't remember a single word that was spoken that evening.

Running Away to Europe

We sailed on the *Normandy* the next day. A number of friends came to see us off, including Tom Wolfe and Andy Whitfield. Andy brought me a dozen gardenias. I asked the steward to put them into cold storage so I was able to wear a fresh one every night at dinner. On the last evening, I used the remaining gardenias to make a lei, which I pinned around the neck of a black dress. I guess I really stood out, for it seemed like everyone in the salon wanted to dance with me that night. I had a marvelous time.

Belinda, John Dewey and I ate our dinners at a table for four that included Dr. Myrtle McGraw, a psychologist who'd been overseeing one of John's educational experiments with identical twins. (One twin was taught under the Dewey system of "progressive" education, the other under the regular system.) Myrtle and Belinda disliked each other immediately. It was partly jealousy, I suppose, because both women seemed to be competing for Dr. Dewey's attention.

Dr. McGraw was engaged to Rudolf Melina, an engineer from Bell Labs who'd been hired to check the ship's vibrations during the crossing with a special machine. He and a colleague named Tweedale (called "Tweedy Pie" by Belinda) were traveling first class, courtesy of The French Line. Every evening they came down to our lowly third-class dining room to escort us up to first class so we could go dancing on the top deck. That was a special treat for us all.

One day, Dr. Dewey was sitting on a deck chair, next to a very attractive young woman with red hair. A single blanket was covering the two of them. At dinner that night, Belinda asked, "John, who's your lady friend you were so cozy with on deck?"

"She's one of my students from Columbia," he said. "She came over to me and we had a very pleasant conversation."

"John," Belinda teased, "are you sure it wasn't more than just conversation?"

"Well," he admitted, "she was good enough for the purpose."

Belinda exploded at that. "What purpose, for God's sake?" she asked.

"*The* purpose," he replied, but that was all he'd say. Belinda later commented on how remarkable John was for "a man who's almost seventy." He was actually 77, but we didn't know that until we received an invitation to his 80th birthday party. He really was a remarkable man.

For years, Uncle Ely had gone abroad almost every summer for a medical congress or to study with Freud and Jung. Belinda usually accompanied him and they always traveled first class on French liners. The head purser on most of these voyages was a man named Villard, who later became head purser on the *Normandy*. When Monsieur Villard learned that Belinda was aboard his ship, he invited us to tea.

We were sitting in the Normandy's glorious lounge, enjoying our tea, when Belinda spoke up. "Monsieur Villard," she said, "the doctor and I have made many crossings with you—on the *Paris* and the *Ile de France*. We've sat at your table and enjoyed your company, but I'll never travel first class again."

The purser drew himself up and asked, "What's the matter, Mrs. Jelliffe? Do you have objections to this ship?"

"Oh, no," she said. "It's just that we have far more interesting people in third class than you have up here. We have artists, writers, directors of art galleries and John Dewey, the philosopher. All you have is a bunch of boring businessmen. And the beards up here are only this long," she added mischievously, indicating a spot just below her chin. "In third class, we have beards down to here," she said, pointing to her stomach. Belinda was referring to two rabbis we'd seen on deck, with their long beards blowing out to sea, but she was just having fun with him.

Another passenger on the *Normandy* was a man named Bignoux, who owned art galleries in New York and Paris. When he heard that John Dewey was aboard, he invited all of us to a delicious luncheon in the Grill Room on the top deck. Bignoux was eager to curry favor with Dr. Dewey because of John's friendship with Albert Barnes, a Philadelphia millionaire who happened to be a major art collector.

John Dewey apparently had a natural talent for choosing the best paintings even though, by his own admission, he knew "very little about art." That didn't seem to matter to Barnes, who bought almost everything John recommended. Today, the Barnes Collection, which includes hundreds of French Impressionists, is world-famous. Housed in the Barnes Mansion in the Philadelphia suburb of Merion, it's now open to the public on a limited basis.

I didn't know anything about Albert Barnes at the time. I was just delighted to be sharing such an elegant luncheon. The main dish was a delicious French bouillabaisse—the first I'd ever had. It was a peak experience on a glorious crossing.

While we were dancing on our last evening aboard ship, a man came around selling chances on the precise time we'd drop anchor in Southampton harbor. (In those days, large ships had to anchor off-shore, with small lighters taking the passengers into the landing pier.) Belinda bought three tickets for five dollars, giving one to me and another to John.

The next morning, as we were waiting on deck to disembark, Mr. Tweedale came up and said, "Mrs. Jelliffe, they're looking all over for you. You won the raffle last night!"

"Oh, don't kid around, Tweedy," she said. "It's much too early in the morning for that sort of thing."

"I'm not kidding," he said. "The raffle was just in first class, so they've been trying to find your name on the first-class passenger list. The prize is a hundred dollars." That was half the price of our round-trip passage!

"Oh, isn't that wonderful?" said Belinda. "I think I'll give the money to Alexandre. He'll certainly need it." She was referring to Alexandre Hellman, a brilliant young pianist and one of her protégés. A Jewish refugee from Russia,

Alexandre was quite handsome. I don't know what kind of relationship they had, but I think Belinda was in love with him. She rarely invited me to join her when meeting Alexandre. In fact, Alexandre was probably the main reason Belinda was so eager to go to Europe at that particular time. Soon after our arrival, he had his first solo piano concert at Wigmore Hall in London—an important step in his career as a professional musician. Belinda didn't want to miss that concert.

After she collected her prize, we got off the ship and went through immigration. I was stopped by a customs officer who asked, "What's that tucked under your arm?" It was a bottle of Scotch that Tom Wolfe had given us just before we sailed from New York. I'd forgotten all about it until we packed our bags. "You can't bring in whiskey," the agent said, "unless you pay twelve and six duty."

That set Belinda off. She said everything she could think of to hang on to that bottle. "Thomas Wolfe gave us that bottle of whiskey," she began. "He bought it in America for much less than twelve and six. He'd just die if he knew you were taking it away; he really loves whiskey." She went on and on in a loud voice, but the agent—who'd probably never even heard of Thomas Wolfe—was undeterred.

"It's going to the Queen's Warehouse," he insisted. "Any time you decide to pay twelve and six, you can have it back." He gave us an unbelievable document, full of official seals, describing the bottle that had been impounded in the Queen's Warehouse. As he finished the paperwork, the man suddenly looked at Belinda and asked, "What's in that box you're carrying?"

"Chocolates," she replied. "Have one!" The fancy box of candy was a bon voyage present from a friend of Belinda's. "We'd better keep these until we get to London," she'd told me. "If no one invites us to lunch, we can sit on a park bench and eat chocolates." She didn't realize they were also on the list of forbidden items. Perhaps the customs agent was content to impound one item or simply reluctant to set Belinda off again, but he let her keep the chocolates.

I find myself remembering that incident whenever I have to deal with officious bureaucrats. Some act as if it's sinful to crack a smile, but I've found that they're usually more flexible if you're friendly and amusing like Belinda. They're also more lenient when you appear to be ignorant of the rules (as we clearly were) than if you're trying to get around them.

After we cleared customs, we boarded the train to London, sitting opposite two very proper ladies wearing flowered hats and gloves. "I think it's the Garden Club ladies from Philadelphia," Belinda muttered under her breath. Then, in a loud voice, she complained about the customs agents, adding that Thomas Wolfe would be so annoyed if he knew they'd confiscated his whiskey. The two ladies gave her a disdainful look, but didn't say a word until it was time for lunch. As the four of us ate together, they gradually became friendlier.

"When you first got on the train," one lady admitted later, "we thought you were both drunk." They didn't believe anyone would talk like Belinda unless she'd had a few drinks. Ironically, Belinda never drank anything but an occasional glass of wine. I was never embarrassed by her behavior, though, because she always made me laugh. I love to laugh and I believe it has contributed to my longevity.

In London, we were guests of C. K. Ogden, a good friend of Uncle Ely's who'd stayed with the Jelliffes in New York several times. Ogden was a Professor of English at Cambridge University and the inventor of what he called "Basic English." He believed you needed to learn only 850 English words to understand the language. As proof of his theory, he'd been translating many classic books into those 850 basic words.

Professor Ogden put us up in a small bed-and-breakfast hotel behind the British Museum. A resident of the same hotel, he owned a town house across the street. He used the house primarily to store his collections (of books, records, photographs, antiques, etc.) and to conduct audio experiments. He invited us over one evening for a demonstration. Wheeling a large phonograph into the marble hallway, he trained the huge speakers up the circular staircase. (This was before hi-fidelity.) After putting on a record, he turned the volume up high. From our seats in the living room, it sounded like we were listening to the symphony in a concert hall. That was fantastic!

It was a beautiful May evening, so Ogden opened the French windows overlooking his little garden. When he played a recording of a nightingale singing, a real nightingale answered from the garden. It was very eerie, but he knew exactly what he was doing. Each time we admired a recording, he'd giggle and put on another, saying, "Listen to this." He was having great fun.

Oggie, as Belinda called him, was a good friend of George Bernard Shaw and James Joyce. He played a recording he'd made of Joyce reading from his new book, *Work in Progress*. It was wonderful to hear that great Irish voice reading his own work. Next, he put the same recording on another machine that played everything backwards, making it sound like Joyce was speaking Chinese. That was very funny.

I was writing post cards in the hotel lobby one morning when Ogden came down. "You've got to do something more interesting than that," he announced. "Come with me." He was an older man and our host, so I dutifully went along to his office where he published books in Basic English. As we entered, I was startled to see a marble statue of the Greek goddess, Nike—with a list of those 850 words clipped to her hand.

Ogden busied himself around the office a while, then announced, "Now we're going to an auction of rare books." It turned out to be an auction of manuscripts by Arnold Bennett, a well-known English writer who died in 1931. Bennett, I learned, had written all of his novels, short stories, plays and journals in long hand. He wrote in a beautiful script, with few corrections. When he finished, he had each original manuscript bound in handsome Moroccan leather. Some of those manuscripts sold that day for hundreds of English pounds each.

I'd never been to such an auction and found it fascinating. The room was dead quiet, with a group of elegant men sitting around a big oval table. (I was the only woman in the room.) As the books were presented, the men kept their eyes on them, never even glancing at each other. I studied everyone carefully because Ogden had told me to watch for bidding signals. It was all so subtle—a wink or a slight finger movement—that I had a hard time detecting their bids.

I didn't know until we left that Ogden was also bidding. He ended up buying a packet of letters between Arnold Bennett and Joseph Conrad, the author of *Lord Jim,* among other popular adventure stories. The two had corresponded for many years—and Bennett had kept copies of all his own letters as well as those from Conrad. Taking the packet, we returned to the office. "Now, why don't you have a spot of tea and look at these letters," Ogden suggested. "I have to meet with some Malaysians doing a translation of Basic English."

A clerk seated me at a desk, then asked, "China or India?" It took me a while to understand that he was asking what kind of tea I wanted. I drank my tea and ate a couple of biscuits while spending an extraordinary hour reading those letters. The correspondence started before the two men ever met and continued into their sunset years. Bennett's letters were more like intellectual essays, while Conrad's were full of sea and adventure stories. As both men became famous, the tone of their letters changed. I felt very privileged to be able to read them.

When Ogden's meeting ended, the letters were shoved back into a manila envelope. He insisted on taking me to lunch at Simpson's on the Strand because "That's where every American wants to go for roast beef." Since Belinda had gone off with Alexandre, I was delighted to have such good company. Before lunch was over, I was calling my new friend, Oggie. I'd learned that older men enjoy having attractive young women speak to them in intimate terms, instead of calling them "Mister."

That was the first time I'd met Ogden, who struck me as an eccentric little man at first. He was a lifelong bachelor almost twice my age so I didn't think we had much in common. I soon realized, however, that age and different interests don't really matter. I kept an open mind and grew to like him so much that I made sure that we continued to get together on my subsequent trips to London.

Several years later, an article in *Life Magazine* listed C. K. Ogden as one of the ten most famous English mystics. I think he was considered a mystic because of his esoteric interests. By the time he died in 1957, he'd distinguished himself in many fields—as a linguist, philosopher, psychologist, editor, art critic and antique dealer, as well as the inventor of Basic English.

My time with C. K. Ogden was certainly more pleasant than my next appointment. A man I'd met on board ship invited me to discuss a role in a movie he was producing. Eager to find work as an actor, I agreed to meet him at his apartment. I'd been there only a few minutes, though, when he propositioned me. I was so shocked that I hardly had time to say, "I'm not interested," as I jumped up and left. I never found out if he really was a producer, but I was more skeptical after that. And I'm pleased to report that I never had such an experience again.

We stayed only four or five days in London because we'd been offered a ride to Paris and Geneva with Elizabeth Allen, an English friend of Belinda's. She was on her way to a secretarial job at the League of Nations and wanted to leave at 6 am to catch the 10 o'clock ferry at Dover. "Bring your bags over to my place the night before," she advised us. "You'll never get a taxi that early in the morning."

She lived way out in a suburb, so we took a taxi to her house and stored our bags in her car. The next morning we got up before dawn and went in search of coffee and a taxi, in that order. Around 5 am, an English bobby came up and asked, "What are you two ladies doing out here so early in the morning?"

"We're trying to find a place to buy a cup of coffee," said Belinda.

"Nothing's open at this hour," he insisted.

"What about Lyons Corner House? Isn't that open all night?"

"Yes, but they don't allow ladies to come in at this time of morning."

"Why not?" Belinda asked. "What's the matter with ladies at this time of morning?"

He gave us a strange look. After some hesitation, he said, "Ladies of uncertain morals are usually the only ones about at this time of day."

"Well," Belinda answered, "my morals aren't too certain at five o'clock in the morning, but they'd be a lot more certain if I could get a cup of coffee." The poor bobby didn't know how to respond to that, so Belinda just asked for directions to the underground. We didn't see any taxis, but London's subway was running so we rode it out to Miss Allen's house.

When we arrived, she said, "Oh, good. I've had my egg and tea, so we're ready to go." Belinda got terrible headaches when she didn't have her morning coffee, but Miss Allen wouldn't let us stop until we got to Dover—about a three-hour drive. After putting the car on the ferry, we found a little hotel where we finally ate breakfast.

It was very rough crossing the English Channel that day. Most passengers got seasick. Belinda and I stayed in the fresh air on deck, so we were OK. But Miss Allen went down into the cabin. When she emerged as the ferry docked in France, she was absolutely green. "I don't think I'll be able to drive," she said. "I feel awful—and I've never driven on the right side of the road."

"I have my license with me, so I could drive," I offered.

"First," Belinda told Miss Allen, "we'll go over to that café and get you a glass of brandy. That'll make you feel better." To my surprise, the brandy worked, so Miss Allen decided to drive after all. We rode along for an hour or two before stopping for lunch at a charming little restaurant. We had a simple meal—an omelet made from fresh eggs, a gorgeous salad of fresh picked greens, and crusty French bread—but I don't think I've ever tasted anything more delicious.

(Now that I've traveled extensively in France, I believe that their excellent cuisine is partly due to their use of very fresh ingredients. I remember one evening when I ordered brook trout at a small country restaurant near Fontainebleau. I was growing impatient by the time the fish was served, but oh what a light, tasty trout that was! I learned later that the owner had caught the fish in the stream behind the Inn while we waited. The French view dining as an experience to be savored, so they're more willing to wait for a meal to be prepared properly.)

After lunch we drove on to Paris. Miss Allen stayed with friends, while Belinda and I stayed with my cousins, Dorothy and Phillipe Le Corbeiller. They had visited the Jelliffes' summer home on Lake George, so Belinda knew them well. Three days later, we were back in the car on our way to Geneva. It was a long drive, so we had to stop overnight in a French inn.

Miss Allen looked like one of those British matrons you see in the movies—a chunky, middle-aged woman wearing flat shoes, a tweedy suit and a pot of a hat. After helping us unload the luggage, she drove the car around back to the garage. In the meantime, we went to the desk to get our rooms. Belinda did not speak French, so I did all the talking.

When we came down for dinner later, we were ushered into the beautiful dining room with great ceremony. I noticed that the waiters were all nudging each other and bowing to Belinda. The three of us conversed in English, of course, but

I did all the ordering in French. The entire staff was very attentive as they served us a delicious meal.

The next morning, I went to the desk to settle the bill. "Would you mind telling me who Madame is?" the cashier asked.

"Not at all. She's Mrs. Smith Ely Jelliffe."

"Is she someone very important?"

"No, I'm afraid not." It turned out that they thought Belinda must be an English duchess or a very rich matron because she was traveling with her private chauffeur and a French-speaking secretary. Belinda roared with laughter when I reported all this in the car.

"Oh, my God," she said. "You two are educated—you know how to speak French and drive a car. I'm just a poor, dumb American, so I kept my mouth shut. And they thought I was the important one! That's so funny!" The moral of that story, I think, is that appearances are not always what they seem—and it often pays to keep quiet.

We drove south through Burgundy, then over to Switzerland, where none of us had ever been. We spent a couple of days touring Geneva, but we didn't know anyone there so it wasn't very memorable. Fortunately, our tickets on the *Normandy* included a rail pass for free third-class travel on European trains. Belinda and I took a train back to Paris where we stayed with Dorothy and Phillipe again. They'd moved from Ile St.-Louis and were living in the same large artist's studio that Dorothy and Honor had shared in the early twenties. Located on the Boulevard Raspail, it had bedrooms on both floors, so there was plenty of space for the four of us.

One day, Belinda turned on the radio and heard a man we soon learned was Adolph Hitler. Although she didn't understand German, she said, "The sound of his voice sends chills down my spine. There's hate in that voice and death here in Paris. I can't stay." This was in June 1936, when Hitler was not well known outside of Germany. Belinda didn't know anything about him, but she returned to London the next day.

I stayed on in Paris another week. My charming old friend, Olivier Regnault had come up from Majorca to see me. He'd been a good friend of my brother's so I felt very sisterly toward him, but he was French and couldn't help flirting. He was a perfect escort, though, who always made sure that I had a good time in Paris.

(That was the last time I saw Dorothy and Philippe in France. After World War II, they immigrated to this country with their son, Jean Patrice. Phillipe had been working as a well-paid engineer for the French government, so I was shocked to learn how much deprivation they'd suffered during the war. Phillipe later became a professor of physics at Harvard so we got together regularly. I grew very fond of their son who settled in New York.)

When it was time to rejoin Belinda, I took the train to Calais. From there, I booked passage on the channel steamer to England. On the boat, I met Roger Diplock, a handsome young Englishman who was returning from a visit to Majorca. It was the beginning of a very long friendship. (In fact, his children are still good friends of mine.)

Roger worked on the editorial staff of a London magazine. He was fascinated with America and disappointed that I didn't use much American slang or speak with a strong American accent. (Being a mimic, I couldn't help adopting an English accent while staying in London.) I introduced Roger to Belinda, though, and she gave him the full treatment–speaking with her North Carolina accent and using every bit of colorful slang she could remember.

At the time Roger was still single, so he took me out a few times while Belinda was with Alexandre. What I enjoyed most were the days we went horseback riding. I especially remember one ride he arranged that took us through some duke's estate. The rhododendrons were in full bloom and it was truly glorious! Roger and I corresponded for a number of years after that.

At the end of another week in London, Belinda and I rode to Newcastle on a train called The Flying Scotsman. At Newcastle, we boarded a ship to Oslo, Norway—the next place friends had invited us to visit. That voyage to Oslo was one of the most beautiful I've ever taken. It was mid June, and we were so far north that the sun never really set. It just dipped below the horizon and came right back up again. All the passengers spent the night stretched out in deck chairs, watching the colorful sky. It was the first time I'd experienced daylight in the middle of the night, so I found it very exciting.

In Oslo we stayed with a lovely couple, Olga and John Larsen. Before marrying John, Olga had spent a number of years as Belinda's housekeeper in New York—and they'd grown very fond of each other. Both Larsens spoke excellent English. They lived in a beautifully furnished apartment on a hill overlooking a fjord. I had to do most of my sightseeing in Oslo alone, though, because it was very hot and Belinda refused to leave the apartment.

Belinda had heard so many women begin a statement with, "My doctor told me..." that she'd begun using that phrase as a handy excuse. "My doctor told me I should never go sightseeing in the heat," she said. "My doctor told me to stay inside and keep cool on hot days." One evening, Olga asked her husband, who was stretched out on the couch, to help with the dishes. "Oh no," John replied. "My doctor told me I should never wash dishes." We were all amused by that.

I was able to get relief from the heat because John took me swimming almost every day. Most of the Norwegians swam in the nude, but I wasn't used to that. John did know a few beaches where the swimmers wore bathing suits, so he took me to those.

Our next stop was Denmark, where Belinda had other friends she wanted to visit. Still using our pre-paid ticket, we got on the train in Oslo and rode to Helsingborg in southern Sweden. We remained on the train as it boarded the ferry over to Helsingor, Denmark. The train's large red spittoons had Belinda's initials, BJ, on them. Knowing that she liked to take souvenir ash trays from hotels and restaurants, I teased her about adding a spittoon to her collection. I think she was tempted, but it was just too big—and too dirty.

We'd planned to stay on the train all the way to Copenhagen, where Fleming Thorlasius was supposed to meet us. His uncle was a psychiatrist and an old friend of Uncle Ely's. Fleming had lived in the Jelliffes' house while working in New York for several years, so I'd gotten to know him then. Belinda also knew his mother, who'd visited her in Lake George. As the ferry approached the Danish shore, we returned to our seats on the train. Suddenly, Fleming appeared like a whirlwind, saying, "Come; you're going to get off here." He pulled our suitcases off the rack, and rushed us off the train. It was only about a five-minute stop, so he had to run through the train to find us.

Once we were settled in Fleming's car, he explained the change in plans. It happened to be June 22, the summer solstice. According to Danish tradition, romantic couples spend that night on the beach, building bonfires to keep the witches away. Fleming had just become engaged, so it was important for him to spend this romantic evening with his fiancée. By picking us up early, he was able to drop us at his mother's home and still go out with his girl friend.

Fleming and his mother lived in Humlebec, a charming little town on the Danish Riviera between Copenhagen and Elsinore. Their home was set back from the sea, but it was only a short walk from there to the beach. The bathing pavilion had separate bath houses for men and women, with a large wooden barrier between them. In the morning, I put on a robe and walked to the ladies' bath house. Once inside, I removed my robe and walked down protected steps into the water. Thus, I was able to swim nude in the warm Baltic, without being seen. It was another new experience—one of the things that makes foreign travel so stimulating.

After my morning swim, I walked back to our hosts' little house, which had a sod roof with flowers growing all over it. We all ate a tasty breakfast on an outside patio before Fleming went off to work. He never drove his car during the week; he'd just ride his bicycle to the station, where he'd catch the train to his job in Copenhagen.

One day Belinda and I also took the train into Copenhagen. Mrs. Thorlasius's sister, the widow of Uncle Ely's psychiatrist friend, entertained us at lunch. That evening we went to the famous Tivoli Gardens in the middle of Copenhagen. To me, it seemed like a combination of Coney Island, Broadway and Carnegie Hall. We passed through one area full of carnival-type games where young people competed for prizes. Next, we watched a ballet of Hans Christian Anderson fairy tales on an outdoor stage. That fascinated me because the sets and costumes were based on illustrations by Kay Nielson—the same ones I had in a book at home.

We stopped for coffee in an elegant restaurant that had an open air terrace on the edge of the gardens. As we sipped our drinks, we heard Lauritz Melchoir singing in an outdoor concert hall nearby. Born in Copenhagen, he was already a famous tenor at the Metropolitan Opera in New York. (Later, during my marriage, I heard him sing in many Wagnerian operas at the Met.) Hearing him sing in Tivoli Gardens in his native land really capped a beautiful evening.

The next night, Fleming and his mother hosted a small dinner party in their home. One of the guests was Fleming's good friend, Thorkield Monk-Anderson, who'd also worked at a bank in New York for a while. I'd gone out with him occasionally during that time, so I was pleased to see him again. After dinner, Thorkield asked to borrow Fleming's car so he could take me to a little road house in the area.

"No," said Fleming, "I don't use my car for such short runs. But you can borrow my bicycle and Faity can borrow the cook's bicycle." We still had many hours of daylight left—and the road house was only about two miles away—so we accepted his offer. I'd never had a date on a bicycle before, but it was great fun to pedal through the countryside that evening with Thorkield. Our destination was a rather intimate little club featuring a young Danish pianist and comedian. His pantomime was so magnificent that it didn't matter what language he spoke. I was so amused and impressed by his clever act that I made note of his name: Victor Borge.

I learned later that his real name was Borge Rosenbaum, and that he was forced to leave Denmark when the Germans invaded in 1940. Victor Borge soon made a name for himself in this country, where he had a long, successful career. (He received an award for lifetime achievement in the arts at the Kennedy Center in 1999.) Whenever I saw Victor Borge perform on TV or in his one-man show on Broadway, I was amused to recall that I'd met him during a date on a bicycle in Denmark. Looking back, I realize that I'd have missed a very special experience if I hadn't been adventurous enough to hop on that bicycle.

On Sunday, Fleming took his car out and drove us around to visit castles and other places of interest. One of the high points was a tour of Prince Hamlet's castle at Elsinore, the model for William Shakespeare's play, *Hamlet*. Like many Shakespearean plays, it's based on real people and events. We had a good time imagining scenes from the play as we toured the castle.

From Denmark we returned to London, taking a train to the coast, then a ferry over to England. This time we landed at Harwich, a port much closer to London. A few days later, we took the train to Southampton and boarded the *Normandy* to return to America.

The ship's vibrations had not improved, but were much worse in the expensive cabins. Whenever we had a drink in first class, the vibrations caused the liquid to rise up in the middle of the glass like a little fountain. But down below in third class, the vibrations were minimal so neither of us got seasick. I already knew that you don't have to spend a lot of money to have a good time, but it was fun to discover that budget travel is sometimes better than first class.

I love boats and the sea, so I was content to relax in a deck chair as we sailed back across the ocean. After all those busy weeks abroad, it was nice to catch my breath and relive a fantastic experience. I felt very grateful to Belinda and to all our generous hosts.

7

Love and Romance

When the *Normandy* docked in New York, I was pleased to find Andy Whitfield waiting. He took me out to dinner that night and seemed very happy to see me after the long weeks apart.

Andy was my first serious beau. Frank Webster, the man I met on board ship when I was 19, was my first love, but that was a short romance. My relationship with Andy was different. I met him at a party in Connecticut during the summer of 1935. A group of us decided to go out on Andy's speed boat after a cocktail party. We didn't consider how much we'd had to drink—or realize how dangerous it was. On the way out of the marina, we hit another boat and Andy actually fell overboard. We managed to fish him out of the water and steer the boat back to the dock, but no one wanted to ride in a car with Andy after that.

They were probably the smart ones, but I stayed with Andy. That's when our romance was born. Later that summer, we took his boat from the marina in Connecticut to Long Island, where we had lunch with his family at their beautiful summer home in Southampton. It was all very nice, but I had the feeling that his parents did not regard me as a suitable match for Andy. Acting was not considered a very reputable career in those days, and I certainly wasn't in the same social strata as Andy's aunt, who lived in the Carnegie Mansion on Fifth Avenue. (That magnificent building, 2 East 91 Street, now houses the Cooper Hewitt National Design Museum.)

Our romance continued, nonetheless, through the winter and into spring. Among other interests, Andy and I shared a love of horses. His family had another lovely home in Middleburg, Virginia, an area that's known for fox hunting. He'd ridden all his life and was an expert horseman. Middleburg is not far from Warrenton, where I'd gone to boarding school, so Andy knew many of my friends and classmates. Riding had been one of my favorite school activities.

Andy also had a spirit of adventure that I found very appealing. One night, for example, we went out with a group of friends that included my brother, Howard.

In the course of conversation, someone mentioned that the Hindenburg, the largest airship ever made, was due to arrive in Lakehurst, New Jersey, around 5 o'clock that morning. We all thought it would be exciting to see it land after its first transatlantic flight from Europe.

It was then about 2 a.m. "I have my car here," said Andy, looking at his watch. "I think we can make it to Lakehurst before the Hindenburg arrives. Let's go." We all piled into Andy's big Packard and took off. The traffic was very light at that hour, so it was a fast trip. As we approached the air field, we noticed a long line of parked cars stretching back from the hangar.

Andy ignored the parked cars and kept driving. He had a set of silver wings on his car that allowed him to park at the private airport where he kept his own plane. Because of that, we were able to drive up to within 100 yards of the landing area. We could see the Hindenburg, which was more than 800 feet long, floating down as we approached. The moon was just setting and the sun was beginning to rise, so the huge silver airship reflected the pale moon on one side and the bright orange sun on the other. It was a magnificent sight that I'll never forget!

We all jumped out of the car and raced toward the reception area. We arrived just in time to see dozens of well-dressed people coming down the stairs. Some of the women were wearing beautiful corsages they'd probably received at a bon voyage party. We found it hard to believe that they'd been in Europe only two or three days earlier. (This was in 1936, several years before transatlantic passenger flights began. The jet planes we take for granted came along much later.)

We were all thrilled to witness that piece of history. On May 6, 1937—the first trip of the following season—the Hindenburg caught fire just as it was landing in New Jersey and blew up, killing 35 of the 97 men and women on board. That horrible disaster—which put an end to that type of transatlantic travel—made me feel even more privileged to have seen the marvelous airship up close on a beautiful spring morning in May, 1936.

The Hindenburg adventure was one of our more memorable dates, but Andy and I had many good times together. I knew he was a heavy drinker, but we all drank a lot in those days, so I didn't give it much thought. What worried me more was his wealthy, imposing family. I was struggling to pay the rent on a small apartment, while his family had luxurious homes all over—in New York City, Palm Beach, Southampton and Middleburg.

Andrew Carnegie Whitfield was my first serious beau.

Andy proposed to me at Christmas, 1935, anyway. I was thrilled and delighted to accept. He said we'd have to keep it quiet for a while, though, so I think he knew his family wouldn't approve. Soon after our "secret engagement," Andy's employer—a new company called International Business Machines (IBM)—sent him to Binghamton, New York, for training. As a result, I didn't see him for a couple of months. That's when my doubts about our future began.

Afterwards, I started running away. First, I took the job at the WPA Theater in Bridgeport, CT., which made it more difficult for us to get together. Then I went off to Europe with Belinda for six weeks. I think I was testing Andy and secretly wanted him to pursue me, but he never did. Deep down, though, I now suspect that I instinctively knew he wouldn't be a very good husband. He'd been very spoiled by his family, among other considerations.

Three days after Belinda and I returned from Europe, I reported to work at the summer theater in Guilford, Connecticut. Andy's job at IBM was his first after graduating from Princeton, so he was eager to prove himself. He worked very hard during the week—and I had performances on weekends. Our conflicting schedules didn't leave us much time to see each other.

One Saturday that fall, I gave a cocktail party at Max Cushing's barn in Connecticut to celebrate the publication of Belinda's book, *For Dear Life*. I asked Howard to be my co-host because Andy said he couldn't make it. About 30 people came, including Max Perkins and Tom Wolfe. I met Tom at the train station and drove him to the Perkins house, where he stayed for the weekend. Tom had great difficulty folding his tall frame into my little MG, but Max thought my car was much more sensible than the huge Cadillac his wife drove. "I see no reason to climb into a hearse just to go out for a pack of cigarettes," he said with a sly smile.

It was a wonderful party and Belinda was very pleased, but I was disappointed that Andy didn't come. I now suspect that he stayed away because his mother had arranged for him to meet her god-child, a charming girl named Betty Halsey. She was one of my classmates at The Brearley School, and we'd been good friends at the age of eight, nine and ten. The Halseys were very close to the Whitfields, so both sets of parents were encouraging that romance.

I was still in love with Andy and continued to see him off and on. I was still dedicated to the theater, too, but the more acting I did away from New York, the less I saw of Andy. It gradually became clear that his interest in me had cooled. His engagement to Betty Halsey was announced the next spring and they were married in August 1937. I wasn't really surprised, but I was heartbroken, nonetheless.

Several months after their marriage, I began hearing from mutual friends that Andy was not very happy. No one really knows what goes on in another couple's marriage, of course, but he was drinking heavily and seemed depressed. His parents had been so concerned about his drinking that they'd offered to buy him a small plane if he'd stop drinking for a year. He got his plane, but he wasn't able to give up alcohol permanently.

In the fall of 1938, Andy went out to Roosevelt Field on Long Island, climbed into his plane and headed out over the Atlantic Ocean. He was never heard from again. His disappearance was in all the papers, of course, because he was the nephew of Andrew Carnegie. The Coast Guard spent days searching for his plane. His family hoped he'd just gotten lost on the way to his sister's summer place in the Canadian wilderness, but no trace of Andy or his plane was ever found.

Some of our friends thought I knew where Andy had gone, but I was just as baffled—and as heartsick—as everyone else. Some time later, a bartender at one of our favorite places took me aside. "Your friend Andy came in alone the night before he disappeared," he told me. "He seemed despondent, so I asked him if anything was wrong. After a few drinks, he told me, "*I married the wrong girl.*"

I don't know if that was true—or if it had any bearing on Andy's disappearance. Either way, it was a tragic loss that made me very sad. In retrospect, I believe the whole experience made me wary of alcoholics, but I was too grief-stricken to think about that at the time.

Unlike my beautiful sisters, I'd never had a lot of beaux. Lee was only 14 when her future husband, Charlie Minor, said he fell in love with her. Nothing like that ever happened to me. I didn't even know any boys during my years at a girls' boarding school. When I moved back to New York after graduation, I went out on more dates, but most of the men were just convenient escorts or good friends. I always felt like an also-ran in my family—but I kept running.

Before Andy, my favorite beau was Dick Redfield, a man I met while we both worked at FAO Schwarz toy store. The store was near Central Park, so we'd often take a picnic lunch and eat in a rowboat on the lake. Dick was very musical, so some days we'd have a quick sandwich, then walk over to Carnegie Hall for the noon concert. In the evenings, we'd go up to the Yorkville area and sing German songs at the beer halls.

Dick grew up in Hartford, so we spent many weekends in Connecticut, going around to all the parties together. He came to see *The Petrified Forest* when we opened in Hartford. Afterwards, he gave me a bottle of champagne to take along to celebrate the Boston opening. We were never serious, but we had great fun together. We developed such a good friendship, in fact, that we eventually went to each other's weddings.

Later on I had a long, serious romance with Oliver Jennings, a tall, good-looking stockbroker. I was still involved with Andy when we first met, so I didn't pay much attention to Ollie at first. His family had a place not far from the WPA theater where I was performing, so he came to Bridgeport and took me out on weekends. As my romance with Andy faded, I began seeing more of Ollie and gradually fell in love with him. He was amused by my theatrical career and enjoyed my perfect opening night on Broadway almost as much as I did. He also had some of the impetuous quality that I'd found appealing in Andy. In May 1938, for example, he suggested we drive to the Kentucky Derby for the weekend—even though we had no tickets and very little money.

We took off in his car, nonetheless, stopping to visit his aunt and my old school along the way. When we reached Kentucky, we were able to stay overnight in Lexington with one of my school friends—a woman who just happened to have a box in the grandstand at Churchill Downs the next day. We went to the races with her and cheered on her horse, Butterbeans, who won an earlier race that day. Everything worked out much better than we had reason to expect, so it was a delightful weekend.

As time went by, I became very friendly with Ollie's mother and father. I'd always been self-conscious about meeting the parents of my beaux—I was well aware that a poverty-stricken orphan in a less-than-respectable profession was not considered a "great catch"—but I felt very comfortable with Mr. and Mrs. Jennings. They seemed to assume that Ollie and I would get married eventually, and so did we.

Ollie and I dated steadily for two years and talked about announcing our engagement from time to time, but neither of us was eager to settle down. I'm not sure why I was so reluctant to formalize our engagement, but I think I realized that Ollie was a little too wild for a life-time attachment. In truth, we were both immature, but we did share a lot of good times.

A few months after I met Ollie, Win Stevenson got married so I had to give up our apartment. Belinda invited me to move into the top floor of the large house she shared with Uncle Ely. The children's rooms on the fourth and fifth floors were no longer used by the family, so she began renting them to young people. Belinda hadn't bothered to convert the house into proper apartments, so my bath tub was in the kitchen and the toilet was in a hall closet. But the rent was only $15 a month and the location—at 64 West 56 Street—was great for me.

The Jelliffes' kitchen and dining room were on the ground floor. Uncle Ely's office and waiting room took up the entire second floor, with the family's private rooms on the third floor. I shared my apartment with Edna Julian, a girl from Kansas who sang at Radio City Music Hall. Often, as we walked upstairs at night, Belinda would pop out of her room to chat. She was always eager to hear about our beaux and everything we were doing.

Belinda met Ollie on various occasions and began to make it clear that she didn't think he was the right man for me. She never explained why she felt that way, but Ollie was another heavy drinker so she probably feared that he—like Tom Wolfe and others we knew—was on the verge of becoming an alcoholic. I tried to ignore her critical comments, but they planted seeds of doubt in my mind.

In November 1939, while still dating Ollie, I received a call from an old friend. I'd known Ann Jones and her sister Jean during my summers in Connecticut. Ann was now living in New York City with her husband, Archie Thatcher. "Jean and her beau are coming for dinner," Ann said, "and we'd like you to join us. Archie's friend, Ben Tuttle, is coming, too," she added. "They went hunting together on Long Island and shot several pheasants, so we're having a pheasant dinner. We can't have the party in our apartment," Ann explained, "because Archie is very fussy about how pheasant is cooked. The oven has to be heated to 500 degrees and our apartment would probably disintegrate if we turned the oven up that high. Archie's friend, Simon, has agreed to let us use an oven in his restaurant on 56th Street, so we're having the dinner there. Can you come?"

I was free that night so I accepted Ann's invitation—and that's how I met Ben Tuttle. I liked him immediately, but I wasn't exactly bowled over. I'd been accustomed to tall beaux, and Ben was just my height (about 5'8"). He had a brilliant mind, though, and was very witty—one of the few truly witty people I've ever known. He'd graduated from Yale at 20 and was interested in the theater, music and opera. Ben was also a mature 38—10 years older than I—and well established in his career. I was flattered that a successful "older man" seemed to find me attractive.

A week after we met, Ben invited me to dinner. When he came to the Jelliffes' house to pick me up, I walked down from the top floor and found him sitting in the waiting room off Uncle Ely's office. He was dressed in evening clothes, with a florist's box on the chair beside him. I was wearing a simple street dress, so I took one look at Ben and said, "Wait a minute, please."

I ran back up to the fifth floor and asked Edna to set up the ironing board. "I have to wear evening clothes," I explained, as I removed my dress and pulled something more suitable from the closet. Everything I owned was made of silk or another fabric that had to be ironed each time I wore it. As quickly as possible, I pressed my prettiest dress, slipped it on and ran back down the stairs. I thought I'd been gone about ten minutes, but Ben said it seemed like an hour to him.

"Where would you like to go for dinner?' he asked as soon as I reappeared. "I thought we'd go to the St. Regis Roof so we can dance." The St. Regis Roof was a beautiful room with a large dance floor and excellent music. I'd been there only once or twice, but it happened to be my absolute favorite place. "That would be wonderful," I replied, and off we went.

We had a lovely evening, dancing all through cocktails and dinner. Ben was an excellent dancer who loved to spin around the floor as much as I did. We had plenty of room to dance, as only eight or ten other couples were on the floor. This was around Thanksgiving, 1939. The war in Europe had just begun and most Americans were still feeling the effects of the Depression.

When Ben took me home that evening, he asked, "Would you like to have dinner with me again next Thursday?"

"That would be lovely," I said, pleased that he'd enjoyed the evening as much as I had. Our next few dates were also on Thursday nights. Like the first, they included dinner and dancing at a beautiful ballroom. Belinda and the others in the Jelliffe house called Ben "the flower beau" because he always brought me a corsage to wear—gardenias, roses, even little orchids.

"I think he always takes you out on Thursdays because that's the cook's night out," said the Jelliffes' cook. "He has to go out because he can't eat at home or invite you to his place on Thursday." In those days, it was traditional for servants to have Thursday night off. The practice was so common that a group of wealthy people started a "Thursday Club" so they'd have a nice place to go for dinner on "cook's night out."

I learned later, however, that Ben had other reasons for taking me out on Thursdays. He and his mother—with whom he'd been sharing an apartment since his father died in 1933—had a regular subscription to the Philharmonic on Friday nights. On weekends he usually went to the Catskills, where he belonged to a fishing and shooting club. Ben was a popular bachelor with many friends, so I became his "Thursday girl."

I didn't mind because he always took me dancing at wonderful ballrooms. We danced to Guy Lombardo at the Roosevelt Hotel and to other big bands at the Persian Room in the Plaza and in the Sert Room at the Waldorf. Our favorite, though, was a Viennese orchestra at the Ambassador Hotel on Park Avenue. They played mostly waltzes, which we both enjoyed.

Belinda was eager to learn more about my "flower beau," so she invited us both to dinner. From that night on she made it clear that she liked and approved of Ben. She appreciated his quick mind and considered him a solid citizen. Uncle Ely also enjoyed Ben's company, for they shared a fascination with the workings of the mind and its effect on the body.

We also talked about foreign travel, which all four of us enjoyed. Ben was so eager to see the world, in fact, that he'd majored in geology at Yale, thinking he'd work for an oil exploration company. That didn't work out, but the American Foreign Insurance Company offered him a job in Trieste, so he spent three years working in Italy. That gave him an opportunity to travel all over Europe and the Mediterranean. On weekends and holidays, he enjoyed visiting such exotic places as Istanbul, Cairo and Tangiers.

Ben returned to the U.S. in 1925 to accept a better offer from the Insurance Company of North America. That got him involved in the inland marine side of insurance, which originally wrote policies on canal boats and their cargo. Next, he was asked to join the Atlantic Mutual Insurance Company as Vice President in charge of the inland marine division. He was only 33 at the time. His division covered all types of inland transportation—boats, railroads, trucks and eventually airplanes, plus their cargo.

A few weeks after Ben and I started going out, his mother went to California for the winter with an old friend. After she left, Ben often invited me to take his mother's place at the Philharmonic on Friday nights—and sometimes at the opera, too. (I'd never liked opera as much as the theater, but Ben's enthusiasm got me so interested that I still enjoy going regularly. I've had the same subscription seats to the Metropolitan Opera for 55 years.)

The more I got to know Ben, the better I liked him. It was soon evident that he was very much in love with me, but he didn't tell his mother about our romance until she returned from California in March. Soon afterwards, I was invited to dinner at their apartment. I was nervous about meeting her, but Mrs. Tuttle was so bright, charming and attractive that she soon put me at ease. A former math teacher, she spoke French and was very interested in music and art, so I couldn't help liking her.

I don't think the feeling was entirely mutual, however. Mrs. Tuttle had been trying for years to get Ben interested in one of the nice girls they knew from church or social events in New York. In those days, "nice" girls were charming, well-educated young women from good, wealthy families. A poor, struggling actress who'd never been to college didn't exactly qualify. But Ben was never attracted to what he referred to as "Mother's nice girls." And perhaps his mother decided to broaden her definition of "nice" by the time her older son was 38.

In any event, it was only a few weeks later that Ben invited me to dinner and a movie. After an excellent meal, we saw *The Baker's Wife*, an extraordinary French film. When he drove me home that April night, he proposed marriage as we sat in his car in front of the house. I was delighted, of course, but not quite ready to make a commitment. "Let me think about it," I said.

Ollie and I had never broken off our informal engagement, so I wanted to talk to him before agreeing to marry someone else. Although we'd been drifting apart, I still went out with Ollie occasionally—just never on Thursdays. Telling him that I'd fallen in love with another man was not easy. He was surprised and rather hurt, I think, but he was very nice about it. We remained friends for the rest of his life (only six or seven years, as it turned out).

Another concern was my understanding that Ben expected me to give up the theater and devote myself to my husband and children. Ben had initially planned to be a doctor like his father and grandfather, but changed his mind, he told me, "because that life is too hard on the doctor's family." Ben's parents had slept in separate bedrooms because Dr. Tuttle didn't want to disturb his wife when he got up in the middle of the night to deliver a baby or treat an accident victim.

Ben's intense concern for his wife's happiness was very appealing to me. He also had all the qualities I admired most, such as intelligence and a lively sense of humor. What really won me over, though, was his declaration, "I want to take care of you." Other beaux had told me, "I need you desperately," but Ben seemed more interested in meeting my needs. That was hard to resist. Suddenly, a career in the theater didn't seem so important after all.

About a week later, Ben took me to the Persian Room. He mentioned marriage again, adding, "Please don't trample on my heart." That time I accepted his proposal. The next morning, I found a big bouquet of long-stemmed red roses on my doorstep. Ben wanted to get married right away, but I persuaded him to wait until June so we'd have time to plan a small wedding. Mrs. Tuttle celebrated our engagement by giving a dinner party for us at the St. Regis Roof.

On June 14, 1940, Ben and I were married at St. Marks Episcopal Church in New Canaan, the same church I'd gone to as a child. Ben's Uncle Tom Worrall, an Episcopal priest in Tioga, Pennsylvania, performed the ceremony. His brother, Tom, was best man and my brother, Howard, gave me away. My only attendants were my two sisters and my ten-year-old niece, Honor Banks, who was the flower girl.

None of us had much money, so it was a simple wedding. Lee wore the same dress she'd worn as a bridesmaid in another wedding, and Honor borrowed a matching dress from another attendant. They both looked lovely. I wore my mother's ivory satin wedding gown. It was a beautiful dress that had turned more ivory with age. I bought white ballet slippers to wear with it, but they looked like giant marshmallows on my feet.

About 200 people attended the church ceremony, but we couldn't afford to invite that many to the reception. Fortunately, it was a beautiful day so we lined up outside the church and greeted everyone as they came out. Afterwards, our relatives and closest friends went on to a joyous reception hosted by my sister Honor and her husband, Roderick Luttgen, at their lovely home on the water on Sherwood Island, Connecticut.

Shortly after the reception began, the sun disappeared under clouds and the wind came up. Suddenly it was so chilly that everyone dove into the warm rum punch. Ben and I finally left the reception in a car that Lee's husband, Charlie Minor, had fixed up with old shoes and tin cans. We drove it to the end of the island where a rental car was waiting for us.

A friend snapped this picture of Ben and me during our wedding reception in June 1940. I wore my mother's satin wedding dress, as had my two sisters.

I drove into New York City because I'd had far more experience on those roads than Ben. I'd had such a good time drinking punch at the reception, however, that it's still a wonder to me that we made it. Luckily, there was very little traffic because every once in a while the Merritt Parkway would turn green. It took me a minute to realize that I was driving on the grassy median, so I had to steer back onto the road. As soon as we reached the city, we returned the rental car and took a taxi to the Plaza Hotel, where Ben had reserved a lovely room.

Champagne and flowers were waiting when we arrived. We celebrated privately while listening to the clop, clop, clop of the horses pulling hansom cabs in and around Central Park. The next morning we boarded a ship for Bermuda. We were invited to sit at the Captain's table, which happened almost every time I traveled by ship with Ben. Most of the steamship lines were insured by his company, so we always received royal treatment on those ships.

We had a marvelous ten days in Bermuda before we had to return to New York. As soon as we got home, Ben's mother moved out and left us their apartment and everything in it—all the furniture, books, linens, china and silver. She took only her clothes, jewelry and personal items. That generosity made my life as a new bride much easier, and I was always grateful to her for that. I also admired the way she bravely started a new life for herself as a 70-year-old widow.

(I couldn't help thinking of her experience years later when I was widowed. I was determined to be as independent of my own children as possible. They're a very loving group who are always there for me when needed, but I don't want to be a burden—either financially or socially. Luckily, Ben's careful planning took care of the financial end so I've been free to maintain my own friends, interests and activities.)

Ben's apartment was in a great location on East 65th Street next to President Franklin Roosevelt's house, but it was old fashioned and not well-suited for modern life. It had three bedrooms, but none was big enough for a double bed—not exactly the ideal arrangement for newlyweds. Ben and I began looking for another place about a month later.

In the meantime, I enjoyed being a "lady of leisure." As a single woman pursuing a career in the theater, I'd spent most of my time working or looking for work—going for interviews and auditions or just trying to learn who was casting. Marriage gave me the freedom to play tennis, attend matinees or go to the beach with friends while Ben was at work. For the first time in my adult life, I didn't feel guilty about taking time to have fun during the week.

On weekends, Ben and I often went to the Trout and Skeet club he belonged to in the Catskills. He taught me to cast flies for fish and to shoot skeet. I'd never been interested in such activities before, but I've always enjoyed the challenge of learning new skills. Eventually I became pretty good—though I was never as good as Ben.

In October, we moved into a spacious two-bedroom apartment on the 10th floor of a new building at 137 East 38th Street. It had a great view looking south over the city. That was where our married life really began. It soon became so interesting and fulfilling that I never had any regrets about giving up my career.

8

Motherhood: The Big Adjustment

Feeling secure for the first time since my mother's death, I was very excited to discover I was pregnant. Ben was a bit worried about becoming a father, but he wanted me to be happy—and I was. We'd just moved into our new apartment and I couldn't wait to become a mother. I was awed by the whole experience of pregnancy and the miracle of the new life I was producing. All of a sudden, I was very interested in what some people call "nest building," sewing curtains as well as baby clothes. When Ben decided to go hunting, I chose to stay home.

In December, he returned from a hunting trip with a string of six black ducks tied together at their feet. "I'd like to serve these at a dinner party," he told me, "but they need to be hung outdoors in the cold for at least a week before they'll be ready to eat." I hung them from the window washer's hook outside my kitchen window. Apparently, I didn't tie the rope very securely because it came off the hook, sending the ducks plummeting down ten flights to the ground!

It seems funny now, but Ben was so proud of those ducks that I didn't know what I'd do if they were no longer fit to eat. I explained my predicament to the elevator man who retrieved the ducks from the back alley. They were well protected by a thick layer of tough feathers and looked OK, so I carefully hung them up again. The butcher who cleaned and prepared the ducks a week later said they were fine, but I didn't want to take any chances. The night friends came over for a duck dinner, I also cooked a beef roast as a backup. The ducks turned out to be delicious, so I saved the beef for later.

I was fortunate to have an easy, healthy pregnancy. When my contractions started only 10 months after our marriage, I went off to the hospital joyfully, wearing my best John Frederick's hat. Everything was coming along fine when I was put under anesthesia (the common practice in those days). When I woke up, though, I was surprised to see a circle of worried faces around me—Ben and several doctors.

"Where's my baby?" I asked, terrified that something had gone wrong with the birth. "Our little boy is fine," Ben assured me. I was not so fine. I'd suffered an allergic reaction, which led to double pneumonia. In fact, Ben told me later, I'd come very close to dying. It was three days before they even let me see my infant son. We named him Frank James, after Ben's father, but we always called him Jimmy.

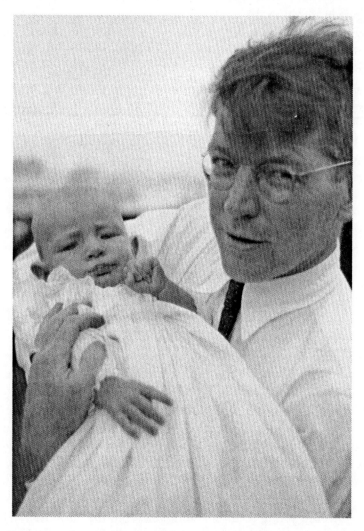

Ben held our first son, Jimmy, on the day he was christened in a dress hand sewn by Ben's mother.

By the time I recovered and returned home, Ben had converted our large dressing room into a nursery. (We used our second bedroom as a library and home office for Ben.) There were no parks near our apartment, but the building had a finished roof garden with a wooden floor, fences and furniture. Another young mother and I often put our babies in their carriages, then took the elevator up to the roof so we could all enjoy the fresh air together.

When Jimmy was almost eight months old, the Japanese bombed Pearl Harbor, plunging us into World War II. I remember that Sunday very well. Ben was an intellectual man who never did any housework. But as he listened to the horrifying reports on the radio that day, he surprised me by washing every window in the apartment. He just couldn't sit still.

Ben had received an ROTC commission as a lieutenant when he graduated from college in 1922, but World War I was over by then. Disappointed at being unable to serve his country in that war, he volunteered for World War II. He was turned down, though, because of his age (40). I was secretly pleased that he was not accepted because Jimmy and I needed him at home.

The war changed our lives in many ways, nonetheless. A variety of goods became scarce so rationing was introduced. We had to stand in line for ration coupons to buy gasoline, leather goods, meat, butter and other foods. As I remember, we were allowed to buy only two pairs of shoes and five pounds of sugar per person each year. The biggest hardship for us was the meat ration: only half a pound per person per week. The doctor who treated Ben's allergies advised him to eat meat three times a day. But even with the extra allowance for babies, we didn't have nearly enough meat for Ben's diet.

We both looked for ways to help the war effort from home. Radar wasn't available then, so Ben worked nights as a plane spotter in a tall building in downtown Manhattan. When he saw a plane, he was instructed to call a central office and describe it. Officials would check their lists to see if it was legitimate. If the plane wasn't listed, air raid sirens would sound until it was cleared.

I volunteered at the USO (United Services Organization) canteen in Grand Central Station, only four blocks from our apartment. The USO provided refreshments and comfort for young soldiers and sailors passing through the enormous rail terminal. If they were tired and had a long wait, we'd provide a blanket and a cot, and wake them up in time to catch their next train. One day, a sailor asked me for "the head," so I led him to the rather pompous woman who ran the USO. "Yes, young man," she told him. "I'm the head here." We were both embarrassed to learn that the sailor was simply looking for a bathroom.

Jimmy was such a delightful child that he soon erased Ben's doubts about fatherhood. When he was only six months old, though, I became pregnant again. Ben was really terrified that time. I'd been so sick after Jimmy's birth that he was afraid of losing me. But I've never believed in dwelling in the past or worrying about "what might happen," so I refused to allow negative thoughts to intrude on my happiness. I just focused on the joys of having another child—and experienced no problems at all with that pregnancy and birth.

Our second son was born on July 18, 1942. He was a robust baby who weighed nine pounds. We named him Woodruff Leeming, after my father. Jimmy was only 15 months old at the time, so he wasn't quite sure what I had in my arms when I came home from the hospital. He watched me put his new brother in the cradle, but mistook the bundle for his beloved teddy bear.

Suddenly, the baby started to cry. Jimmy came running to me. "Dear Teddy crying," he said. "Dear Teddy crying," he repeated with growing distress. We thought this was so cute that we started calling our new son "Teddy." I must admit that Woodruff Leeming was a rather imposing name for an infant, so he's been Teddy Tuttle ever since.

Like all parents, I have favorite stories about my children when they were young. One involved the Third Avenue Elevated Train (or the El, as it was known) which we could see running on tracks ten floors below our apartment. Jimmy was fascinated by that train and spent hours watching it out the window. When he was almost three, Ben bought him a small electric train for Christmas. After setting it up, Ben explained how it worked and showed Jimmy where to plug it in. Suddenly, the El roared by. Jimmy ran to the window and looked down at the El. Then he glanced up and asked, "Where do they plug in that train, Daddy?"

When Jimmy first began to talk, he had difficulty pronouncing the letter T. If he wanted to say "train," it came out sounding more like "frain." One day, I took him out to lunch in a new restaurant with his grandmother. Shortly after sitting at a table near the window, Jimmy saw a big truck go by outside. "Mommy," he said, "look at that big fruck." It sounded like he'd used a four-letter word, causing a well-dressed woman at the next table to give us a very dirty look.

Like most boys, ours became increasingly active as they grew. Although a joy to be around, they were little imps who got into all kinds of mischief. One day when I was nursing Teddy, Jimmy toddled into the bathroom and shut the door. By the time I was able to follow him, he'd gone to work with Ben's black liquid shoe polish. He used it to "polish" his white shoes and socks and to "paint" the bathroom walls. My lipstick was another of his favorite decorating tools.

The apartment that had seemed so spacious when we were newlyweds suddenly felt crowded and confining with two little boys running around. I yearned to live near a large park where the children could play outside and run off some of their excess energy. Ben was feeling cramped for different reasons. He missed his private office and library, which we'd turned into a nursery after Teddy was born. We also needed more space to store all the paraphernalia that comes with children—carriages, strollers, tricycles.

When Teddy was about 18 months old, we began looking for a new home—either a larger apartment or a house near a major park. Ben didn't want to spend more than 15 minutes traveling to work in lower Manhattan, so that eliminated the suburban towns where my siblings and many of our friends lived. His 15-minute rule also disqualified upper Fifth Avenue, where I'd seen an appealing apartment overlooking Central Park.

We'd been searching for several months when Ben suggested looking in Brooklyn. Just a short subway ride from his office on Wall Street, it still had many single-family houses. I'd lived there as a child, of course, and still had relatives residing in the borough. Ben had also lived in Brooklyn, sharing an apartment on Garden Place with his brother, Tom, after graduating from Yale. "I liked the small town feeling of our neighborhood," he remembered.

One of my first cousins, Helen Leeming Thirkield, suggested that we look at houses in her Brooklyn neighborhood, an area known as Park Slope. "It borders Prospect Park," she said, "which has wonderful playgrounds and children's programs." We were tempted by a charming house near the water in Brooklyn Heights, but it needed a lot of work. Early in 1944, at the height of World War II, building materials were scarce, so major renovations were out of the question.

We finally bought a house in excellent condition at 633 Second Street in Park Slope. A three-story brick Georgian Revival with five fireplaces, it had a beautiful staircase lit by a huge skylight. The finished basement, with Spanish tile floors, was probably the original kitchen, but it made a wonderful playroom for the kids. On rainy days, they could roller skate on the tile floor.

The living room, dining room and kitchen were all on the main level. A small office was on one side of the front door, with a cloakroom on the other. The master bedroom was on the second floor, along with a smaller bedroom and a large, 22-foot drawing room. The third floor had three bedrooms, plus a maid's room and bath, so there was plenty of space for a growing family.

The house was near Helen's home, around the corner from Prospect Park—and only a 12-minute subway ride from Ben's office. (He did have to walk a few blocks to the nearest station, though.) After we had closed on the house, the boys and I went to our farm for the summer. The lease on our apartment didn't expire until October, so Ben used the time to move our things over to the new house gradually.

The Family Grows in Brooklyn

After we were settled in Park Slope, we invited Ben's mother to live with us. A doctor she respected had told her, "Do not live with your children until they've been married at least four years," and she took that admonition seriously. In the meantime, she'd moved around a lot—living with Ben's brother, her sister and various friends. We'd been married exactly four years—and Granny Tuttle was 74—when she took over a large, sunny room on the top floor of our house.

We've all heard horror stories about mothers-in-law, but mine was a remarkable person. "Having two women in the kitchen never works out," she told me soon after she arrived. "You're a better cook than I am so I won't offer to help you prepare meals. I'll just do all the cleaning up afterwards." She stuck to that agreement, which was great for me. As soon as dinner was over, I was free to spend time with the children—discussing their troubles, helping with homework, putting them to bed. Sometimes I'd just relax in the living room, listening to music with Ben. It was really wonderful.

I remember only one time when I had second thoughts about our arrangement. Ben's mother always changed her clothes and fixed her hair before coming down for dinner. On this occasion, she was wearing one of her prettiest dresses. I looked pretty grubby by comparison. As I stirred bubbling pots in the kitchen, I heard her laughing with Ben in the front room. They were having a cocktail and enjoying themselves immensely. I felt a twinge of jealousy because I wanted to be there, too, but I'm sure she often felt the same way after dinner.

Granny Tuttle had lived with us less than a year when I gave birth to our third child on March 28, 1945. We named her Mary Worrall Tuttle after Ben's mother. Granny was thrilled because she'd always wanted a baby girl of her own. Ben's father was an only child, his mother had two sons, his brother had three sons, and we had two sons before this little girl came along. In short, she was the first miss in the Tuttle family in three generations, so we called her Missy. Like the other childhood nicknames, it stuck.

With three children under four, I didn't have much time to get out and make new friends. Fortunately, my cousin Helen—who was about ten years older than I—was a big help in that regard. She gave a delightful party to introduce us to the neighbors soon after we moved in. I met some marvelous people through Helen and learned a lot from her, too.

One of the most helpful activities Helen introduced us to was called John's Club. A group of parents paid a man named John Duda to take their boys into Prospect Park for two hours of organized games after school every day. That sounded great to us, so we signed up our sons. I was always amused when John lined up the boys and said, "Come on, men!" though they were only 6, 7 or 8 years old. On rainy days, he took them to a church gym where they played basketball. I think Teddy enjoyed it more than Jimmy, but both made good friends in the club.

Teddy (left) and Jimmy during the summer of 1945.

Helen also recommended the schools that she and her children had attended. Jimmy started kindergarten at The Berkeley Institute in 1946. Ted followed the next year and Missy enrolled in 1950. It was a private school within walking distance of the house, but I had to walk with the children in the morning and pick them up again at noon or at three. Kindergarten and the first three grades at

Berkeley were co-educational, but it was limited to girls after that. Missy continued at Berkeley for nine years.

In the fourth grade, the boys transferred to Brooklyn Polytechnic Preparatory School, an excellent country day school in the Ft. Hamilton section of Brooklyn. "Poly Prep" has a wonderful campus with tennis courts, football and soccer fields, even an indoor swimming pool, but the boys could no longer walk to school. They rode the subway with a group of friends. It was a ten-minute walk to the nearest station, so their trip to school usually took an hour each way.

My uncle Ely Jelliffe thought so highly of Poly Prep that he'd sent his son Leeming there, even though his commute from Manhattan was much longer. (Leeming was an excellent swimmer and diver who went on to become the captain of the swimming team at Yale University. He and Ben were classmates at Yale, though I didn't know Ben at the time.)

The six of us settled into a very happy life there in Brooklyn. It was a warm, cheerful house with all those fireplaces. In the evening, we'd often have tea or drinks in the drawing room, then sit and tell stories in front of the fire. Granny Tuttle added a wonderful extra dimension to the children's lives. She was always eager to hear about their activities and had the patience to sit and play all their favorite games. A former math teacher, she offered experienced help with their homework, too. She handled the children so effectively that her example helped me to become more patient and understanding with them, too.

Some of my friends couldn't believe that I'd invited my mother-in-law to live with us, but we got along very well. The fact that I hadn't had a mother of my own for so many years probably made it easier. Ben's mother didn't have to compete with another mother or grandmother. She also kept her opinions to herself and never criticized the way we ran our lives or reared our children. I was very grateful for that.

Mother Tuttle's presence in the house made my life easier and more fun. If one child was sick in bed, I could still go shopping or to a meeting because Granny was home. When one child had a dentist appointment or a scout meeting, I could leave the others behind knowing that they were safe with a grandmother they adored. Sometimes, Mother Tuttle and I even went out together in the evening when Ben preferred to stay home. She was very witty and had a wonderful laugh, so I enjoyed her company.

I also appreciated her help with numerous projects. I made all the draperies in the house, as well as clothes for Missy and myself. Granny was much better at fancy work than I was, though, so she often added the trimming. She crocheted beautiful bedspreads and made Scout uniforms, pajamas and costumes for the boys' Teddy Bears as well as intricate clothes for Missy's dolls. We spent many pleasant hours sewing together.

Ben's mother, Mary Worrall Tuttle, was a remarkable woman and a beloved grandmother.

Having a live-in mother-in-law was also a great help when I had to go to the hospital for an emergency hysterectomy. As it happened, we had house guests from England at the time, but my doctor said he could not guarantee my survival if I postponed the surgery. My tumor ("the size of a grapefruit" according to my doctor) was benign, but I still spent ten days in the hospital. I'd suffered an allergic reaction to a blood transfusion that made me very ill. I was relieved to know that Ben and the family were well taken care of at home during that time.

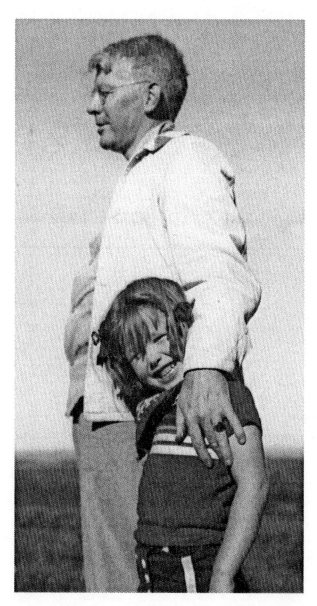

Ben put a protective arm around our daughter Missy in the early 50's.

Ben's mother enjoyed excellent health for most of her eighteen years with us, but she did have a hearing problem. That proved to be fortunate because I didn't have to worry about the children disturbing her when they became rowdy. Like most siblings, they had many noisy disagreements and minor skirmishes. Jimmy generally tried to avoid fights, but Missy and Teddy were terrible teases who liked to annoy each other.

When the boys were around 12, we sent them to Miss Hepburn's Dancing School in the parish house of Grace Episcopal Church in Brooklyn Heights. Most of their school friends went to the same dancing school, so they didn't object. In fact, I think they secretly enjoyed socializing with girls after classes in an all-boys school. Their teacher, Elsie Livingston Hepburn, was a small woman with ramrod straight posture who barked out sarcastic orders like a drill sergeant. "Go ahead and step on the girls' toes," she'd say. "They won't be in the way the next time."

I have no idea how old Miss Hepburn was, but she taught my sister Honor to dance back in 1915—almost 40 years earlier. Despite her strict discipline, however, she made the classes fun. She always ended with the Mexican Hat Dance, the Lindy or another spirited dance that the students enjoyed. By the time Jimmy and Teddy started going to teenage dances, they knew how to dance the waltz, fox trot, cha cha, Lindy and other popular dances.

Two other mothers and I formed a car pool to drive the boys from Poly Prep to dancing school. The kids ignored me as they chatted among themselves, so I usually kept quiet. But when I overheard one boy say, "I don't like to dance with her because she stinks," I couldn't resist speaking up.

"That's not a very gentlemanly thing to say," I protested.

"Oh, it's not what you think, Mrs. Tuttle," he replied. "It's just that she reeks of her mother's awful perfume." I had to laugh at that. (By the time Missy was ready for dancing school, the boys had graduated, so I joined a different car pool. Missy enjoyed dancing school, too, especially after she met a cute boy named Woody in class.)

Jimmy and Teddy were close enough in age to travel to school and other activities together. But Missy was almost three years younger than Teddy, so I spent more time taking her places. When the boys came home from school, one inevitably asked, "Where's Mother?"

If Granny said, "She took Missy to her Girl Scout meeting," Teddy would sometimes sling his book bag across the floor and say, "That stinking Missy!" Both wanted to find me waiting at home and were jealous of the time I spent with their sister. Perhaps they were right in thinking that Missy was spoiled—especially by Granny, whose bedroom was next to hers. As the only girl, Missy probably received extra attention, but she never got additional toys or clothing.

In truth, none of our children received a lot of material things. Ben and I were both old-fashioned Yankees who'd developed frugal habits during the Depression, so we were never extravagant with our children. Each received an allowance of 25 cents a week—and was expected to put 10 cents of that into the collection plate at the Dutch Reformed Church where they all went to Sunday school.

Teddy told me later that he always thought we were very poor because he never had enough money to buy chocolate bars—and he loved chocolate bars. The boys never complained; they just accepted the situation. Jimmy's high school classmates must have thought we were very poor, too, because he wore the same corduroy jacket to school for several years. The sleeves kept getting shorter and shorter, but he didn't seem to care or I'd have bought him a new jacket.

Poly Prep allowed seniors to bring cars to school. As soon as they acquired driver's licenses, a number of students came sailing out to the Fort Hamilton campus in Porsches or other fancy sports cars. Jimmy stood out because he drove to school in a big Chevrolet pick-up truck, which he'd driven in from our farm.

Perhaps because we'd lived through the Depression, Ben and I didn't spend a lot of money on ourselves, either. I hired a nice Irish woman named Nora Daly to help with the cleaning and laundry, but we never had live-in servants like many of our friends. We didn't take taxis very often, either. Ben was still riding the subway to work when he was President of The Atlantic Mutual Insurance Company.

When Ben was promoted to Chairman of the Board, Miles York (the man who replaced him as President) insisted that executives in their positions should live on Park Avenue and ride in chauffeur-driven limousines. Ben wasn't about to leave Brooklyn, but his firm did acquire a car and a driver after that. Miles was driven between his office and his Park Avenue apartment every day. The same chauffeur picked up Ben in the morning and drove him back home in the evening. If I had a meeting or an appointment in Manhattan, I'd go along for the ride. After dropping Ben at the office, the driver would take me on to my destination, a luxury that was a real treat for me.

Ben was seldom interested in going out after working all day. His idea of a perfect evening was to play with the children, eat a good dinner, then listen to music or play the piano. He also liked to read and play chess or bridge. As the boys got older, though, Ben got involved in more of their activities. He especially liked to take his sons fishing, which both enjoyed.

When the boys were about 12, we started taking them to a cabin Ben had bought at The Triton Fish and Game Club, about 100 miles north of Quebec City, Canada. It was a great adventure just to get there. My knowledge of French often came in handy. We'd drive to Quebec City where we'd leave the car and board a one-track railway destined for Chicoutimi. Around 2 am, we'd get off the train and spend the rest of the night on sleeping bags in a small cabin near the Sanford station. In the morning we'd meet our Blackfoot Indian guides, then pick up four or five canoes that Ben kept in the club's shed over the winter.

We carried all our luggage, groceries and gear for a two-week stay because it took about six hours to reach our cabin. The journey took us through a chain of lakes, so we'd paddle for a while, then get out and portage the canoes and provisions to the next lake. Fortunately, the guides handled all the portaging. Once we reached our rustic cabin (which had no plumbing, electricity or telephone), our extraordinary guides chopped wood, hauled water and cooked our meals over the wood stove in the cook shack.

Our cabin was the only one on that section of *Lac des Passes*, so it was very peaceful—and a great escape for Ben. Sometimes we traveled to other lakes nearby. We caught and ate numerous brook trout during those vacations. (Luckily for me, the guides cleaned all the fish.) The boys really loved the fishing, while Missy and I enjoyed swimming, hiking and canoeing. Ben also taught the boys about hunting on those vacations.

(Jimmy still takes his family to that cabin, but he usually flies in on a pontoon plane. His wife cooks their meals on a wood-burning stove, using water hauled from the lake. The fishing is only fair these days. After 100 years, the Canadian government decided not to renew the Triton Club's lease on the land, so the whole area has been opened to the public. It's advertised in France as a wilderness experience, so many visitors come over from Europe, flying in to the main clubhouse on pontoon planes. The lake gets fished more heavily now that motor boats and all types of lures are allowed.)

By and large, our children did very well in school. But aside from the boys' shared love of fishing, they had very little in common. Jimmy was a slight, elfin child who never liked to play games very much. (This was partly due to a vision problem he developed after being hit in the eye with another child's arrow.) Jimmy enjoyed science projects and loved to build things at his cellar workbench. He and his best friend, Robert Martinson, were so handy with tools that the minister of the Dutch Reformed Church where they went to Sunday school gave them a small office at the church. He called on them when lighting projects and certain other maintenance work was needed.

Teddy, on the other hand, was always bigger and tougher—even though he was a year younger than Jimmy. He enjoyed playing football and other contact sports. He also liked games of all kinds—board games, chess, puzzles, bridge.

Since the boys had such different personalities and interests, we thought it might be uncomfortable for them to compete with each other in the same high school.

Jimmy wanted to stay in Brooklyn, so he continued at Poly Prep until he graduated in 1959. But Teddy liked our suggestion of boarding school, so he went away to a small boys' school in Millbrook, New York, at age 15. He was a little homesick at first, but soon grew to love it—especially the hours he spent helping out at the school's private zoo.

As Jimmy was getting ready for college and Teddy was about to start his senior year in boarding school, we thought Missy might benefit from going away to school, too. She was too old to be chaperoned, but we didn't think she was really safe wandering around Brooklyn on her own, without her brothers. After researching numerous schools, we settled on Emma Willard in Troy, New York, less than an hour's drive from the farm where we spent our summers.

In addition to an excellent academic reputation, Emma Willard had a good horseback riding program back then. Missy loved horses and learned to ride English saddle at school. From time to time, girls from Emma Willard rode with the Old Chatham Hunt, to which we belonged, so Missy and I were sometimes able to ride in the hunt together on fall weekends.

Unlike her brother, Missy really hated being away at boarding school. In retrospect, I think it was a mistake to send her there because she was terribly homesick. She especially missed her grandmother, to whom she was very close. During Christmas vacation in 1962, Granny told Missy about a problem she'd had with her kidneys. Ben and I were both unaware of any difficulties, so we didn't take her to a doctor.

A few weeks after Missy returned to school in January, she wrote Granny a letter. Suddenly, she burst into tears. "My grandmother is never going to get this letter," she told her roommate as she tore up the pages and threw them away. Missy was soon sobbing so hysterically that her worried roommate called a teacher to come to their room.

"What's the matter?" the teacher asked.

"Something is wrong with my grandmother," Missy replied, tears streaming down her face. The next morning, she learned that Granny had, in fact, died that night—some 200 miles away. She was 92 and had enjoyed a good, long life, but Missy was only 17 and took it very hard. Ben, the boys and I were all very sad over losing Mother Tuttle, but Missy was so close to her that I think she suffered the most.

Looking back, I'm very grateful to my mother-in-law for being not only a very unselfish person but an outstanding role model, too. Her high standards and fine examples helped me to become a better mother, grandmother and mother-in-law. Watching how she worked to stay mentally and physically active into her 90s also inspired me to do the same.

Moving On

In what now seems like a very short time, our sons and daughter grew up, went off to college, fell in love and got married. Ben and I were pleased that each of our children managed to acquire a bachelor's degree before getting a marriage license. We were also delighted with the extraordinary people they chose to marry and spend their lives with.

Jimmy decided to go to Denison University, a small liberal arts college in Granville, Ohio. He participated in the ROTC and was commissioned a second lieutenant in the Air Force when he graduated in 1963. The Air Force sent him to a base in Mountain Home, Idaho. That Christmas he became engaged to Nora Varess, a Denison classmate. Ben and I liked her immediately. Born and raised in Budapest, Hungary, Nora and her prominent family (whose noble title dates back to 1640) had suffered greatly during the communist occupation. She'd won a dancing competition when she was seven, so most of her schooling was at the Grand Opera House, where she danced in many operas as part of the children's Corps de Ballet.

Jim and Nora on their wedding day in June 1964. On Nora's right is her mother, Piry Varess, then my big hat and Ben.

Nora's father, a military officer, was killed during World War II when she was very small. During the Hungarian Revolution of 1956, the whole family—Nora, her sister, Christa, their mother, grandmother, aunt and uncle—managed to escape to England. Aunt Ellie and Uncle Louis Deak were the first to immigrate to the United States, settling in Cleveland. Both found good jobs so the rest of the family joined them in 1957.

Nora and Jim were married in June 1964, at the Magyar Catholic Church in Cleveland. It was a beautiful wedding, followed by a delightful reception at a nearby country club. Their "honeymoon" was a cross-country drive to Jim's Air Force base. Our first grandchild—named Franklin Benjamin Tuttle after his grandfather—was born there on July 4, 1965. Ben and I flew to Idaho to welcome little Ben into the world. I was pleased to become a grandmother—and I've always enjoyed playing with my grandchildren—but I've never wanted to be a baby sitter or responsible for their care.

A few months after Ben was born, Jim and Nora were transferred to Kaiserlauten, Germany, for three years. Their second son, Thomas Louis Tuttle, was born in Germany on October 21, 1966. When Tommy was a year old, Ben and I went abroad to see him. We had a lovely visit with our two grandsons before departing on a two-week trip through Germany and Austria. An American woman on the air base took care of the little boys so their parents could come with us. It was our first visit to that part of Europe and we felt very fortunate to be able to travel with Nora, who spoke excellent German.

We had a wonderful time visiting castles, museums and other places of interest. I loved the Heidelberg Museum and the beautiful city of Salzburg. What I remember most about that trip, though, was arriving in Vienna, Austria. Nora looked at the Danube River—somewhat wistfully, I thought—and said, "Just think; this same river flows through Budapest, where I was born." We were only about 100 miles away, but Hungary was under communist control at the time. Nora's American passport listed her birthplace as Budapest, so it was risky for her to visit. Since Jim was on active duty with the U.S. military, he was not allowed to go there anyway.

When Jim completed his Air Force duty in 1968, he returned home and started graduate school at the State University of New York (SUNY) in Albany. He received his MBA in December 1970. He started work at Key Bank in Albany in January 1971, shortly after Nora gave birth to their third son, Christopher.

Jim spent his career at Key Bank, staying more than 30 years. A senior vice president, he worked mostly in the Albany office, but was transferred to Cleveland in 1994. By then, all three of their sons had finished school and Nora had launched her own career. After receiving a master's degree from Russell Sage College in 1981, she taught biology and health education to high school and college students. She continued to teach at Cuyahoga Junior College in Cleveland, so they enjoyed a good life there until Jim retired in the summer of 1999.

In the meantime, Teddy graduated from Millbrook in 1960 and enrolled in Hobart College in Geneva, New York. In his sophomore year, Ted's roommate arranged a meeting with Dawn Henion, his girlfriend's roommate at nearby Oswego College. Dawn was a beautiful girl with enormous blue eyes who soon stole Ted's heart. They became engaged shortly after he graduated in 1964. Rather than wait to be drafted, Ted enlisted in the Army and went to Officer's Candidate School in Ft. Sill, Oklahoma.

Ted received his commission in August 1965. The following March, he called Dawn from Fort Bragg on a Monday. "Will you marry me next Sunday?" he asked. "I've got orders to Vietnam." Dawn bravely said, "Yes," then called her mother who managed to get a beautiful wedding together in less than a week. They were married in the Methodist Church of Sloatsburg, New York, where Dawn had taught Sunday school and her father, a prominent Rockland County judge, had served as deacon. Unfortunately, Judge Herbert Henion died during the couple's engagement, but Dawn's handsome brother Herb gave her away. During the morning service that Sunday, the minister invited the entire congregation to the afternoon wedding ceremony.

The church was full, but only about 35 of us—mostly family—went on to the Henion home for the reception. The bride and groom flew off to Bermuda for a short honeymoon before Ted had to report to Vietnam for a one-year tour. In the interim, Dawn returned to Sloatsburg to live with her mother. She was happy to discover that she'd become pregnant on her honeymoon, but she had to get through the entire pregnancy and birth without her husband. Ted was still in Vietnam when Tamzine Esther (Tammy), our first granddaughter, was born December 11, 1966.

When Ted returned home in April 1967, he flew immediately to New York to see Dawn and his beautiful little daughter. After a joyous reunion, they drove to Ted's next assignment at Ft. Lewis, Washington. When Ted was discharged from the Army in August 1967, they took a leisurely drive across the country, camping along the way, until they reached our farm in Kinderhook, New York.

Ted enrolled in graduate school at SUNY Albany in January 1968, receiving his MBA and CPA certification in January 1970. His first job was with Price Waterhouse in New York City. He and Dawn started out in an apartment on

Staten Island, with Ted commuting to work by ferry. They had two more children—Elizabeth (born December 7, 1970) and Jefferson (May 17, 1972).

Dawn and Ted drink a toast at their wedding, shortly before Ted left for Vietnam.

When Jeff was about two, Dawn and Ted bought a charming little house on Albemarle Terrace in the Flatbush section of Brooklyn. Ben and I were delighted to have them nearby where we could watch the children grow up. All attended The Berkeley Institute where I served on the board. Ben had retired by then, so we both enjoyed going to Ted and Dawn's home for dinner and bridge. They were also frequent visitors to our place when Ben's health began to fail.

In 1983, Ted was offered a good job with the real estate department of Merrill Lynch in Stamford, Connecticut, so he moved the family to Weston. They loved the town and their lovely home so much that they stayed on after Merrill Lynch closed down the real estate operation. Ted had a long commute to his next job with Greenpoint Savings Bank in Flushing, New York. In 1995, after all three children were married, Ted took on a new challenge and accepted a transfer to San Diego. When he retired in November 1999, he and Dawn returned to Columbia County, New York, and began making plans to build their dream house.

Missy didn't move around nearly as much as her brothers. After graduating from Emma Willard in 1963, she enrolled at Wells College in Aurora, New York, to study for her BA in English. In 1966, a good friend of Teddy's gave Missy's phone number to his cousin Alonson Conklin, a student at Cornell University in Ithaca, New York. Both Wells and Cornell border on Lake Cayuga, one of the longest "finger lakes."

One day Norwig Debye and his friend Bill Fabens (Alonson's roommate) decided to paddle Norwig's kayak up Lake Cayuga. It was a long, cold trip in the middle of February, so they agreed to stop in Aurora, about 30 miles north of their starting point. Eager to find a place to spend the night—and perhaps some companionship for the evening—they pulled out a phone number Alonson had given them. When they reached Missy at Wells College, she told them about a farm house where they could get a room. She and her roommate then agreed to join the boys for dinner.

It wasn't exactly love at first sight, but Missy and Norwig began corresponding after that evening. Before long, they made arrangements to get together again. As their romance began to flower, Missy learned about Norwig's unusual background. His maternal grandfather, Peter Wilhelm Debye, won the Nobel Prize for Chemistry in 1936. As Director of the Kaiser Wilhelm Institute in Berlin, he worked with many top scientists (including Albert Einstein). But when Hitler rose to power, Dr. Debye was eager to leave Germany. He had a Dutch passport, so he was able to immigrate to New York, where he accepted an offer to chair the Chemistry department at Cornell.

Ben carries Missy's train as they enter the church for her marriage to Norwig in June 1967. Missy is wearing a 125-year-old veil from my mother's family.

Meanwhile, Dr. Debye's daughter, Mayon, had married an Austrian, Gerhard Saxinger, and given birth to two sons, Norwig and Nordulf. Post-war Germany was not a very good place to raise children, so when the boys were 8 and 10, their

Debye grandparents brought them to Ithaca. In their mid-60s at the time, the Debyes put their grandsons through school. (The boys' parents divorced several years later.) Both graduated from Ithaca High School, then went on to college—Norwig at Cornell, and Nordulf at Rice University in Houston.

As time went by, the relationship between Missy and Norwig developed into a serious romance. About eighteen months after they met, they became engaged. They were married in June 1967, just after Missy graduated from Wells. (Norwig was in graduate school at Georgetown University by then.) Their beautiful wedding was at the Episcopal Church in Kinderhook, with the reception under a tent at our farm. Dr. Debye died during their engagement, but Norwig's charming grandmother attended the wedding, along with his mother and his uncle, Peter Debye.

Missy and Norwig also received masters' degrees from SUNY, Albany. Missy worked at the State Library for the Blind during the day, going to school at night. She and Norwig usually commuted together. After Norwig received his masters' degree in public administration in 1970, he began working for the state government in Albany. He was Acting Commissioner for Substance Abuse when he left to work for Phoenix House, a drug rehabilitation center affiliated with the state.

A few years after their marriage, Norwig and Missy traveled to Germany and found Norwig's father, whom he hadn't seen since he was nine. It was a happy reunion that led to a close friendship between father and son. Later on, Norwig and Missy named their first child Gerhard Debye-Saxinger after his grandfather.

Two years before Gerhard was born in 1973, however, Missy was trying on a dress in my kitchen. I noticed a mole on her back—one that a local doctor had insisted was harmless. "I think that mole has grown," I told her. Ben overheard my remark and became alarmed. "I want you to see my dermatologist, Dr. Lowry Miller, immediately," he insisted. "I'll make the appointment."

The next day, Missy and I went to New York City to see Dr. Miller. He took one look at her mole and sent us to a renowned specialist in skin cancer. Dr. Ju was equally alarmed. "I'd like to put you in the hospital tonight so I can do a biopsy in the morning," he said.

Missy burst into tears. "I don't want to be in a New York City hospital," she said. "It's too far away from my husband, who works in Albany." To calm her down, Dr. Ju called an Albany colleague to make an appointment for the next day. As soon as Dr. McCumber saw Missy in Albany, he admitted her to the hospital and removed the mole. His diagnosis: *melanoma, the deadliest form of skin cancer.* "I think we got it all," he told Missy. "Just get on with your life and don't worry about it."

Missy did exactly that. After getting her masters degree in library science, she worked at several libraries before finding a job close to home at the Kinderhook Memorial Library. She went on to have three terrific children: Gerhard (born December 19, 1973), Honor (November 11, 1975) and Peter (April 18, 1979). She and Norwig had a loving marriage and Missy was one of the happiest people I knew.

In 1983, twelve years after her surgery, the cancer returned. This time it started in her lymph glands, spreading quickly to her liver. There wasn't much the doctors could do. Sadly, Missy died at 10 o'clock in the morning on Christmas Day, 1983. She was only 38. Even more tragic, her children were 10, 8 and 4—and Christmas will never be the same for them.

Missy's death left a big hole in the lives of all of us who loved her. Ben was really devastated, but it was particularly tough for Norwig, who had three young children to rear on his own. He also had a whole menagerie of farm animals—including horses, cows, ducks and chickens—to look after. He struggled for several years with baby sitters and others who came in while he was at work. Ben was seriously ill at the time, so I was too busy to offer much help.

In July 1986, Norwig married a charming young lady who'd been executive secretary to one of his colleagues. Michele Johnston was not yet 25, so it was courageous of her to take on the responsibility of Norwig's children, then 12, 10 and 7. She also defied her own parents, who were very upset when she broke her engagement to a young man they'd selected for her and decided to marry Norwig instead.

The marriage of Norwig and Michele in July 1986 was a happy occasion.
Honor (right) was a junior bridesmaid.

It was a beautiful wedding at St. John the Baptist Church in Valatie, just a few miles from our farm. Michele's parents refused to attend, so her maternal grandfather gave her away. Her sister, Paula, served as maid of honor. All three of Norwig's children participated in the ceremony: Gerhard as an usher, Honor as a bridesmaid and Peter as ring bearer. The guests included Michele's grandmother, all three of her sisters, her brothers-in-law, a niece and one of her aunts.

When Ben and I entered the church, I asked to be seated in the place usually reserved for the mother of the bride. It was a spontaneous gesture on my part, but Michele told me later that it made her feel welcome and very proud. I was pleased to see the marriage get off to a good start because I knew the adjustment would not be easy.

At first, Gerhard and Honor resented having a young stepmother—no matter how kind and loving she was. But they gradually learned to appreciate her many fine qualities. Michele soon had two children of her own: Maria (born April 3, 1987) and Tristan (April 24, 1989). The three older ones adore their half siblings, who are terrific youngsters.

I've always considered Michele to be my daughter-in-law and feel privileged to have Maria and Tristan as my grandchildren. Since Norwig's parents are dead—and the family continues to be estranged from Michele's parents—I'm the only grandparent Maria and Tristan have. I love them both dearly and we have a good time together.

9

Ichabod Crane's House at Merwin Farm

When we were first married in 1940, I was happy to live in the city so Ben wouldn't have a long commute to work. But I thought our children would benefit from having an opportunity to get away from the city and enjoy the outdoors. I also wanted to keep a horse so I could continue to ride. "A horse requires a place in the country," Ben said, so we began looking for a suitable summer house soon after Jimmy was born.

We had friends living in Kinderhook, New York—a small town about 25 miles southeast of Albany. While visiting Ed and Dorothy Lewis one weekend, we found a derelict little farm house with 100 acres of land around it. A sign in front of the house, erected by the New York Education Department in 1932, read "*Merwin Farm House, where Ichabod Crane lived.*" We were enchanted by the history of the place.

Although Washington Irving placed *The Legend of Sleepy Hollow* near his home in Tarrytown, it was actually based on Jesse Merwin, an itinerant school teacher who moved from Connecticut to Kinderhook. I'm pretty sure of that because we have a letter signed by President Martin Van Buren in 1846 confirming that Jesse Merwin was, in fact, the prototype for Ichabod Crane. It seems that Washington Irving had been hired around 1810 to tutor the children of Judge William Van Ness at a Kinderhook farm known as Lindenwald. (Later the home of President Van Buren, Lindenwald is now a National Historic Monument.) During his stint as the Van Ness children's tutor, Irving often went fishing with Jesse Merwin. The two young men enjoyed swapping stories while they fished.

According to local historians, Merwin told Irving about a Halloween party he'd attended at the home of Katrina Van Alen, the girl he was in love with. (She is Katrina Van Tassel in Irving's story.) A big burly man named Brom Van Alstyne (called Brom Bones in the story) attended the party, dressed as the ghost of a Hessian soldier, or the "headless horseman." Mounted on a large horse, Brom chased Merwin as he left the party, throwing a pumpkin at him as he disappeared through the covered bridge into Kinderhook.

Merwin didn't really disappear; he continued to teach in a small local school outside Kinderhook. Like many teachers of that time, he lived with a local family, the Van Dykes. He ended up marrying their daughter and spending the rest of his life in the house the Van Dykes had built. Members of the Merwin family still owned the property when we first saw it.

We bought the house and 100 acres in 1942 for only $3,000, which is a good indication of the shape it was in. The house sits at the end of a narrow lane, about half a mile from a quiet country road. Back then, a stream that was sometimes a foot deep passed over the lane. It was not a problem for the old farmer who'd been living in the house. He always traveled by horse and wagon—and the horse simply walked through the water. But we couldn't get any workmen to drive across that stream, so one of the first things we did was hire a mason to build a stone bridge.

Once the bridge was completed, we went to work making the place habitable. We had the foundation shored up and columns put under the beams in the basement to make the floor level. (It's still not exactly level, but it's much better than it was.) We put on a new roof and replaced the plaster that had been ruined by leaks. (I think the old farmer had lived entirely in the kitchen, for he kept a cot behind the wood stove.)

The lintel of one of the old barns on the property is dated 1797, so we believe that's the year the Van Dykes began building the house. In those days, people started with one room, adding others as they could afford to buy the materials. The house still had no electricity, running water or telephone when we bought it. I told Ben we couldn't bring a baby to a place with no running water, so he rigged up a gasoline motor in the cellar. It pumped water from an old outside well into an enormous holding tank.

Ben always kept a watchful eye on the pump while it was working in case something went wrong. As soon as the boys were old enough, he'd take them down in the cellar with him. He'd sit on a large wooden box, with one arm around each son, telling them stories until the water tank was full. He had a wonderful imagination, so the boys have fond memories of those hours in the basement with their father. Some of Ben's stories came from books, such as *Ivanhoe*, that he remembered, but others were his own yarns about fishing and hunting and the wild woods.

Ben's ingenious little pump provided running water in the kitchen and bathrooms, but we had to limit the children to three inches of water in the bath tub. It was also difficult to cope when the boys were in diapers. Disposables didn't exist yet, so water had to be heated on the stove to wash their cloth diapers.

We managed to pump enough water to get by, but we spent four summers on the farm without electricity or a telephone. We bought kerosene lamps for reading and an old oak ice box that was cooled with huge blocks of ice. The ice man wouldn't deliver on our lane, so we had to wait for him at a neighbor's house a mile away, then lug the ice home and heave it into the box.

We devoted our first few summers to working on the house—scraping, painting, hanging wall paper, fixing up the rooms. It was hard work, but it gave us a great deal of satisfaction to renovate the place with our own hands. The children loved the farm, which provided endless places for them to play. As they grew older, they slept outside in a tent—and Ben often visited the tent to tell bedtime stories.

In 1946, when rural electrification came to America, we finally got electricity and a telephone in the house. "All the ruggedness has gone out of life," Ben complained, but I was pleased to have the extra conveniences.

Like many 19th century farm houses, ours had a pair of magnificent maple trees out front. More than 100 years old when we bought the place, they dominated the landscape until around 1951 when I decided to test a local legend. We'd been told that the two marble slabs in front of our doors were actually tombstones from the graves of Jesse Merwin and his wife. They'd been moved to the property around 1900, when some of Jesse's descendents decided to erect a more imposing monument to their famous ancestor in the Kinderhook cemetery.

"Don't ever move those tombstones," we were cautioned after buying the house. "If you do, the headless horseman will ride again," insisted local residents. The exposed surface of the marble slabs was smooth and unmarked, so I couldn't help wondering what was on the other side. One day when a strong young man was mowing our lawn, I said, "Joe, let's get a crowbar and lift up that slab so we can find out if it's really Ichabod Crane's gravestone."

Joe heaved the stone up high enough so we could see the other side. Sure enough, it was carved: *J. Merwin, Esquire, life-long friend of Washington Irving. Died November 8, 1852, aged 68 yrs, 3 months, 8 days.* "Put the stone back the way it was," I told Joe, "and please don't say anything about this little discovery of ours."

I'm not really superstitious, but as that day turned into evening, I kept my eye out for the headless horseman. I saw nothing. Just around sunset, however, a terrible thunderstorm blew up. A bolt of lightening hit one of the giant maple trees, splitting it down the middle. Nothing could be done to save it. I was so distraught over losing that beautiful tree that I told my family about turning over the slab. "Nobody is going to move those tombstones again as long as I own this property!" I added. My grandchildren give me funny smiles when I tell this story, but I don't think they'd dare tempt the fates.

Legend also says that our house is haunted, but I'm not sure about that, either. We had only one bedroom restored in time for our first summer, so we put the boys to bed on a screened porch with big windows. Teddy, age one, was in his crib and Jimmy, two and a half, slept on a cot. One night, after telling the boys a story and singing one of their favorite songs, I went back inside the house. Jimmy suddenly jumped out of bed and knocked on the door between the porch and the living room. I put him back to bed, but he came to the door again and screamed. "There's terror in that scream," Ben said. "He's clearly afraid of something." Then, turning to Jimmy, he asked, "Do you want to sleep in the house, son?"

"Yes," Jimmy gasped. He was so frightened that we moved both boys into the house and put our own bed on the porch. We found it a heavenly place to sleep so we stayed there. Once inside, Jimmy had no more scares. After we returned to the city for the winter, however, Ben was telling the boys a bedtime story about the little farmhouse and its lovely sleeping porch. Suddenly, Jimmy sat straight up in bed and said, "I didn't like the white Mommy on that porch."

"What white Mommy?" Ben asked. "Was it Elizabeth?" he said, naming our baby sitter.

"No, no," Jimmy insisted. "It was a white Mommy who wouldn't sing a song for us." Ben felt chills go down his spine, but decided not to upset Jimmy any more by pursuing it.

The following summer, we received a visit from two elderly members of the Merwin family. They told us that the sleeping porch had been added to the house so their beautiful sister, Nellie, could sleep in the fresh air. She was very ill with consumption, a serious lung disease. In those days, sleeping on an open porch was believed to be beneficial to lung patients. Sadly, it didn't help poor Nellie who died on that porch around 1917.

As far as we know, Jimmy is the only person who ever saw the "ghost," but Ben's mother believed she'd heard her. "In the middle of the night," she told us, "the thumb latch on my bedroom door clicked up, and the door swung open. I didn't see anyone, but it was unnatural. The same thing happened several other nights, too, so I'm sure I wasn't dreaming."

Whether haunted or not, our old house certainly has a lot of atmosphere which makes it a fun place to live. It all began, of course, because I wanted a place to keep a horse. The next summer we bought two horses that we shared with our neighbors. We've had horses on the farm ever since. For 60 years I've enjoyed riding, driving horse carts and teaching my children, grandchildren and great grandchildren how to ride and appreciate horses. It has been a wonderful hobby—and a stimulating change from city life, too.

The Good Old Summertime....

From the time we bought Merwin farm, we spent summers there. When gas was rationed during World War II, we'd take the Albany Day Boat from Manhattan at 9 am. We paid $5 for a cabin, which had a private bathroom and a place for the children to nap. The boat also had a charming dining room, so we ate a delicious lunch on board. Ben and I enjoyed the gorgeous scenery along the Hudson River while the boys ran around having fun. Around 3:40 in the afternoon, we'd land in Hudson and walk to the garage where we kept our car during the winter. Then we'd drive about 15 miles north to the farm.

The children and I stayed at the farm for the entire summer, with Ben coming up by train on weekends. We'd drive to Hudson on Friday evenings to meet him. The train was due at 7 pm, but it was often late. We always took a picnic supper to eat while we waited. In early September, we'd all take the boat back to the city. It was a wonderful way to travel in the days before parkways. Now, of course, we go back and forth to New York City by car, making the trip in about two hours. No matter what transportation we used, though, we were always happy to return to the farm.

It was a healthy life for young city kids. They spent most of the summer outdoors, playing with the neighbors' children, helping me take care of the horses or doing chores with their father. I think it gave them a real appreciation for the value and satisfaction of working with your hands. When Granny Tuttle joined us at the farm, the children also learned a lot about nature. She'd search the woods and fields for wildflowers, then teach them the names. She also taught them how to recognize all the local birds by their songs as well as their feathers.

Ben taught Jimmy and Teddy carpentry skills, so they were able to help him build a small rowboat that we kept on one side of Merwin Lake. The three of them also built a float that Ben anchored in the middle of the deep lake. On summer mornings, we'd row the boat out to the float for swimming lessons. In addition to my three children, I taught several of their friends how to swim. Once they became good swimmers, we had races and played games in the water. They also began fishing in the lake after receiving instruction from their father.

In the late afternoon, when our chores were completed, we'd go horseback riding. All three children learned to be pretty good horsemen. Unlike my formal training on an English saddle, my boys joined the local 4H club and rode western style, often bareback. They also played games on horseback, pretending to be cowboys rounding up herds of cattle or getting into skirmishes with Indians. Jimmy's good friend Danny Warner had a terrific horse. While riding uphill at full gallop, Danny would suddenly cry, "Oh, the Indians got me." Then he'd pitch off the horse onto the ground and play dead. Danny had learned how to dive and roll so he wouldn't hurt himself—and his horse always stopped and waited for him to climb back on.

Around 1953, we decided to participate in a 4-H Club exhibition at the Columbia County Fair, held every Labor Day weekend. We didn't have a horse trailer, so we had to get up early and ride the horses to the fairgrounds in Chatham, seven miles away. We usually spent the entire day there. The horses stayed in the stable when they weren't participating in rodeo games for 4-H kids.

One year, young children were asked to bring their ponies to the ring in front of the grandstand. Missy, age 8, came out leading her old spotted pony, Champ. Most of the other ponies had learned a few tricks—such as counting by nodding their heads—but we'd never trained Champ that way. After several children had demonstrated what their ponies could do, the judge came over to Missy.

"What tricks does your pony know, little girl?" he asked.

"Oh, he used to know lots of tricks," she replied. "But he's so old he's forgotten them all now." The whole grandstand roared with laughter. I was amazed that she'd managed to come up with that answer on the spot.

A few years later, we bought Missy a younger, jazzier pony that she named after Jesse Merwin. She loved that pony and spent a lot of time with him. She could hardly wait to take Jesse to the 4-H horse show at the next county fair. Although she'd never won any ribbons before, she won first prize at her first event that day! She was so happy that tears were streaming down her face as she left the ring. Missy and Jesse went on to win two more blue ribbons that day. At the end, Jesse was named Champion Pony of the Day. We both dissolved in tears over that.

The boys also competed at the fair, but in more dangerous events, such as barrel racing and pole bending. Teddy was particularly ambitious and worked very hard at the shows. Both boys spent the whole day racing around the fairgrounds seeing the exhibits, riding on the Ferris wheel and taking advantage of everything the fair offered.

It was nearly dusk by the time we began our long ride home. The horses had been working all day, so we rode slowly, taking about two hours to make the seven-mile journey. Danny Warner's mother took the three boys' saddles home in her car so they could ride bareback (which they preferred) on the return trip to the farm. After we'd ridden about six miles one evening, Danny's horse sensed that we were close to home and started to trot. He was in the lead, so my horse and the others began to trot, too. All of a sudden, I heard Teddy cry out, "Mommy!" I looked around and saw him sprawled in a ditch.

"Teddy, what happened?" I asked.

"I fell asleep," he said. "When you started to trot, I tumbled off." He was so exhausted that he'd been sleeping most of the way, with his feet curled under him as he sat on his big fat horse. It's no wonder he bounced off, but he didn't get hurt because he was sound asleep when he fell.

Haying is serious business at Merwin Farm, but it's also good fun.
Norwig gave me instructions on driving our tractor while my son
Jim and several grandsons relaxed on top of the stacked hay.

The boys continued to participate in fairs with other members of the 4-H Club until they were 14 or 15. Neither one developed much skill at tennis or golf because they preferred hanging around the farm. They even seemed to enjoy cleaning stables, mending fences, making hay and all the other chores—especially when they were old enough to drive a tractor. (Even today, in middle-age, they still enjoy working with their tractors.)

I was usually too busy at the farm to have much social life in summer. I did a lot of gardening, raising both flowers and vegetables, including peas, beans, beets, carrots, corn, potatoes and herbs. I also raised puppies. One summer we had a litter of six dachshunds, ending up with dogs from three generations of the same family.

From time to time, though, I did manage to participate in community events. When a large central school was built in the late 1940s, all the one-room school houses in the area were abandoned. A group of local women, led by our neighbor Julia Fisher, decided to convert our little school—the one where Jesse Merwin taught—into a social center for young people. Everyone worked very hard to get the building repaired and painted.

Another neighbor, Dorothy Lewis, was friendly with Mary Margaret McBride, the host of a popular radio show at the time. Both women knew Eleanor Roosevelt, so they described the project to the former first lady and UN delegate. She seemed interested, so they invited her to the dedication on October 11, 1952. When Mrs. Roosevelt agreed to come, Ms. McBride arranged for her radio show to be broadcast from the new Ichabod Crane Community Center that day.

After the dedication, Dorothy invited a group of friends—including the rector of St. Paul's church and his wife, Granny Tuttle and me—to lunch at her home. It happened to be Eleanor Roosevelt's 68th birthday, so we celebrated with a cake. After blowing out the candles, Mrs. Roosevelt described her family tradition: they re-light all the candles, giving one to each guest who makes a wish for the birthday celebrant before blowing it out again.

When it was Mother Tuttle's turn, she said, "I wish you as many happy years as I've had." Mrs. Roosevelt seemed surprised at that, not realizing that Ben's youthful-looking mother was actually 82 at the time. It was a wonderful day—and a great beginning for the new center, which became the meeting place for the local 4-H club and Girl Scouts, among other groups.

Our old farmhouse becomes inaccessible when snow and ice coats the road, so we've always closed it up for the winter. I don't mind that because I think a change of routine is stimulating. I also enjoy a variety of city activities during those months. It seems to me that people who do the same things all the time get into ruts—and that takes the fun out of life. I'm determined not to let that happen to me.

Retiring to the Farm

The children were always so happy at the farm that Ben and I began thinking ahead to future grandchildren. As neighboring farms and adjacent land became available for purchase, we began expanding our property. We now own almost 390 acres. In addition to our original house, the family owns five others, including two that are currently rented to non-relatives.

It has been deeply satisfying to see our children, grandchildren and great grandchildren enjoying this place that Ben and I loved for so many years. Although my husband and I never lived on the farm year-round, all our children have been full-time residents at one time or another.

After Ted left the Army, he enrolled in graduate school about 30 miles from the farm. He and Dawn spent that winter of 1968/69 in our little farm house with their daughter, Tammy. Later on they moved into a new house we built about half a mile from our little cottage. They left the farm after Ted got his MBA in January 1970, returning only for brief visits during the next 30 years or so. In 1999, however, Ted retired and moved back to the area. He and Dawn are now building a retirement home on the farm.

When Jim and Nora returned from Germany with their two sons, he joined his brother in graduate school in Albany. They spent their first winter roughing it in our little farm house. Next, they moved into the house that Ted and Dawn vacated when Ted took a job in New York City. Their third son was born there in December 1970.

During Jim's two years in graduate school, he enjoyed living on the farm so much that he decided to seek work in Albany so he and his family could stay put. Jim and Nora's three boys—Ben, Tommy and Christopher—all attended local schools and grew up mostly on the farm. This gave Ben and me a wonderful opportunity to develop close relationships with our grandsons during summers and weekends. Although Jim and Nora spent six years in Cleveland after the boys were grown, they returned to their home on Merwin Farm when Jim retired. I feel very fortunate to have both sons back in the area again.

Missy also loved the farm. She even chose to have her wedding reception under a tent in front of our house. By that time, Norwig had fallen in love with the place as well. "I'm going to get a job in Albany so we can live here on the farm," he said. Soon after he and Missy were married in 1967, they moved into a house by Merwin Lake, which we'd bought from Ed and Dorothy Lewis. Their three children grew up on the farm and attended schools in the area until they went off to college.

(I thought Norwig might move away after Missy's death, but he didn't want to disrupt his children from their home. When he remarried, Michele moved to the farm and is raising their children, Maria and Tristan, in the same house. It has undergone major renovation and expansion during the 36 years that Norwig has lived there. He's done most of the work himself, with the help of family and friends.)

Missy was an excellent rider who really adored horses. Early in their marriage, she and Norwig decided to raise Morgans. An American breed from Vermont, Morgans are beautiful, utilitarian horses that many farmers use for plowing and pulling carts as well as riding. Morgans are so calm—even in traffic—that they're popular with mounted police in New York City.

Missy and Norwig started with two mares, which they bred. At the high point of their breeding operation, they were taking care of 17 Morgans at the farm. Being around all those horses—and sometimes helping with the foals—was great fun for us all.

One summer, Missy and Norwig took their children on a fishing trip around the time a new foal was due, so I offered to look after the pregnant mare. When I noticed her walking restlessly in and out of the lake, I cleaned out a big stall and put down fresh straw. Fearing that she'd drop her foal in the lake or the pasture where I wouldn't be able to pick it up (I was in my early 70's at the time), I led her into the barn and locked her in the clean stall, well away from the other horses.

Once the mare was comfortable, I returned to the house. A short time later, Nora happened to walk past the barn. "I think the mare is having her baby," she reported. I called Jim Borden, a friend who is also a professional horse breeder, before we returned to the barn. It was dark, so we lit a kerosene lantern hanging from a peg. Sure enough, the foal's two front feet were already visible. The head came out next, then the body. Completely covered by the caul or birth sac, the little horse looked like a beautiful package wrapped in cellophane.

I was preparing to cut the cord when the foal beat me to it, pushing his sharp little hoofs forward. As I grabbed the sac and pulled it back, his flattened ears shot up and his eyes opened. The mare went to work immediately, licking her baby all over. As she licked, that little foal looked at me so intently that I immediately fell in love. A few minutes later, Jim Borden arrived with an enormous towel he used to dry off the foal. Soon the newborn was staggering around on his wobbly little legs, trying to figure out where to find his mother's milk. It was a perfect birth—and a special experience for me.

Missy registered all her Morgan horses under the names of herbs and spices. Her farm was called "Echo Lake," so the new foal was named Echo Lake Ginger. He had siblings called Parsley, Cinnamon, Cardamom, Rosemary and Juniper. All the Morgans were trained by Jim Borden to pull a cart before they were broken to ride. Ginger became my special favorite as a driving horse after I played "midwife" at his birth. We took a number of ribbons together in driving shows.

The opportunity to become intimately involved with animals and nature is one reason the farm has played such a big role in my life. I've found that nothing relieves stress better than a horseback ride or a long walk in the woods on a sunny day. Even more important, Merwin Farm is the place to which my children, grandchildren, great grandchildren and some of their cousins return when they want to relax, recharge and relive happy memories.

Although Ben and I didn't plan it, I believe the farm has been instrumental in developing a genuine closeness among the various branches and generations of our extended family. Seeing so many loved ones getting together for holidays and special occasions fills my heart with joy.

My horse, Donna, and I often teamed up for carriage driving shows.

10

Close Calls

My most memorable experiences at Merwin farm were not always as delightful as those I've already described. About eight years ago, for example, Norwig came home with a new pet: a pot-bellied Vietnamese pig that he'd been told could be trained like a dog and kept in the house. He envisioned it sleeping by his chair near the fireplace. The training was never very successful, though, so the pig was banished to a dog kennel behind the house.

Confucius, as the family named him, didn't like being cooped up in the kennel. As he grew bigger and stronger, he broke through the kennel door and wandered down the road to the barn. A friendly little animal that never harmed anyone, he apparently decided he'd rather live with the horses. He settled into the horse barn and wouldn't leave. When the weather turned cold, he just burrowed under the hay to keep warm. Confucius seemed especially fond of my horse, Donna, a very friendly mare.

A beautiful black cat also lived in the barn. One of the children had named him "Killer," because he kept the barn free of mice. The cat, the pig and the four horses lived happily together for a year or two. Every morning, I'd walk from my house to the barn to tend to the animals. I usually fed Confucius first because he was the most aggressive. The horses came next, then the cat. I put the cat's food up on the hay wagon so the pig wouldn't get into it if Killer decided to finish eating later.

One fall morning on my way to the barn, I noticed a tree full of wild apples, so I picked a few as a treat for the horses. When I reached the barn, I placed the apples on the hay wagon. Killer jumped up on the wagon and nuzzled my arm, so I began stroking his silky fur. As long as he was there, I decided to feed him first. Suddenly, I felt such a sharp pain in my leg that I thought I'd been struck by lightening. Confucius, who was hungry and probably jealous of the attention I was giving the cat, had charged across the barn and rammed the side of my leg with his tusks.

The blow took my breath away. As soon as I recovered a little, I pulled up the leg of my jeans to check the wound. To my horror, I found a big triangle of flesh dangling from the side of my leg. It wasn't bleeding very much—and nothing felt broken—so I limped back home and washed my leg under the tap in the bath tub. The wound looked quite alarming under the light, so I called Michele. She rushed over.

"I think we'd better take you to the emergency room," she said. "Something has to be done about that." She bundled me into her car and quickly drove me to the nearest hospital.

"What happened to you?" the intern asked when he saw my wounded leg.

"I was gored by a boar," I replied. Judging by the look of disbelief on his face, he probably thought I was either senile or had a vivid imagination. But suddenly everyone in the hospital wanted to see "the old lady who'd been gored by a boar."

After cleaning and examining the wound, the young doctor said, "Fortunately, the pig just missed a blood vessel or it would have been very hard to stop the bleeding. He did hit a nerve, which explains why you didn't feel much pain. But it's a nasty wound, so I'll have to stitch it closed." After giving me a shot of Novocain, he started stitching away. We sat there chatting the whole time as if he were doing needlepoint. I didn't feel a thing, but I went home with a huge bandage on my leg. When the stitches came out, I was happy to see the wound had healed nicely.

Soon after that, Confucius decided to join us whenever we went riding. Although pigs and horses don't usually get along, he'd made friends with our horses. Each time Nora and I went on a trail ride, Confucius would run along beside us like a dog. Sometimes we rode so fast that the pig fell behind, but he always caught up later.

One beautiful day, Nora and I returned from a particularly long ride and couldn't find Confucius. We thought he'd show up soon, but he never came home at all that day, or the next. Finally, a neighbor drove up and asked Norwig if he owned a pig.

"Yes, we have a pet pig," he replied.

"I really must apologize," said the neighbor. "The pig was chasing my dog the other day. My brother thought it was a wild boar, so he shot it. He was so proud of his shot that he took the head to a taxidermist to be stuffed and mounted on the wall."

"'That's not a wild boar,' the taxidermist told him. 'It's a Vietnamese pot bellied pig! You've shot somebody's pet, so you'd better find out who it belonged to.' I'm really sorry," the man repeated.

Confucius, the pot-bellied Vietnamese pig, tags along as Donna and I
prepare for our morning ride.

"I'm sorry, too," Norwig told him. "Do you want to tell my children what happened to their pet or shall I do it?"

Later on, I learned that most people who keep pigs as pets have their tusks removed. Vietnamese pigs are usually very friendly, but they do use their tusks whenever they feel threatened or, as I learned, jealous of another animal. I decided to be more careful around animals—even my beloved horses—after that. You never really know what they might do.

Survival Instinct

In the fall of 1996, when I was 85, I had an experience that was even more dangerous than being gored. During my early morning walk, I decided to see what progress had been made in cleaning out our man-made pond in the woods. A few months earlier, a man named Felix had cut a channel through the dam so he could drain the pond. After letting it dry out most of the summer, he'd returned with his bulldozer to clear all the weeds and muck from the bottom. I hadn't been near the site since the clearing had been done.

As I approached Peachy Pond, I could see that Felix had filled in the channel with sludge he'd removed from the bottom. It looked solid, so I started to walk across, unaware that it was just gooey muck, about six feet deep. My right foot quickly sunk in so far that I couldn't pull it out. I kept my left foot stretched out behind me, lying on top of the mud. As I tried to free myself, the right foot kept sinking in deeper. The sludge was already over my knee and getting higher.

It was a cold day, so I was wearing a warm, fleece-lined jacket, a wool hat and gloves. I tried pushing the mud away with my gloved hands, but they just sank in until one glove disappeared. Next, I tried using the visor of my hat to push away the mud, but that didn't help, either. Peachy Pond is about half a mile from a country road that has very little traffic. My grandchildren were all in school and their parents had gone to work. I knew Felix wouldn't be back for a few days because he'd told me everything had to settle before he could finish the job.

Suddenly it hit me: *I'm really stuck. It will be at least seven hours before anyone in my family gets home—and even then no one is likely to come down this trail They probably won't miss me for a while, and they won't know where to look when they do notice I'm gone. It's pointless to call out for help, so I'll just have to get myself out of this mess.*

My predicament brought to mind the time I'd seen a horse, ridden by a teen-aged neighbor, stuck in a drainage ditch full of similar muck. The horse's feet kept sinking in deeper as he struggled to get out. The boy ran for help, but it wasn't until his uncle came with a tractor that we were able to pull the horse out of the ditch.

As I pictured that scene in my mind, it suddenly occurred to me that the horse's feet had sunk into the mud quickly, but his body had not. That's when I decided to try using my torso for leverage. The nearest firm ground was behind me—and the channel was about 15 feet wide—but my position forced me to try going forward. I threw myself down on my chest and stomach, with my left leg stretched out in back and my arms spread on either side. Then, using my hands as paddles and squirming slightly, I began trying to swim and wiggle my way through the muck like a giant reptile.

It was hard work pushing against the heavy sludge. After struggling about ten minutes, I was gasping for breath and my heart was thumping. *This is no place to have a heart attack,* I thought. *If I die and sink into the mud, it might be spring before they find my body. I'd better stop and rest.* Lying on top of that cold, slimy mud was not exactly pleasant, but it allowed me to catch my breath. My right leg was still imprisoned, but I knew I was making progress because it was inching forward with me.

I continued twisting and paddling, stopping to rest, then twisting and paddling again. After struggling about an hour, I finally got across the channel and crawled up on the bank. As I lay there, totally exhausted, I felt (and looked) like a monster that had slithered out of some primeval ooze. *This is a new beginning*, I thought. With the frightening ordeal behind me, I felt that I'd received a special gift from God. That gave me renewed faith in my ability to go on, help others and enjoy life again.

I was thinking only about life as I lay on the ground, slowly recovering from the combination of fear and exertion. The incident had made it painfully clear that we're all in charge of our own lives. We can't always count on others for help, so we must be prepared to get out of whatever situation—social, emotional, economic or physical—we've gotten ourselves into.

It took me 10 or 15 minutes to regain enough energy to get to my feet. My clothes were so saturated with heavy mud that it was hard to walk. My sneakers squished with each step and I felt like a zombie. The shortest path to my house was blocked by the channel full of muck, so I walked around the far side of the pond. From there, I had to climb a fence into the horse pasture—not an easy task for an exhausted 85-year-old weighted down with mud. The horses came over, smelled the muck and backed off. I think they were frightened until they heard my voice, but they still wouldn't come near me. I went through another fence before I was able to begin walking back home. It was a slow, cold trek in those wet, muddy clothes.

When I reached the house, I pulled everything off and dropped it all on the front porch. Then I took a hot shower, put on a warm robe and climbed into bed under an electric blanket. It took about an hour to get warmed up again—but I felt very grateful to God for giving me the mental and physical strength to escape from that muddy trap.

Once I recovered enough to crawl out of bed and make a pot of coffee, different emotions took over. I began to feel lonely and frustrated because I was eager to share this tale of horror. Yet I still had a long wait before my family got home. As I sipped my coffee, I couldn't help thinking about the "what ifs." *What if I hadn't extricated myself? How long would it have been before someone started searching for me? What if they couldn't find me or even my body? What would my family think then?* I was pretty sure they wouldn't think of foul play, because mischief is so rare in our area.

My theatrical background came into play as my thoughts turned to Jesse Merwin and the headless horseman. Maybe "The Disappearance of Faity" would have become a new legend in Columbia County, with people thinking the headless horseman was at it again. I was momentarily amused by these thoughts, but it was very obvious to me that I was not ready to die. Relief at having survived flooded over me.

The whole experience was a dramatic reminder that I'm not invincible. We all know that, of course, but we often act as if we don't believe it. I think it's good to be reminded of our vulnerability from time to time so we don't become careless.

When I finally told my children about my ordeal, I tried to make light of it all, but they were more distressed than amused. After that, new family rules were established:

- Always carry a cell phone when walking alone;

- Never swim, ride or ice skate without a companion;

- Tell someone where you're going—or leave a note on the door describing your route and destination—if you go off alone.

I certainly don't want to give up my independence or my daily rambles in the woods, so I try to follow these sensible rules. If I should break a leg or experience some other disaster, I want to make sure my family knows where to look for me. It's a small price to pay for the immense pleasure I derive from living on the farm in the summer and fall months.

11

Giving Back

From the early days of my marriage, volunteer work has played a major role in my life. Ben didn't want me tied down to a paying job—and we didn't really need a second income—but he was very supportive of my volunteer activities. He knew I had a lot of energy and it pleased him to see me using my talents to benefit the community.

Helping others has always appealed to me—partly because of the relatives who did so much for Howard, Lee and me after our parents died. I knew I could never repay Aunt Mamie, who provided a home for us, or Aunt Gertrude, who paid our boarding school tuition. But their generosity inspired me to seek ways to make a meaningful contribution of my own.

Over the years, I became almost a professional volunteer, but I didn't plan it that way. It just happened as various opportunities came along. Soon after I was married, for example, Dorothy McFadden, the wife of one of Ben's good friends, asked me to help with a project she'd initiated. Called Junior Programs, it produced good children's theater around the country, using a touring group of professional performers. I'd been interested in children's theater since I performed as a child, so I agreed to join the board of Junior Programs and help promote the organization.

During World War II, it was impossible to get enough gasoline to keep touring, so Dorothy arranged performances for children in schools, parks, theaters and other places in New York City. In the two years that I worked on Junior Programs, I became close friends with two other board members: Dottie Teegan, who'd worked on children's theater at the Chicago World's Fair, and Helenka Panteleoni, who went on to start the United Nations International Children's Educational Fund or UNICEF. (Later on, I spent about ten years helping to sell UNICEF Christmas cards, which provide funds for many wonderful children's programs around the world.)

While working with Junior Programs, I met a woman at the Brooklyn Academy of Music (BAM) who invited me to join their Women's League, a group trying to promote larger audiences and more programs. My family had a long history with the Academy—my Uncle Tom Leeming had been president from 1901 to 1926—so I was eager to help. Not long after joining the Women's League, I was asked to be president. When I told Ben about it, he said, "You pop up to the top of these groups like a cork in a barrel of water." But it wasn't really a big honor; I was chosen because I was willing to work. The League disbanded after a few years when Harvey Lichtenstein became the director and changed many of BAM's programs for the better.

My free time was more limited after I had two babies so close together, but I continued to volunteer whenever I could. I was eager to have a role during World War II so I worked at the USO, rolled bandages for the Red Cross and became a part-time plane spotter near our farm.

Once our children started school, I was eager to know their teachers, what projects they were working on and what was going on. I joined the PTA at Berkeley Institute, the private school they all attended for a while. I was elected president of the PTA in 1946 and invited to join the Board of Directors several years later. I served as board secretary, taking notes and typing them up for 25 years. I was still on that board when my granddaughter, Tammy, enrolled at Berkeley. When I left in 1976, they gave me a lovely certificate for 26 years service.

The Brooklyn Botanic Garden

About two years after we moved to Brooklyn, the mother of one of our sons' friends told me about an excellent course at the Brooklyn Botanic Garden (BBG) on making Christmas decorations. I signed up and found it so interesting and practical that I took other BBG courses in flower arranging and landscaping.

I loved spending time at the Garden, a beautiful 52-acre oasis in the middle of Brooklyn. One day I was asked to help with a mailing for the Women's Auxiliary. That involved a lot of folding and licking which wasn't very exciting, but it led to an invitation to join. As usual, I said, "yes." After working with the Auxiliary for more than a decade, I became President in 1961.

When I began volunteering at the BBG, I was feeling a bit lonely at home. Most of my neighbors were much older than I, and my darling children were too young to provide very interesting conversation. When Ben came home from work, I was at my busiest, cooking dinner and dealing with the kids. I didn't get a chance to talk with my husband until the children were in bed, so I yearned for more adult companionship during the day. Thanks to the wonderful help I received from Ben's mother and from Nora Daly, the Irish woman who came in to clean and do laundry, I had time to devote to volunteer work.

I've always enjoyed meeting new people, but those I've met at the Botanic Garden have been truly special. Clementine (Clem) Kastendieck, for example, has been a close friend for decades. We got to know each other while working on the annual fund-raiser for the Auxiliary. Instead of the traditional bridge party (which included the sale of a few plants) Clem and I decided to put on shows in the auditorium. We sold "Patrons Tickets" to the performances, but continued to sell plants as well.

We created a one-hour show, complete with costumes, music and narration on a garden theme. Clem did the writing and I did the narration. The hard-working Garden staff helped build the sets, while talented members of the Auxiliary performed or helped out backstage. The first show was such a success that it became an annual event. The 50th Anniversary Pageant, written and directed by Clem in 1960, was an outstanding production that covered all aspects of the Garden's first 50 years.

Within a few years, though, what had begun as a sideline sale of a few plants grew into the BBG's large Spring Plant Sale open to the general public. The sale became so popular that Clem and I decided to skip the entertainment and devote all our efforts to selling plants. That important event now raises thousands of dollars for the BBG every year. In fact, the 2002 Plant Sale grossed $280,000. Some of the plants are still grown in the BBG's greenhouses, but others come from wholesale nurseries.

One plant sale I'll never forget occurred in 1959. The union representing city employees, including many of our gardeners and maintenance workers, was on strike at the time. Members of the Auxiliary stepped in to rake, water and prune so the Garden would continue to look beautiful. But the nurseries that supplied plants for our sale were unable to deliver because their drivers were afraid to cross the picket lines.

I volunteered to pick up some of the plants, using the farm truck that Jimmy was driving to school that year. With 1,000 pansy plants massed together, the bed of our old truck looked like a handsome Oriental rug. When I arrived at the Garden's back gate, however, the pickets surrounded the truck and refused to let me pass. "What nursery are you from?" they demanded.

Fortunately, Alys Sutcliff, the Head of Horticulture at the Garden, recognized me and opened the gate. With her commanding voice and charming British accent, she announced, "That's Mrs. Tuttle, one of the leaders of our Auxiliary.

You just step aside and let her pass." And step aside they did. Volunteers quickly unloaded the truck.

In 1965, Dr. George Avery, Director of the Brooklyn Botanic Garden, suggested that the Women's Auxiliary make a film about the BBG. Clem and I were a team by then, so we agreed to take it on. We asked the Auxiliary to appropriate $10,000 from that year's plant sale for the film. (It was customary to use those profits for a special project. One year the Auxiliary donated money to buy a sorely needed back-end loader for the Garden; another year it bought a coke machine for the Garden staff.)

We began interviewing film makers, but were disillusioned to learn that professionals charged at least $1,000 a minute for a finished film. We planned to make a 20-minute documentary, so we couldn't afford to pay that rate. Our next step was to approach all the New York colleges that had film departments. New York University posted a notice on their bulletin board, but we got no response. A graduate student at City College of New York expressed interest in filming our gardens—until budget cuts forced CCNY to close its film department.

Finally, we contacted the film department at Columbia University's Center for Mass Communication. In return for a $10,000 grant, they arranged for a talented young graduate student, Stuart Chasmar, to make our film. Stuart came to the BBG for an interview and made a good impression on us. He loved the beauty of the Garden, but knew very little about horticulture so we assigned Daphne Drury, one of our instructors, to guide him.

At George Avery's suggestion, we planned to make an educational film based on one of the Garden's popular handbooks. We thought pruning had the broadest appeal, so Stuart set off to film the BBG gardeners pruning trees and bushes in spring, summer and fall. Late that autumn, Stuart showed us two hours of beautiful shots of the Botanic Garden in all phases of pruning. They ranged from close-ups of small rose bushes being trimmed to dramatic shots of gardeners working with saws in tall trees.

By the time Stuart finished that first screening, we knew that our most difficult task would be to condense those two hours into 20 minutes. We asked Frances Miner, the head of the BBG's Education Department, to write the script and help us choose the shots that best illustrated correct pruning techniques. We all spent hours going over the film, cutting, editing and rearranging pictures. We even worked at Columbia's film lab on the day before Thanksgiving, when we should have been home stuffing turkeys and making pies. We kept at it because we were determined to finish in time to enter an important film festival.

The final version of *Pruning Practices at the Brooklyn Botanic Garden* was 22 minutes long. The first horticulture film produced by a Botanic Garden, it was entered in the American Film Festival, where it won the prestigious Gold Eagle Award for short documentaries. In the spring of 1966, Sumner Glimscher of Columbia University, Clem and I traveled to Washington, DC, to receive the award. We also received a silver cup from a film festival in Salerno, Italy.

Later on, I showed our little movie to Brendan Gill, film critic of *The New Yorker*. "It's a wonderful film," he said, "but where did you get that awful title?"

"Well, what do you think we should call it?" I asked. "Cutting up at the Brooklyn Botanic Garden?"

"Well, that might have more appeal," he said. In any event, the pruning film launched a new business for the Auxiliary—making educational films for and about the Botanic Garden. Profits from selling our first endeavor to film libraries, garden clubs and private individuals enabled us to make a second film, *Planting and Transplanting,* in 1969. It was also shot by Stuart Chasmar and produced by Columbia University Press, under Sumner Glimscher's guidance.

I share a laugh with Celeste Holm at the Brooklyn Botanic Garden on the day she received the Forsythia Award for outstanding service to New York organizations.

The BBG subsequently made five other educational films. Ian Clark, an Australian film maker, had called the BBG for permission to use some of our beautiful Bonsai plants in a film he was planning. When Clem and I interviewed Ian and saw samples of his work, we decided he was just the person to make our next film. *Bonsai—the Art of Training Dwarfed Potted Trees* was completed in 1971. It was so successful that we asked Ian to make other films: *The Art of Dyeing with Plants, Herbs—Use and Tradition, Dried Flower Designs,* and *Get Ready, Get Set, Grow—a teaching video for children.* Most of the films were later made into videos that were sold in our gift shop, but they're no longer available—and the BBG has stopped producing films.

After serving as president of the Women's Auxiliary for several years, I was elected to the Governing Board of the BBG in 1965. Five years later, I became Chairman of the Board. I didn't know anything about running a board, but my husband had served on the boards of several public companies, so I was able to tap his expertise. (In fact, someone once told me that Ben ran the best board on Wall Street.) Although he never had time to do volunteer work himself, Ben always supported my efforts and provided invaluable advice when I needed it.

One major undertaking during my seven years as Chairman of the Board was to establish a pension plan for employees of the Brooklyn Institute of Arts and Sciences, the parent organization of the Botanic Garden. At the time, Ben was on the board of TIAA/CREF, an investment company that provided insurance and retirement plans for teachers. Our previous director, George Avery, was a former teacher who had a policy with TIAA/CREF. "Their pension program would be a great model to follow in setting up a retirement plan for Garden employees," he told us.

At my request, Ben spent a full day with Tom Donnelly, who handled financial matters for the Brooklyn Institute. Together they mapped out the Cultural Institutions Retirement Plan, which was soon adopted by our board. Gradually, other cultural institutions in New York City joined, too. That plan is still going strong, so I'm proud of my role in getting it started.

Much more difficult for me was overseeing the incorporation of the Brooklyn Botanic Garden as a separate entity from the Brooklyn Institute of Arts and Sciences. This was a controversial move opposed by some of the old, traditional Brooklyn families who'd been friends of my parents. I was criticized for going against local tradition. The Institute had launched the Garden as its scientific arm (with the Brooklyn Museum and the Academy of Music on the art side), so some old-timers thought it should remain a single institution.

As I acquired more knowledge of the business side of the Garden, though, I became convinced that separate incorporation would be very beneficial to us. It was, as George Avery had pointed out when he retired in 1970, the best way to protect our endowment and enhance our ability to raise money for the BBG. The first step was taken in 1975 when the Institute's board agreed to form a tax-exempt Brooklyn Botanic Fund for gifts and grants to the Garden. I appointed board member Lois Carswell to head this fund. She and her husband, Donald, were instrumental in helping us become The Brooklyn Botanic Garden, Inc. in 1976. The BBG and the Brooklyn Museum have both been more successful in fund raising and other activities since becoming separate entities, so I'm very glad we got it done.

The Garden Guides program was also begun during my tenure, under the leadership of Clem Kastendieck. We trained volunteers to lead visitors on tours of the Botanic Garden and to answer their questions. This program has been so successful that many other gardens have copied it, so getting that started was very satisfying as well.

I was also delighted when my BBG activities inspired some of my relatives to become involved with the Garden. One was a favorite cousin, Helena Jelliffe Goldschmidt, who'd fled Holland with her two sons when World War II broke out. Her husband, Carel, worked for a Dutch company that sent him to Sumatra to bring a ship load of tobacco to the United States, so the family was reunited in New York. Their home and everything they owned in Amsterdam was seized by the Nazis, but Carel was able to continue his work in this country, so they never returned to Holland to live. Once he got back on his feet, they bought a beautiful home in Mt. Kisco.

Helena was devoted to her own garden, which featured a spectacular array of Dutch tulips, so I invited her to a plant sale at the Kitchawan Research Center, the BBG's 250-acre outreach station not far from Mt. Kisco. Soon after that, Helena and some of her friends from the Bedford Garden Club started a Kitcha-wan Auxiliary of the BBG. Later, Helena served on the BBG Board.

Helena's son and daughter-in-law, Ely and Ann Goldsmith (who anglicized their surname), also became interested in the Brooklyn Botanic Garden. Ann joined the Auxiliary and eventually served on the BBG board for about ten years. She was instrumental in introducing her aunt, Helen Froehlich, to the BBG. Helen was a loyal member and a generous donor who left a marvelous bequest, in the form of a trust, to the Brooklyn Botanic Garden.

After my term as Chairman of the Board ended, I continued as a Trustee of the Garden and an active member of the Auxiliary. In 1988, I was thrilled to become the 36th recipient of the Brooklyn Botanic Garden's Forsythia Award for "outstanding service to organizations throughout the New York area." Previous recipients of the annual award include Helen Hayes, Celeste Holm, Danny Kaye, Dr. Howard Rusk and Mrs. David Rockefeller, so I felt very honored to join this distinguished group.

As I look back at all I've received from the Botanic Garden—the recognition, the satisfactions, the friendship of many wonderful people and the sheer joy of being in such a beautiful place—I believe that my years as a volunteer have done as much for me as they have for the BBG. I certainly have no regrets about all the time I've devoted to the Garden. Although I resigned from the Board in 2002, I continue to be an active supporter.

The Girl Scouts

Soon after Missy was born, my mother's first cousin, Emma King Gray, said, "Now that you have a daughter, you must get involved with the Girl Scouts." That sounded like a good idea to me, so Emma introduced me to some of the Brooklyn women active in scouting. After helping with fund raising, I was invited to join the Board of the Girl Scouts Council of Greater New York—before Missy was old enough to become a scout. My title was Staff and Office Person, but I was actually in charge of all the Girl Scouts in Brooklyn. We had more than 30,000 scouts in our borough at the time, so it was a big job.

I served as a liaison between the Board, the paid staff in Brooklyn, and the volunteer coordinators in each of Brooklyn's eleven districts. I chaired a monthly meeting with all these leaders, bringing them information from the Board, which met in Manhattan. I also helped them plan and run various events, including the annual sale of Girl Scout cookies. This was the major fund-raiser that helped make all the programs for the girls possible.

At one point, I was chairman of the cookie sale in Brooklyn, which meant that all the money came to me at the end of the sale. One night I sat in Ben's little office at our house in Park Slope, tallying cash, checks and money orders on a borrowed adding machine. When I saw the total—$137,000—I got nervous. Ben was in California on business and the children were asleep on the top floor. *It's ridiculous to have all this money in one place*, I thought, *but at least no one knows that it's here.*

My relief was short-lived. As I put the proceeds in a box, I glanced at a bulletin that had gone out to all the Girl Scouts in Brooklyn. I was startled to see this notice: *If, by October 13, you have not turned the money over to the commissioner, send it directly to Mrs. F. B. Tuttle, 633 Second Street, Brooklyn.* I decided to put the box of money underneath the chaise lounge in my bedroom. Then I allowed our two little dachshunds to sleep on the chaise that night. They weren't exactly guard dogs, but I knew they'd alert me if anyone came near.

The next morning, I stashed the box under a rug in the back seat of my car and drove into Girl Scout Headquarters in Manhattan. At the board meeting, I voiced my concerns. "This is a foolish way to handle so much money," I said. "I think each commissioner should deposit the cash and checks as they come in, keeping careful records along the way." After that, the procedure was changed and I was elected Assistant Treasurer of the Board.

Following a meeting of the board of the Girl Scouts Council of Greater New York, I chatted with fellow members Helen Hayes (left), Kitty Carlisle Hart (second from right) and Mrs. Itman.

Each new responsibility I took on helped me acquire new skills and more self confidence. One of my duties, for example, was interviewing young women for paid positions with the Girl Scouts. Since they were all college graduates and I'd never been to college, I began to wonder about the fairness of the procedure. When I voiced my concerns to the head of personnel, who had a Ph.D., she put my mind at ease. "Don't worry about that," she said. "I'd hire you in a minute. You have solid experience and leadership abilities that most of these young girls lack." I was surprised—and very pleased—to hear that.

Scouting is no longer as popular as it was in those days. The main problem, I think, is the difficulty of finding leaders who can meet with scouts after school. Mothers of today's school-age children often have full-time jobs—and the Girl Scouts can't afford to hire staff to replace all those volunteers. But even in the 1950s and 60s, it wasn't easy to find reliable scout leaders.

As part of my effort to recruit volunteers at Brooklyn schools, I remember going to a contentious PTA meeting in Bedford-Stuyvesant, a poor and predominantly black section of Brooklyn. The meeting began with a group of parents complaining about the condition of the school—a leaky roof, faulty plumbing and rooms so cold the children had to wear heavy coats to class. I turned to my colleague and said, "How can I ask these parents to volunteer for Girl Scouting when they're struggling to keep body and soul together?"

"You just have to do it," she insisted. "You're listed on the program and they've already seen you here in your Girl Scout uniform."

Reluctantly, I got up and described the scouting program, then asked for volunteers to help form Girl Scout troops in the neighborhood. Six women approached me afterwards. "We desperately want scouting here," they explained, "so our daughters will have something to look forward to after school. We're prepared to volunteer so we can form a scout troop in Bed-Stuy." They turned out to be some of our best volunteers, even though it was difficult for them to take time away from their jobs to do it.

We also had a problem finding places to hold scout meetings. The schools usually provided a room where we could meet after classes were over for the day, but the school custodians suddenly started demanding two hours' pay just to keep one room open. That was typical of the obstacles we faced as we tried to keep a scouting program going.

I saw how much scouting meant to Missy and the other girls, though, so that made the work very rewarding. My involvement with the Girl Scouts also introduced me to many wonderful people, such as Helen Hayes, the famous actress who served on our board, and Ellin Mackay Berlin, the wife of the eminent composer and song writer.

Irving Berlin had joined the board of the Boy Scouts of America because he believed he'd gained a great deal from being a scout in his youth. He arranged for all the royalties from his song, "God Bless America," to go into a charitable foundation, The God Bless America Fund, with the Boy Scouts as a major beneficiary.

I got to know Irving through his wife, Ellin. Her former roommate, Harriet Price Phipps, was Chairman of the Girl Scout Council of Greater New York. Ellin, the mother of four daughters, joined our board and did a great job as public relations director. She also persuaded Irving to add the Girl Scouts to the list of The God Bless America Fund recipients. Both Ellin and Irving Berlin actively promoted scouting for many years.

While chatting with Ellin after one of our board meetings, I told her a favorite story about my sister's first meeting with Irving Berlin. "When Honor was studying art in Paris in the twenties," I explained, "she happened to see Mr. Berlin at the Four Arts Ball. She boldly went up and introduced herself, saying they'd met at some function in New York City (which was not exactly true). Mr. Berlin did not remember her, of course, but graciously admired her gown. 'Would you like to meet the designer?' Honor quickly asked. 'He's a classmate of mine at Parsons and he's here tonight.'

"Mr. Berlin was so taken with Honor's dress—and with her friend who designed it," I continued, "that he arranged a meeting with the designer. His name was Adrian and Mr. Berlin hired him to design all the costumes for *The Music Box Review* on Broadway."

"Oh, was that your sister?" Ellin asked. "Adrian was talking about that recently. He told us he owed his start to a beautiful young woman who introduced him to Irv in Paris. As you probably know," she added, "Adrian has become the most popular costume designer in Hollywood. He designs clothes for all the most glamorous movie stars."

That evening, I related our conversation to Ben who surprised me by saying he knew Adrian, too. "We went to high school together in Naugatuck, Connecticut," he said. "He was Adrian Greenberg then. His mother owned a hat shop where Adrian helped out after school."

Honor introduced me to Adrian when they first returned from Paris. I never owned any of his dresses, but I know many women who've worn his clothes. For example, Kitty Carlisle Hart, the singer and widow of playwright Moss Hart, told me that one of her favorite dresses was designed by Adrian. Kitty was also a Girl Scout board member when we first became friends.

I served on the Board of The Girl Scouts Council of Greater New York for more than twenty years, spending about ten years on the Executive Committee.

In 1970, I was flattered to be considered for President of the Girl Scouts Council, but I declined. "I've just become Chairman of the Board of the Brooklyn Botanic Garden," I explained, "and I really can't handle both." The Girl Scout job was more demanding because it involved visiting troops all over the city's five boroughs. I'd enjoyed my years with the Girl Scouts, but it was time to move on. Ben had retired and I wanted to be free to travel with him.

Volunteering Just for Fun

I've always loved acting, but I wanted to be a good wife and mother, so I had no regrets about giving up the theater when I got married. By then, I'd learned what a difficult and demanding career it is. Professional actors not only deal with constant rejection, they have to work nights and weekends and make long-term commitments. If the producers decide to take a play to San Francisco or on a long tour around the country, the actors have to go along. I wasn't willing to do that once I had a family.

Still, I must admit, I sometimes missed performing for an audience. I was delighted, therefore, when Dottie Teegan introduced me to The Snarks, Ltd., an amateur theatrical club for women. The name comes from Lewis Carroll's nonsense poem, *A Hunting of the Snark*, which was popular when the group was founded in 1910.

The club was started in response to the exclusionary practices of the men's Amateur Comedy Club, established around 1885. The men put on plays in their own little theater and at other places in New York City. Wives and girl friends are invited to play female roles, but women have never been allowed to become active members. They can only be "associates." The Snarks have, nonetheless, been allied with the Comedy Club for many years. They now use the Club's 100-seat theater on East 36th Street for all their productions. Members of both groups perform in each other's plays, an arrangement that works well.

The Snarks is a totally volunteer group with one exception: a professional director is hired for each production (unless a talented director happens to be a member who volunteers for the job). Members and other volunteers not only perform all the roles, they design and build the sets, make the costumes and do all the other backstage work for two major shows every year, with eight performances of each.

I joined the Snarks in 1952 and have remained active for more than 50 years. In May 2002, for example, I played the mother in *The English Teachers*, written by the young playwright, Edward Napier. Ben encouraged my work with the

Snarks because our plays run only one week and we stay in New York. He always sent me flowers on opening night and came to every show I appeared in while he was alive. My children also enjoyed seeing many of the shows.

As an amateur group, the Snarks can't sell tickets, so we just perform for ourselves and our subscribers. To join, a woman must be proposed by a member and perform at an audition. Candidates for membership are also required to work back stage on two shows before being formerly proposed. We currently have 90 dues-paying members, plus about 100 subscribers who support the group with annual contributions. In return, they receive six tickets to each show.

My Snarks membership has been very important because it provides an opportunity to satisfy my need to perform without neglecting my family or other responsibilities. I find it very exciting to get an audience with me during a performance. Shedding my own skin for that of another person gives me a great sense of satisfaction and accomplishment. Members of Snarks generally take acting seriously, and I like that. I also enjoy working with professional directors to create new roles. Over the years, many successful actresses, such as Julie Harris and Hope Williams, have belonged to the Snarks. I've also made many good friends in the group.

When I was appearing in one Snarks' production, Peggy Conklin was in the audience. This was about twenty years after we appeared together in *The Petrified Forest* on Broadway. When I came on stage, she whispered, "Oh, that's Esther Leeming," to her companion, Betty Schwarz.

"No, it's not," said Betty, who happened to be an old friend of mine. "That's Faity Tuttle." It wasn't until they came back stage after the final curtain that they realized both were right. When I learned about their argument, we all had a good laugh together.

Betty and I used to organize private children's parties at FAO Schwarz, the large New York toy store started by her grandfather. We had great fun interviewing all the magicians, clowns and other performers. The parties featured giant gift pies, with ribbons coming out of every section. Each guest pulled a ribbon and received the surprise gift attached to it. That project came to a tragic end when Betty fell off a horse. She was injured so severely that she spent the rest of her life in a wheelchair. Before her injury, Betty had been active in the Snarks, so she continued to take part in our meetings.

My children also got involved in Snarks' productions from time to time. Jimmy was primarily interested in back stage work with lighting and sets. But when Teddy was 11, he played the role of Cupid in our production of *Venus and*

Adonis. He wore a Grecian robe we made for him and carried a beautiful gold bow and arrow.

The woman playing Venus was quite beautiful, but very nervous and stiff. The director, a charming older man named José Rubin (who'd been Sarah Bernhardt's leading man), kept trying to get her to loosen up. He'd say, "Look at Teddy. See how relaxed he is? Just forget yourself the way Teddy does." She was trying so hard that I couldn't help feeling sorry for her. At the same time, I was very proud of Teddy. He learned every line in the play and spoke very clearly. His whole performance was natural and graceful.

Two of my Snarks friends, Dottie Teegan and Virginia Williams, along with Harriet Phipps from the Girl Scouts, proposed me for membership in the Cosmopolitan Club. We were still living in Brooklyn at the time (1962) and the Club is on East 66th Street in Manhattan, so I hesitated to join. When I discussed it with Ben, he said, "If friends urge you to join a group like that, do it. The day will come when you'll have time to enjoy it, but you may be too old to join then." He was right, of course, and I've enjoyed being a member for 40 years.

The Cosmopolitan Club is a private social organization just for women. It was started in 1911 to provide a social life for the young governesses working for wealthy New York families. They gathered so many interesting people at their first club house (a rented stable in Gramercy Park) that other women—including those who employed the governesses—wanted to become members, too. To this day, the Cos Club is a haven for professional women. The talented membership includes doctors, lawyers, writers, actors, musicians, educators and others who've achieved prominence in their fields. It's a diverse group, ranging from the singer Marian Anderson to the *New Yorker* cartoonist Helen Hokinson.

Over the years, more than 200 writers have belonged to the Cosmopolitan Club. They've included Rumer Godden, author of *Black Narcissus* and other novels, and Phyllis Levin, who wrote well-received biographies of Abigail Adams and Woodrow Wilson. I especially enjoyed getting to know Cornelia Otis Skinner and Emily Kimbrough, co-authors of *Our Hearts Were Young and Gay*, a very amusing book about their youthful adventures in Europe.

It was at the Cos Club that I renewed my childhood friendship with Ethel Barrymore Colt. We worked together to produce two delightful skits: "Brush up Your Shakespeare" with Peggy Wood, and "A Night at the Opera." I've served on the Drama Committee with various other actresses, too, including Mildred Dunnock and Mildred Natwick. Both had careers spanning more than 40 years on the stage, in the movies and on television.

Over the years, I've heard many fascinating speakers and enjoyed a variety of other programs at the Cos Club. A few years ago, for example, the actress Patricia Neale gave an inspiring talk. Ben enjoyed the Cos Club, too, saying it had the best food of any club in New York. We often took friends there for dinner when he was working in Manhattan. When our daughter Missy made her debut, we had a tea dance for her in the Club's beautiful ballroom. Now that I live only two blocks away, I'm spending more time at the Club. I often go there to meet friends for lunch or to take lessons in yoga, tap dancing or French conversation.

I've also enjoyed being a member of Mrs. Field's Literary Club on Brooklyn Heights. It's a group of 100 women who, to my delight, are involved in dramatic as well as literary pursuits. Although they've never had their own clubhouse, the members have continued their activities for nearly 120 years. I've always found that participating in such clubs is mentally stimulating as well as a great social outlet, so I was pleased to read that mental stimulation and social connections are both considered important factors in aging successfully.

Branching out

During my first fifteen summers on our farm in Kinderhook, I stayed close to home. When I wasn't busy working on our old house and grounds, I loved spending time with the children. As they reached their teens and became involved with their own friends and activities, however, I became more involved in the community.

We joined the Old Chatham Hunt Club, a local group that organizes fox hunting and various other activities. At first, I just went beagling (walking behind a pack of hounds that chase rabbits) with other members of the club. I enjoyed that so much that I decided to try something more challenging. My horse was not trained to hunt, so Prince and I learned to jump fences together. I had some pretty scary experiences as a beginner, but it was still fun to ride to the hounds with the other fox hunters.

I also began driving a cart with my pony, Bucky. Through my involvement with pony carts, I formed a friendship with Wiggy Cox, a wonderful woman who loved horses as much as I did. Wiggy introduced me to John Williams who'd turned his large collection of Shaker furniture and artifacts into the Shaker Museum. It was housed in a group of restored barns across the road from his house in Old Chatham. I've loved that Museum since it was opened to the public in 1950. When it became accredited in 1972, it was the largest collection of Shaker artifacts in the world.

In 1966, John invited me to join the Shaker Museum Board. Back then, the Museum's entire staff was three people: John, his secretary (Muriel Collins) and the curator (Phelps Clawson). They relied heavily on help from neighbors and board members. Before long, I was in charge of publicity. That meant dreaming up picturesque events—such as antique automobile exhibits, fashion shows and Shaker dances—to enhance and attract more people to the annual Antiques Festival, a major fund-raiser.

We also tried to arrange special exhibitions by local artists and book signings by famous writers living in the area. Our most successful special attraction was a book signing by the famous *Saturday Evening Post* illustrator Norman Rockwell and his wife, Molly. Both autographed copies of a charming children's book *(Willie was Different—The Tale of an Ugly Thrushling)* that was written by Molly and illustrated by Norman. A record crowd of more than 6,000 people lined up at the Museum most of the day to meet the Rockwells and get their autographs.

The Shaker Museum is open only in summer, so my board responsibilities were easy to fit in with other activities. I served on that board until 1990—nearly 25 years. I made new friends and became better acquainted with Columbia County, where I've lived for 60 summers. Once again, I gained a great deal from being a volunteer.

As my nest emptied, I became involved with new activities in New York City, too. My cousin, Helena Jelliffe Goldschmidt, introduced me to The Colonial Dames of America and the charming Abigail Adams Smith Museum and Garden which they own and run at 421 East 61st Street in Manhattan. I was so delighted by the place that I became a volunteer docent. I especially enjoyed explaining the building and its contents to groups of New York City school children. (Most were shocked to learn that people in colonial times did all their cooking over an open fire and managed to live without bathrooms, telephones or television.)

Once I got involved with the museum, Helena urged me to join the Colonial Dames. The major requirement: being able to trace your family back to an ancestor who held an important position in colonial times. Helena, whose mother was a Leeming, had already done the tedious work. She'd traced the family of our mutual great-grandmother, Arethusa Helena Dewey, back to colonial times. (Arethusa married Isaac Ogden Woodruff in 1836. Their daughter Helena married Thomas Lonsdale Leeming of Montreal and became our grandmother.) It wasn't hard for me to bring that history up to date and qualify for membership in The Colonial Dames of America.

Working in the little museum and its lovely colonial garden (designed by my friend Alice Ireys, a noted landscape architect) is really a pleasure. I became chairman of the garden committee in 1992. Later on, I was invited to join the Colonial Dames' Board of Managers, where I served as Corresponding Secretary. (I was National Vice President, too, for a while.) In the fall of 2002, I had the honor of co-chairing, with my friend Julie Bird, the annual fund-raising gala, "Designer's Fare." We raised more than $8,000 for our museum, which has reclaimed the name it had in the 1830s: "The Mount Vernon Hotel Museum and Garden." My apartment is just a few blocks away, so it's easy for me to help in the garden and participate in other Colonial Dames activities.

Needless to say, I got involved in some of these groups—such as The Snarks and the Cos Club—just for fun. But I was attracted to others because I wanted to make a contribution to organizations that benefit the community. In every case, however, I've enjoyed the work and received great satisfaction from being useful to others. I've never felt that my time was wasted because I continue to develop new skills and to grow as a person with each new challenge.

My life has also been enriched by all the fascinating people I've met and the good friends I've made along the way. Putting on a play or working on a major project together can really cement a friendship. And the older I get, the more I treasure these special friends.

12

Shifting Gears

We all have to adjust to new realities when our lives enter a different phase—marriage, career, parenthood, the empty nest. Some adjustments are easier than others, of course, and they vary from one person to the next. But for me, the most difficult ones came early in life. Those I experienced in middle age or later were much easier.

If I'd had a choice, I would have happily skipped all the painful adjustments of my childhood. I've come to believe, however, that those experiences helped me cope with other difficulties that came later. They also taught me a valuable lesson: change is scary, but it's also exciting and can even be beneficial in the long run. When one door closes, another often opens.

Ben and I were proud of our children and loved them dearly, but we were happy to see them cut the bonds of home and childhood. Ben believed it was a mistake to try to hang onto children. "Give them their independence and they'll want to return home," he said. He proved to be right about that. They not only came home from school and college regularly, but they often brought friends with them. And now, all three families are living on our family farm.

I missed my children when they moved on, of course, but by the time all three were away at school, I'd taken on so many responsibilities with the Girl Scouts, the Brooklyn Botanic Garden and other groups that I was simply too busy to feel the loss as keenly as some parents do. And those commitments helped me to avoid the debilitating loneliness and depression that plagues many women when they reach middle age.

To be honest, I wasn't usually thinking ahead when I got involved in various projects. Once in a while, I even wished I had fewer responsibilities and more free time. Ben's job required him to make a series of business trips each year, visiting branch offices around the country. He also made annual trips to England to meet with "names" at Lloyds of London, which handled Atlantic Mutual's reinsurance.

Some of Ben's trips sounded so appealing that I was eager to join him, but I was generally too busy at home.

In the spring of 1955, however, when Missy was 10 and the boys were teenagers, I decided to go away with Ben for a week. I hired a middle-aged widow to shop, cook and look after the family during our absence. Nora Daly continued to come in every day to do the laundry and heavy work, of course. Since Granny Tuttle was also on hand for emotional support, I felt confident that everyone would be fine.

Ben and I flew to St. Louis to begin a trip down the Mississippi River. We boarded a large diesel-engine craft called a tow boat, though it actually pushed barges full of cargo ahead of it. At one time, six large oil barges were strung out in front of us. Tow boats don't usually take passengers, but Ben's company provided their insurance so he was allowed to travel as an agent. We were guests of the ship's captain, who turned over his comfortable cabin to us. During the day, we'd go into the wheelhouse and watch the captain navigate treacherous parts of the river. We could see that it required a great deal of skill.

The current was so swift and carried so much debris down the river that the navigable channel changed constantly. The captain received radio bulletins about its status each morning and was in regular communication with pilots of various other ships plying the river. In addition, the words "mark twain" were called out to indicate the depth of the channel on each side. I was surprised to learn that these signals—which my grandfather's friend Samuel Clemons had appropriated as his pen name—were still being used.

When we reached Cairo, Illinois, where the Ohio River joins the Mississippi, it started to rain. It continued to rain heavily all night. By morning, the skies had cleared but the captain's eyes were as red as the sweater I was wearing. He explained that he'd been forced to keep the windshield tilted open all night because the wipers didn't work fast enough for him to see clearly as he struggled to steer the boat.

I was on deck admiring the scenery along the river when the captain received a radio message from another boat: "Who's the lady in the red sweater?" Women are not seen on tow boats very often, so I stood out. The captain chose not to satisfy the other man's curiosity, though. His reply: "Please don't say anything about her. My wife has a radio and might be listening in."

Most of the shoreline was pretty rugged with muddy banks, but we did see a few of the antebellum plantation homes with their lovely lawns and gardens as we neared Memphis. While sailing along the border between Arkansas and Tennessee, the captain showed us a chart indicating that an island about a mile long was now to the west of us, even though it was part of Tennessee, the state on our eastern side.

Ben and I left the ship when it docked in Memphis. From there, we flew on to Houston, where he had an appointment. While he worked, I was entertained by wives of his colleagues. They took me to museums and other interesting places in the area. All in all, it was very enjoyable trip and I looked forward to joining Ben more often.

When we returned home, we found that the kids were all fine, but not very happy—especially Teddy, then 13. According to him, the woman I'd hired was "a nasty lady" who disciplined him constantly. While mulling that over, I noticed that the ironing board was broken. "How did this happen?" I asked Nora.

"Missy was riding on it," she replied. "She was pretending it was a horse. I knew it might break, but I didn't care. That Miss High Horse you hired was so mean to the kids that I let them break a few rules." That was the last time I dared to leave the children with a stranger. A few years later, my cousin, Barbara Stragnell, offered to run the house while I was away. She managed beautifully, so I was able to travel with Ben again.

One of our more memorable trips came during the spring of 1959. By then, Missy and Teddy were away at boarding school and Jimmy was finishing his senior year at Poly Prep. I decided to accompany Ben on a business trip to London. He always went to Europe by ship; it was good public relations for a marine insurance executive. But even if he'd been in another field, I think he'd have still traveled by ship because he really enjoyed being on the water. Ben needed at least a week in London—and crossing the Atlantic took about a week each way—so he was usually gone three weeks or longer.

I'd never felt comfortable being away that long when the children were home, so this trip was an exciting change for me. We had a fine crossing on the *Mauritania*, one of the Cunard line's smaller, more elegant ships. When we reached London, we checked into a beautiful suite at the Connaught Hotel near Grosvenor Square. That was a great neighborhood for me to explore during the day while Ben was working.

I called Larry and Hubert Parker, old friends of Honor's and mine, who had a lovely house in London. Larry and I got together several times. We'd have lunch, followed by a visit to a museum or a matinee at the theater. On another day, I picked up a pass at Hubert's office so I could visit the Old Bailey, the court where he presided as Lord Justice in his long white wig and red robes. All the barristers in that court wear white wigs, so seeing them in action was like going to the theater for me. It was so stimulating and entertaining that I returned to the Old Bailey on subsequent visits to London.

Roger and Frankie Diplock, also old friends, invited us for a weekend at their country home in Kent. They kept horses, so I had the immense pleasure of joining them on a ride through the English countryside. Ben always enjoyed talking to Roger, a magazine editor, who provided a very different point of view—and a pleasant change—from his conversations with insurance executives. The Diplocks belonged to the local beagle pack, so we followed the English hounds as they chased rabbits. We'd enjoyed the same sport with our own hunt club, but we found the English hunt was longer and swifter.

For our return trip, Ben arranged to sail on the *Brittanic*, another small Cunard ship that sailed from Liverpool. On reaching the pier, though, we learned that our departure had been delayed by a dock strike. That meant spending a full day in Liverpool, which is not exactly a sightseer's delight. We walked around until we found a lovely cathedral to visit. After admiring the stained glass windows, we discovered that the Liverpool Stock Company was performing *The Confidential Clerk* by T.S. Eliot. We enjoyed being able to see that performed by one of England's best regional theater companies.

We returned to the ship for dinner, only to learn that our sailing would be delayed another day. Ben arranged for a taxi to pick us up in the morning and take us to Chester, an historic town on the sea, about 30 miles from Liverpool. Much of Chester is still enclosed by ancient stone walls built by the Romans, so it was a fascinating place to visit. After driving us all over the town, our friendly taxi driver chose a different route back. Along the way, he suggested stopping at a charming pub for a drink.

It was after 5 pm when I asked the driver, "How far are we from the harbor in Liverpool?"

"About an hour," he said.

"But we're supposed to sail at six," I told him. At that, we all jumped into the taxi and went on a wild ride back to the dock. We were relieved to find our ship was still there. In fact, the officers admitted that they still didn't know when the strike would be settled, so they'd decided to transfer us to another Cunard liner. The next morning, we took a train to Southampton and boarded the *Queen Elizabeth*. It wasn't due to sail until the following day, so our small group had the big ship to ourselves.

By that time, Ben and I had become quite frustrated by all the delays because we were trying to get home for Jimmy's graduation from Poly Prep. Unfortunately, we didn't make it, which was a big disappointment for us all.

We decided to allow more time for possible delays after that, but I continued to join Ben on business trips to London. We usually traveled in the fall, when ocean liners were less crowded. Thanks to Ben's position, we were often invited to sit at the Captain's table, where we met many interesting people. The food was delicious, so we always enjoyed our days on board ship. While Ben worked in London, I played—sightseeing, visiting friends, going to plays and concerts. I loved exploring London on foot and eventually got to know the city quite well.

One year we traveled on the *SS United States*. The head of that shipping company served on Ben's board at the Atlantic, so we received VIP treatment in a lovely double cabin with its own sitting room. As soon as we arrived in our stateroom, we received an invitation to sit at the Captain's table. Just before dinner, a beautiful corsage was delivered to our room. (We dressed for dinner every night, in long dresses and dinner jacket.)

Dinner with Captain Alexanderson and the other passengers at his table was delightful. I was fascinated to learn that only two items on the entire ship were made of wood: the chopping block in the kitchen and the Steinway piano in the lounge. The next night, we were invited to the captain's private quarters for cocktails. When I mentioned living in Brooklyn, the captain asked, "What part of Brooklyn?"

"Park Slope."

"My son just married a young lady from Park Slope," he said. "She lived on Third Street."

"What's her name?" I asked.

"Nancy Baier. Do you know her?"

"I've known her since she was a baby," I told him. "Her brother, Lee, is my son's best friend. They all went to The Berkeley Institute together." By the time he pulled out Nancy's wedding pictures, we felt like old friends. After that, the captain invited us for cocktails in his quarters regularly—and we dined at his table every night. It all added up to one of our more memorable crossings.

Later, I accompanied Ben on a few business trips in this country, too. In the summer of 1961, for example, he had several appointments out West so Missy and I went along. Our first stop was Spokane, Washington. While Ben was busy with meetings, Missy and I drove a rental car to Coeur D'Alene, Idaho, about an hour away. It's a magnificent spot in a high valley surrounded by peaks of the Cascade Mountains.

A national Girl Scout roundup was in progress, with troops from all over the country. I knew some of the scout leaders who'd come from New York, so they introduced us around. Neither Missy nor I had ever been to such a large camp gathering, so it was a special experience. We stayed for a cookout supper and were inspired by the group singing around the bonfire.

The next day, all three of us drove to Yellowstone Park. It was our first visit to Yellowstone, but at the end of August the tourist traffic was fierce. All we saw for miles was the back of the car or van ahead of us. We did manage to see Old Faithful spout on schedule—and to spot a few bears in the distance—but it was a relief to reach the cabin we'd reserved for the night.

Feeling quite hungry by then, we were pleased to find a rustic dining hall near our cabin. But it was very crowded and we were told the wait for a table would be at least 30 minutes. To pass the time, we headed to the bar for a drink. A severe-looking man stopped us at the door.

"How old is your daughter?" he asked.

"She's sixteen, but she'll have a ginger ale," Ben replied.

The man looked sternly at Missy and said, "You may not come into this room. That's Ranger law." At that point, a very frustrated Missy burst into tears and left, running down the trail to our cabin. She refused to come back for dinner and Ben refused to leave her alone, so I made several trips to and from the cafeteria to feed the hungry Tuttles. We made a final stop in Denver before flying home in time for Missy to return for the fall term at Emma Willard.

After Missy graduated from college and got married in June 1967, our nest was truly empty. We no longer needed such a big house, so we decided to sell it and move to a smaller place. My cousin Helen told us about a large apartment that had just become available at 35 Prospect Park West, the building where she'd been living since selling her own big house. We loved the apartment with its magnificent views of lower Manhattan, the harbor with the Statue of Liberty and several beautiful bridges. It didn't take long to decide to buy it.

Located just a few blocks from our house on Park Slope, the apartment was well designed and well appointed, with mirrored closet doors, built-in bookcases and other special features. It had a large living room with a fireplace, a large dining room, a big kitchen with a butler's pantry, and two spacious bedrooms. Each bedroom had its own bath, as did the "maid's room" which became Ben's home office.

We still had all the advantages of being close to Prospect Park for our morning walks, but were spared the upkeep problems of home ownership. We looked forward to taking long trips in the winter without worrying about the pipes freezing, the roof leaking or snow piling up on the sidewalk. It was so much easier to go away after the move that we ended up staying in that apartment for more than 20 years.

Ben's Retirement

Ben had been Chairman of the Board of Atlantic Mutual Insurance Company for about 10 years when he retired on his 65th birthday in September 1966. We'd both looked forward to that day—not as a chance to take a much-needed rest but as an opportunity to pursue different interests and activities.

Retirement did not end Ben's business career, either. He remained on the Atlantic's board until he was 80 and continued to serve on three other boards—Bank of New York, Seaman's Bank for Savings and TIAA/CREF—until he was 75. Each board of directors met once a month, with various committee meetings in between. Ben found the work stimulating and enjoyed keeping in touch with his Wall Street friends and associates.

Unlike the wives of many new retirees, I didn't mind having Ben around the house all day because he was always busy with his own projects. For years, he'd been studying the human mind. "Now that NASA has put a man on the moon," he said, "the last great frontier is the human mind. How we operate, why we think the way we do—that's what we know the least about."

Eventually, Ben wrote a book based on his years of research into all the great thinkers, philosophers, psychologists and others who'd studied the human brain. He wrote his manuscript in long-hand and I typed it. He decided not to publish it under his own name "because everyone in the insurance business will think I'm crazy to write about such an esoteric subject." Instead of Tuttle, he used his grandfather's middle name, Maynard.

The Nature of Ego by Benjamin Maynard was published by The Philosophical Library, Inc. in 1962. Ben believed his book was never given serious consideration in the academic community because he lacked the proper credentials. What one critic called "an extremely interesting treatise" was generally overlooked because Ben's only academic degree was a BS in geology. He enjoyed the research and writing, though, and was proud of his accomplishment. Such projects made his life more interesting—and they probably lengthened it as well.

Despite his intellectual interests, Ben had a great sense of humor and was always fun to be around. He continued to enjoy dancing, going to concerts and the opera—all of which provided enormous pleasure for me, too. More than anything else, though, we were eager to travel together.

Ben's retirement gave us the freedom to take longer trips—and the flexibility to go by freighter, which he'd wanted to do for years. Freighter travel is risky for anyone on a fixed schedule because you never know exactly when the ship will sail, what stops it will make or when you'll get home. Freighters are much smaller than tourist ships and usually carry only 6 to 12 passengers. (If they take more than 12, they're required to have a doctor on board, so few are willing to assume that extra expense.)

Our first freighter voyage was from New York to California, by way of the Panama Canal. Ben was fascinated by the Canal's engineering and wanted to see it in action. We spent an entire day going through it, even eating lunch on deck so we wouldn't miss anything. Although the trip from the Atlantic Ocean to the Pacific is only about 50 miles, the water is at different levels. The ship moves through a series of locks which are slowly filled with water (or emptied, if you're traveling in the other direction). Being able to observe all of that activity up close was a unique and fascinating experience.

Although we passed through the Canal on New Year's Day, 1969, it was quite warm. As we reached the Pacific, we saw lights coming on all over the large U.S. Army base that guarded the Canal back then. It was a quite a show! The trip up the Pacific Coast, past all the Central American countries and Mexico, was really beautiful, too. We saw many whales of various kinds, as well as enormous sea turtles in the ocean. The ship docked in San Diego, where we spent an enjoyable day touring their famous zoo and the beautiful old Coronado Hotel.

The next day we sailed up to Los Angeles, where we left the freighter and stayed in a hotel for several days. Ben's firm insured several Hollywood production companies, so he was able to arrange a special tour of Universal Studios for me. My guide was the Studios' fire chief, a man who knew exactly what was being filmed on every one of the numerous stages and sets. "How do you know so much about what's going on?" I asked.

"I have to," he replied. "Every script and shooting schedule must be submitted to me so I can alert my team whenever there's any danger of a fire—even if it's just from cigarette smoking."

"Well, I think you've got a wonderful job," I told him.

"Yes, I do," he agreed. "I inherited it from my father, who was also the fire chief. When I was a little boy," he continued, "I hung around the studio a lot. A terrific actor named Will Rogers taught me how to swing a lariat when he had time off between scenes."

After two delightful nights in Hollywood and a good visit with my former roommate, Edna Julian, and her family, we flew home. It was a beautiful clear day so we could see the Grand Canyon and the Mississippi River clearly as we flew over on our way back to New York.

Ben and I enjoyed that first freighter trip so much that we quickly signed up for another one. A Norwegian ship, the *Concordia Tadj*, was heading to the Mediterranean in 1969. After boarding in Brooklyn, we had a long sail of about nine days to our first stop, Las Palmas in the Canary Islands.

Two other passengers in our age group were both traveling alone: Bob Mills, a retired yachtsman, and Lura Cushman, a dear little lady whose grandfather had been a sea captain. She still lived in his house overlooking the sea in Duxbury, Massachusetts, but she loved to travel. Something made me say, "I bet you were a school teacher, Miss Cushman."

"Yes, I was," she said. "I taught at Miss Farmer's Cooking School in Boston." That school was started by the same woman who wrote the famous *Fanny Farmer Cookbook*. When the steward who provided the delicious smorgasbord for our daily lunches learned that a cooking teacher was on board, he invited Lura into the galley to help him. From then on, we ate glorious hors d'oeuvres and desserts all across the Atlantic.

Freighters take passengers along primarily to provide companionship for the officers. The protocol of the times did not allow the captain, first mate, chief engineer and purser to socialize with other crew members. In those benighted days, freighters had three dining rooms: one for the officers, another for the white crew, a third for the rest of the crew. Passengers ate in the officers' dining room which had delicious food. Our cabins were almost as luxurious as those we'd had in first class on the Cunard line.

Nine days is a long time between ports, but we found plenty to do on board. Sometimes we'd go up on the bridge where the captain explained all the instruments and showed us how the ship was navigated. We enjoyed the ship's library, which had an assortment of games as well as a collection of interesting books. None of the officers or other passengers played bridge, so we learned to play pinochle with the captain and first mate. Having time to ourselves just to read, write and think was pleasant, too.

When we reached Las Palmas, a pair of South American newlyweds got off, leaving only six passengers on board. Las Palmas is not a very exciting place, but we did enjoy going out to the desert where we saw camels for the first time. We also visited the charming old Spanish house where Christopher Columbus stayed when he was outfitting his ships, the *Niña*, the *Pinta* and the *Santa Maria*, in preparation for his brave voyage across the Atlantic Ocean to the "new world."

The next morning we watched the crew loading cargo onto the freighter. Open crates full of green tomatoes were stacked on a giant sling. A young man turned a hand crank that raised the load from the dock up to the ship's deck. Once it reached the right level, he'd swing the cargo over to the hold for unloading. But a young woman walking by in a mini-skirt distracted him so much that he swung the sling over too soon. It hit the edge of the ship and sent hundreds of tomatoes flying in every direction. We all got a big laugh out of that—except, of course, the mortified young man who was responsible.

To reach our next port of call, we sailed through the majestic Straits of Gibraltar into the Mediterranean Sea. It was amazing to see how close Europe is to Africa at that point. When we docked in Genoa, another couple disembarked. They each had Fulbright Fellowships to study early Italian music.

The Captain told us we'd be staying in Genoa for two full days, so we requested permission to take a train to Florence. We checked into a small hotel near the Arno River, not far from the famous Ponte Vecchio. Our room provided a delightful view of the Duomo, the Ufizzi Gallery and other palaces and courtyards of that beautiful city. The next morning, an old friend who'd gone to school with our kids in Brooklyn joined us. She lived nearby with her Italian husband, so she graciously guided us through all the art galleries. Ben and I had a marvelous time.

Instead of taking the train back to Genoa, we decided to drive a rental car so we could stop along the way. After visiting the Leaning Tower in Pisa, we went on to Carrara to see where the famous marble is quarried. Then we drove along the coast, passing through Portofino and other charming fishing villages on the sea. We both enjoyed that drive immensely.

As soon as we reached Genoa, we returned the car and took a taxi to the pier where we'd left the ship. The *Concordia Tadj* wasn't there! That was a real shock because we'd left most of our luggage on board, taking just a small overnight bag to Florence. Ben was still fluent in Italian from the three years he'd worked in Trieste, so he walked around asking questions until someone told us our ship had moved to the other side of the harbor. We took another taxi and were relieved to find the freighter was still there. It sailed the next morning.

We traveled south along the coast of Italy, sailing into the magnificent Bay of Naples just as the sun was setting behind the mountains ringing the harbor. Lights were starting to come on all over the city and wispy trails of pink smoke were rising from Mt. Vesuvius, the volcano in the background. It was a magical sight that I'll never forget!

The next day we hired a Mercedes with a driver to take Lura Cushman, Bob Mills and the two of us along the Amalfi Drive, south of Naples. I'd heard so much about that drive that I was eager to experience it. The incredibly narrow road winding along the coast is cut into the mountain on one side, with a steep drop off to the water on the other. As we drove, we could see houses both above and below us, with orange trees and flowering shrubs in their gardens. The car had to make so many quick, sharp turns, though, that I began to feel sick—even though I never get seasick on rough water. I had to ask the driver to stop so I could get out and walk a while to restore my equilibrium. Still, I was glad I'd gone because the views were truly spectacular.

(When I returned home, I pulled out a journal written by my great-grand-mother, Susan Raymond Howard. The description of her trip on the Amalfi Drive in 1860 is what first made me curious to see it. But she rode in a horse-drawn carriage—and did not get sick. "The horses flew like the wind!" she wrote. We were "flying like the wind" at about 25 miles per hour in our Mercedes. Per-haps it was less frightening when the road had little traffic and no cars coming around curves from the other direction.)

Back on the freighter that night, we were buffeted by such heavy winds that I was reminded of Biblical stories about shipwrecks in the Mediterranean. As we sailed through the Straight of Messina at the toe of Italy's boot, the wind whistled through the ship's rigging, stimulating my imagination so much that it was diffi-cult to sleep. But we weathered the storm and went on to dock in Beirut, Leba-non, another lovely harbor ringed with orange trees. (When war broke out between Lebanon and Israel a few years later, I was glad I'd had the opportunity to visit that beautiful city before so much of it was destroyed.)

The next day, we four—the only remaining passengers—hired a car to take us to the historic ruins at Ba'labakk. Since we had not been permitted to stop in Israel (because of cargo destined for Lebanon and Syria), I was especially eager to see this city that dates back to Biblical times. We drove through a series of primi-tive villages that reminded me of scenes from the Bible. Men were cultivating the fields with primitive plows pulled by donkeys. The villages still had communal wells, but in one place it was just a large faucet—and women were carrying the water in huge cans instead of clay pots.

Our driver stopped at a communal beehive oven, where each family was tak-ing turns baking their unleavened bread. As we watched children work the dough the same way their ancestors had for centuries, I noticed an amusing incongruity: one little girl had bright red nail polish on her fingers. We enjoyed sampling the delicious bread fresh from the oven, but it made me sad to see those people living in such primitive conditions.

The ruins of Ba'labakk are quite magnificent, with many well preserved towers and columns reminiscent of Greek and Roman ruins. But instead of white mar-ble, the temples were made of red sandstone that gave the whole city a rosy glow. The remains of the Palace of Nebuchadnezzar, the king of Babylonia, were especially beautiful. The old city was in the early stages of restoration, but we had a fascinating tour, nonetheless.

The next day we sailed on to Latakia, Syria. Unlike the sophisticated city of Beirut, it was quite primitive. Our freighter was unable to get into the port, so a lighter full of dock workers came out to unload the cargo. Suddenly, we heard a raucous chorus of shouts and yells. A bunch of wild-looking Arabs, wearing voluminous striped robes pulled up between their legs and tucked into belts, came running up the gangplank. They looked like a gang of pirates wearing oversized diapers. Apparently their pay was based on how fast they unloaded because they really attacked the cargo in the hold. I quickly retreated to my cabin where I watched the scene from above. A man with wild eyes looked up and began blowing me kisses. It was all rather weird.

Once the cargo was unloaded, we took a lighter to shore and hired a car to take us out to a castle used by Saladin, a 12th century Moslem warrior and opponent of the Crusaders. The driver stopped in a village to pick up a little boy, the son of the castle's guardian, who had the key. The four of us, plus the driver, filled the car, so the boy had to ride in the propped-open trunk. He didn't seem to mind—perhaps because he thought it would lead to a bigger tip.

The red sandstone castle was remarkably well preserved considering its age (Saladin died in 1193). It was fascinating to see how it dominated the narrow mountain pass. Our guide pointed out huge clay jugs that had once been filled with boiling oil to be poured down on invaders. The castle's lowest level had a big cistern, which was still full of water. Its two largest areas were the stables and the room where Saladin kept his large harem of women—which shows what was important to him, I guess. It reminded me of an old Arab saying: *Never lend your horse or your wife to any man.* Note that the horse is mentioned first.

After that excursion, we stayed on board the ship until it reached Piraeus, Greece. The freighter went into dry dock for repairs, so we got off and spent several days in Athens, touring the Acropolis and other fascinating ruins. From there, we headed home, making one brief stop in Zurich, Switzerland. Ben talked to bankers about investing in gold bars, while I visited the local Botanical Garden. We flew out on a beautiful clear day, so we enjoyed incredible views of the snow-capped Alps from the plane.

In 1972, Ben and I took another freighter from Brooklyn Harbor. We could see the ship from our window as we ate lunch. When we finished eating, we just took a taxi to the end of our street and climbed aboard. Soon after getting settled in our stateroom, we met the other passengers, including Hugh Franklin and his wife, Madeleine L'Engle. Hugh was an actor who'd had leading roles in two soap operas, *As the World Turns* and *All my Children*, as well as other TV shows. Madeleine, a former actress, is a well-known author of children's books. Her book, *Wrinkle in Time*, won the prestigious Newbery medal in 1963. She later won an American Book Award for *A Swiftly Tilting Planet.*

Ben and I liked Hugh and Madeleine immediately. When we reached our first port in Haiti, we invited them to join us on a sightseeing tour. We hired a car and driver to take us around the island, stopping for lunch at a charming place on a hill overlooking Port au Prince. The four of us had such a good time together that we continued to share a hired car at every port.

In Maracaibo, Venezuela, our driver took us on a tour that included stopping at a lovely hotel in the mountains. As the four of us entered the lobby, I noticed three American women in pastel pants suits nudging each other. We walked straight out to the terrace, which had a spectacular view of the hills and valleys beyond. The three women soon followed us to our table, where we'd ordered drinks.

"Is he...is he...?" they asked Madeleine.

"Yes," she replied. "He is."

"Oh, Dr. Tyler," they screamed. "We recognized you from *All My Children.*"

When the women finally left, I asked Madeleine "Does this happen often?"

"Not usually in places as remote as this," she said. "The last time was at the Oracle of Delphi in Greece. But Hugh is recognized all the time on the subway in New York." Despite his fame, Hugh still took the subway to work every day from their apartment in upper Manhattan, near Columbia University.

As our journey continued, Ben and I found much in common with Hugh and Madeleine. Hugh and I discussed acting, while Madeleine shared many of Ben's intellectual interests. In the evening, we often played bridge together. Such congenial companions made everything more fun, no matter what we did. To me, the opportunity to become acquainted with a variety of interesting people from all over the world is one of the great joys of travel.

Our next stop was the island of Aruba in the Dutch Antilles, where we all enjoyed a swim in the ocean. A few days later we docked at Port O'Limon, Costa Rica, where we decided to fly up to San José, the capital. We rode to the airport in a former New York school bus. Still painted bright yellow, it had a red stop sign that shot out to the side each time we stopped. We were all amused by the incongruity of riding that bus in Costa Rica.

The primitive airport had just one small building with a wind sock on top. A bird had built a nest in the wind sock, so it didn't do much good. We were told that the planes landed on the beach, so Madeleine and I ran along it, removing orange crates and other debris that we feared would interfere. When our plane finally arrived, the four of us were followed aboard by a local woman carrying a crate full of live, squawking chickens she planned to sell in San José. That made it a lively flight, to say the least. It took only an hour to reach the city, so we were able to tour an interesting museum before dinner. Service at the restaurant was very leisurely, though, so we didn't eat until 9 pm. After a tasty dinner, we spent the night in a hotel.

The next morning, Hugh and Madeleine flew back to New York because Hugh was due at NBC. We promised to get in touch when we returned home—and we did. Shortly afterwards, Madeleine invited us to join her at the opening of *The Play's the Thing*, a Broadway show in which Hugh had a leading role. We knew he'd been rehearsing before the freighter voyage, so we were delighted to see what an excellent actor he was "live" on stage.

(Although we all had busy lives going in different directions, we continued to get together for dinner about once a year. Hugh died in 1986, but I still hear from Madeleine. In fact, I attended her 70th birthday party in the garden of the Cathedral of St. John the Divine, where she served as librarian for many years. At that party, Madeleine mentioned her latest book, *Two Part Invention*, which she thought I'd enjoy. She was right. I did enjoy reading about her marriage, which had many similarities to my own.)

After Madeleine and Hugh flew home from Costa Rica, Ben and I returned to the ship. We'd hoped to travel back to port on a narrow gauge railroad through the jungle, but the captain called us to report that our freighter would be sailing that afternoon. (We always left a number where we could be reached so we wouldn't miss a departure.) The rail trip took about six hours, so we flew back to Limon instead. "I'm sorry," the captain said as we climbed aboard, "but we're not going to sail this afternoon, after all. A young sailor has disappeared. He's only eighteen—and I'm responsible to his parents when we get back to Holland—so I don't want to leave without him." (It was a Dutch ship, so most crew members were Dutch.) Local police reported seeing the young man heading into the jungle with a young lady.

The captain kept blowing the ship's horn, but the sailor did not return. "He's not going to be very comfortable on the way back to Holland," he told us. "We'll put him in irons for delaying us like this." In the meantime, a French banana boat was loading next to us, so we went over to watch. A giant canvas conveyor belt was moving huge bunches of green bananas onto the ship. We were interested to learn that the temperature on board was carefully controlled so the bananas would not ripen before reaching France.

It was growing dark by then, so our captain made a decision: "We'll continue to make every effort to find the missing sailor," he announced, "but we're going to sail with the tide at eleven a.m., with or without him."

The whistle was still blowing at eleven the next morning, but the sailor had not returned. "If you find him," the captain told the local police, "please send him on to New Orleans, our final stop before we return to Holland." Needless to say, the captain—and everyone else on board—worried about the safety of the missing sailor. The ship made an interim stop on the Texas coast before going on to New Orleans. We spent two days touring Houston while cargo was unloaded and replaced. The highlight of that stop was our tour of NASA headquarters at the Houston Space Center. Five days after leaving Costa Rica, we pulled into New Orleans and saw a blond young man, with a policeman on either side, being escorted toward our ship. As promised, the captain put his troublesome sailor into solitary confinement.

It was time to leave the freighter, so we checked into a hotel in New Orleans. At the suggestion of my friend, Marion Ascoli, we decided to visit Longvue, an old plantation north of New Orleans owned by her sister. She gave us a letter of introduction, so we rented a car and drove there. Although Marion's sister was not home, we were welcomed into her magnificent garden. It was beautifully landscaped, with a ring of live oak trees all around the edges. After taking in the view from the plantation's porch, we walked down paths through the beautiful, well-maintained flower beds.

That night we had an outstanding dinner at Antoine's, reputed to be the best French restaurant in New Orleans. The next day we toured some of the most famous sites in the French Quarter before flying back to New York.

In 1973, Ben and I decided to visit South Africa, where my good friend Betty Scholtz grew up. She helped us arrange a wonderful trip. At her suggestion, we broke the long flight into two legs, stopping at Rio de Janeiro, the colorful Brazilian city I'd heard so much about. Ben's brother had worked in Rio for four years, so Mother Tuttle and I had studied Portuguese together in preparation for a visit. I never made it during Tom and Laura's stay, but Ben's mother told me all about the fun she had visiting them in Rio.

Ben and I toured Rio's Botanical Garden, where we were surprised to see water lilies with leaves as big as coffee tables. We visited Corcovado, the majestic mountain-top statue of Christ that is inset with red stones indicating a trail of blood. And, of course, we walked along Copacabana Beach where I was fascinated by the mosaic walkway. After three days in Rio, we took another direct flight on to Johannesburg.

Betty had arranged for her sister-in-law, Penny Scholtz, to pick us up at the airport and drive us to Pretoria, the South African capital. Penny was a very gracious guide who escorted us all around that modern city. Since this was our first visit to Africa, we were eager to see some wild animals. We spent several days at the Mala Mala game reserve, a very comfortable camp, complete with its own library and swimming pool. Visitors stayed in individual round huts with thatched roofs and full baths, so we weren't exactly roughing it. After riding around in a Land Rover all day, we were treated to a real feast at night, with a variety of wild game on the menu.

One day our Land Rover was totally surrounded by a herd of water buffalo. The driver had to stop and wait until the buffalo decided to move on, but I found it exciting to be so close to those large and surprisingly calm animals. I also loved watching the stately giraffes move through the grass, but the biggest thrill was seeing so many lions. When we noticed two male lions pursuing the same female, we asked the guide if they'd fight over her. "No," he replied, "they share and share alike."

Late one afternoon, we were taken into a barn-like structure with a long, narrow section cut out of one wall. From there we had a clear view of a family of lions coming to dine on a freshly-killed impala. Everyone was very quiet as we watched the papa lion eat first, followed by the cubs and finally the mama lion. The only sound in our enclosure during this encounter was the tinkling of ice in our drinks. Ben leaned over and whispered, "This is the damnedest cocktail party I've ever been to." He had a good point, but it was great fun.

At Betty's recommendation, we booked passage on the renowned "Blue Train" from Johannesburg to Cape Town. That was the most luxurious train ride I've ever taken. Our cabin—actually a suite—had regular twin beds that were much more comfortable than the usual bunks on trains. It also featured a full bath with a tub, and had a music console underneath a large picture window in the sitting room. The dining car served gourmet French food—the best meal we had in South Africa. It was a slow overnight trip, but we relaxed and watched the beautiful countryside go by outside our big window. Our only stop was at Kimberly, where we made a brief visit to the famous diamond mine.

Betty's best friend, Julie te Groen, met our train as it arrived in Capetown around 11 in the morning. Another gracious host, Julie showed us through the Botanical Garden in Cape Town. We were surprised to see how many of the plants and flowers grown in nurseries are native to South Africa. Julie planned to take us on the cable car up to Table Mountain (named for its unusual flat top), but the mountain was hiding under its table cloth (fluffy clouds) until we were ready to leave, so we missed that.

Another friend of Betty's, Wim Tiemans, picked us up in Cape Town one morning and drove us out to Stellenbosch. Wim was director of the local Botanical Garden, so he not only gave us an expert tour but he took us through several beautiful private gardens, too. A quaint old city in the wine district, Stellenbosch is known for its many charming Cape Dutch houses. We felt privileged to see it with such a knowledgeable guide.

Instead of flying straight home, we booked passage on a Union Castle Liner sailing from Cape Town to England. It was a very elegant ship and we had a festive sailing. A band was playing as passengers tossed paper streamers to their friends waving from the dock. Julie came to see us off, presenting us with a bottle of delicious South African wine.

Sailing from Cape Town Harbor was a magnificent experience. The city is spread all around the crescent-shaped harbor, with the majestic Table Mountain in the background. We had a spectacular view as the ship pulled away from all the waving, cheering people on the pier.

We had a most pleasant two-week sail up the West Coast of Africa to the Canary Islands, then on to Southampton, England. We were seated at the Purser's table with a group of very congenial people. Most of the passengers were either South African or British. The Pilkintons, a couple we'd met at the game park, were also on board, so we enjoyed spending more time with them. (He was the head of a large glass company and had just been knighted by the Queen.)

My old friend, Kay Nicholetts, and her husband, Chris Newman, met us at the dock in Southampton and drove us to their lovely home in nearby Ipping. After a delightful visit with them, we drove up to London to spend a few days at the Connaught Hotel. We returned to a few favorite spots—and visited our friends, the Parkers and the Diplocks—before flying home. It was a long trip, but we'd enjoyed a great variety of exciting experiences.

Slowing Down—for a time

Although I was attracted to Ben partly because he was more mature than my other beaux, I was seldom aware of our 10-year age difference once we were married. Ben was always very youthful in his thinking and in his capacity for having fun. It wasn't until his eighties that age became a factor in our relationship. Ben woke up on his 80th birthday with a bad case of shingles. Then he contracted pneumonia, followed by severe back pain from disintegrated discs. It seemed that we were always going to Lenox Hill Hospital as Ben suffered one health problem after another. Finally, the doctors diagnosed his major problem as Parkinson's, a chronic, progressive disease. The tremors and other effects were minor and sporadic at first, but easy access to medical care suddenly became important. We had to stop traveling on freighters and going to third world countries.

We did visit my sister Honor for several weeks every winter, though. She'd settled on Manasota Key, near Sarasota, Florida, after her marriage to Savington (Savvy) Crampton in 1970. We arranged to rent their charming guest house so we'd feel comfortable staying for long visits. Ben was the same age as Honor and Savvy, so we all got along well. We usually got together for dinner every night. (I continued to visit Honor and Savvy until Honor's death at age 96 in 1997.)

As the months and years went by, Ben became less mobile and more frustrated by his limitations. His mind was still going strong, but his body gradually failed him. He continued to walk slowly around our apartment, but it was increasingly difficult for him to shuffle along.

He still liked to go to Merwin Farm, so I'd help him into the car and drive there. We always took our time, stopping for a picnic lunch along the way. September is one of the prettiest months in Columbia Country, so we drove up to our farm toward the end of September 1987. Ben was shuffling across the dining room of our little farm house when he fell and broke his hip. The rescue squad came and took him to the hospital, where he had to undergo surgery on his hip. Within hours, it seemed, he had contracted a serious case of pneumonia.

Two days later, on September 27, Ben died peacefully. I wish he could have died at home, but he was in traction and couldn't be moved. I tried to take comfort in the fact that he was in the hospital for only two days. He would have been miserable if he'd been forced to go into a nursing home to recover from the broken hip.

Ben's funeral service was at St. Paul's Episcopal Church in Kinderhook, the only church he attended during our marriage. Jim and Ted each gave beautiful talks about memories of their father. That wasn't easy to do, but it was a very touching tribute that I'll never forget. (Later on we had another service at Trinity Church near Wall Street so Ben's business associates could honor his memory.)

The day of Ben's funeral (October 2, 1987) was warm and beautiful. We served lunch outside for everyone who came from the church service to the farm where we buried Ben's ashes. ("I never want to leave this place," he'd told me, so he was buried in our family plot, along with our daughter Missy. Honor and her husband, Savvy, are now buried there as well.)

That night, I slept in the farm house—the first time I'd ever been completely alone there at night. I was awakened early by a sharp CRACK! It sounded like a gun was being fired behind the house, so I jumped up to tell the shooter to go away. When I opened the kitchen door, however, I was shocked to see that more than a foot of snow had fallen—and was still coming down.

The noise I'd heard was the treetops breaking off from the weight of all that wet snow on the branches. It was only October 3, so the leaves were still on the trees, making them far more vulnerable to snow than in winter. I noticed several trees had fallen across power lines, so I tried to call my children, but I couldn't get through. The electric power was out, too, so I had no heat—and the house had grown quite cold during the night.

I dressed in warm clothes and boots and went out to collect firewood. I lit one fire in the coal stove in the kitchen, another in the living room fireplace. Next, I went to the hand pump outside and pumped pails of water to use in the house. While I was still busy with these chores, my grandson Gerhard, then 12, glided up on cross country skis (the only means of reaching my house at that point). I'd been feeling terribly alone, so I was very happy to see him.

The oldest of Missy and Norwig's children, Gerhard had been particularly close to his grandfather. During Ben's illness, he used to come over and ask, "How ya doing today, Grandpa?"

"Just hanging by a thread," Ben sometimes replied.

The next day, Gerhard would ask, "How's that thread holding up, Grandpa?" But on this occasion he was more solemn. "You know, Granny," he said, "something about this storm is very strange. The day of my mother's funeral, we had a terrible ice storm. The priest was late getting to our house because his car kept spinning around on the slick ice.

"Now, the day after Grandpa's funeral," he continued, "we have an unprecedented snow storm. There has never been a storm like this on the third of October!" He hesitated a moment, then asked, "What's going to happen around here when you die?"

"It will have to be a tornado," I answered. "Nothing less than a tornado will do for me, Gerhard."

13

On My Own Again

Ben's death was very sad, but the last three or four years of his life had not been very happy. He never complained, but sometimes he'd bang his fist on the chair in frustration, so I know it was difficult for him. I couldn't help feeling relieved that his suffering was finally over.

I missed Ben's company, and I still do—more than 16 years later. But what I've missed is the healthy Ben and the many good times we had together. In truth, I began mourning for my husband while he was still alive. His debilitating illness made the adjustment easier than it might have been if he'd died suddenly while still active and enjoying a good life.

I was pleased that so many friends drove up from New York City for Ben's funeral. Among them was Betty Scholtz, my dear friend who'd been appointed Director of the Brooklyn Botanic Garden shortly after I became Chairman of the Board. We'd enjoyed a great working relationship for many years as we ran that wonderful institution together.

One of Betty's favorite BBG projects has been organizing and leading special tours of public and private gardens all around the world. That October, just two weeks after Ben's death, she was scheduled to guide a group of about 20 BBG members through Japan, visiting some of their most beautiful gardens.

After the funeral, Betty came up to me and said, "One of the women scheduled to take our Garden trip to Japan has just canceled. Why don't you come along in her place?"

"Heavens no," I said. "I have much too much to do—and too many adjustments to make—to go so far away right now."

"Don't make a hasty decision," Betty said. "Just think about it." When I mentioned her invitation to my children, they urged me to go. "You've been tied down with Daddy's illness for so long, you need to get away," Jim said. "We'll take care of everything here until you get back."

When I learned that another good friend from Brooklyn, Alice Ireys, was going on the trip, I signed up. I knew several other participants, too, but only Betty and Alice had known my husband. I'd never been to Japan so I knew the journey wouldn't trigger any bittersweet memories, but I still had mixed feelings about taking a pleasure trip at that time.

My doubts continued as I boarded the plane for Tokyo, but it soon became clear that I'd made the right decision. Meeting new people and making new friends while traveling in such a beautiful country was very therapeutic. We flew the polar route, non-stop from New York to Tokyo. It was a twelve-hour flight that grew tedious at times, but the Japanese flight attendants taught me some valuable techniques for coping on long flights.

They put strips of split bamboo on the floor of the cabin. "If you stand and work your bare feet back and forth over these strips," they told me, "it exercises your whole body." I gave it a try and it seemed to help. I also did yoga stretches periodically and drank large quantities of water and other beverages—all of which helped to make the long flight less tiring.

I was very excited about finally going to a country that had fascinated me since my childhood. An uncle who'd visited Japan shortly after World War I had intrigued us with tales of his adventures. He'd brought Lee and me lovely Japanese kimonos, complete with the wide sash (or obi) and wooden sandals with white split-toe socks. We'd spent many pleasant hours wearing our kimonos and pretending to be Japanese ladies drinking tea while kneeling on cushions. We even made up plays to go with our costumes.

Years later, I was delighted when Missy asked to bring a Japanese friend, Yoshiko Kusakawa, home for the Christmas holidays during her senior year at Emma Willard. Yoko, who seemed much more mature than Missy, was so pretty and charming that we all became very fond of her. She also taught us about Japanese customs. When I'd go upstairs after dinner to kiss the kids goodnight, for example, Yoko would say, "Please don't kiss me Mrs. Tuttle; that's considered a dirty habit in Japan."

Yoko wore a beautiful kimono to a Christmas party at Asia House and to several debutante teas to which she and Missy were invited. But for the Cinderella Ball, the high spot of the holiday season for my children, Yoko wore a simple, Western-style silk party dress. I'd invited the handsome son of a friend to be her escort. He happened to be in the Navy ROTC at college, so he wore his dress uniform instead of a tuxedo. When Yoko met him at our home, she turned white and fled to my bedroom.

"What's the matter, Yoko?" I asked.

"My mother told me, 'Never go out with an American sailor!'" Shades of *Madame Butterfly,* I guess. But when I explained that he was just a college student, she felt better. And Jimmy and Teddy made sure that she had a good time at the ball. We then celebrated the New Year at the farm, where Yoko was thrilled to be able to play in the snow. It was the first big snowfall of her first winter in New York, so it was all new to her.

When Yoko finished school, she returned to Kyoto. Her English was so good that she got a job with Japan Airlines as a hostess and interpreter. We kept in touch via Christmas cards over the years, so I looked forward to seeing her again in her own country. One of the great pleasures of foreign travel, I've found, is the opportunity to see how people of other cultures actually live.

Our first stop was Tokyo, where I shared a room with Alice Ireys at the elegant Omni Hotel. The first morning I took an elevator up to the restaurant on the hotel's top floor (the 40th) for breakfast. Much to my delight, I had a clear view of Mt. Fuji, with the morning sun shining on its white cap. It was a spectacular sight, even though the mountain was at least 50 miles away!

Eager to continue my usual early morning walks, I asked the concierge if it was safe for old ladies to walk the streets alone. "Certainly, Madame," he replied. "In Japan, we honor old ladies." After hearing that, Alice and I spent many happy hours exploring the crooked little side streets near the garden of the Imperial Palace. We were taken aback, though, when we noticed school girls pointing to us and giggling. It seems that tall women with white hair are an unusual sight in Japan. We saw very few elderly Japanese women out in public—and they were very small ladies with completely black hair.

One of my most memorable experiences in Japan was visiting the nursery of Saboru Kato, the keeper of the Emperor's Garden and one of the most famous creators of Bonzai in the world. He was a gracious host, showing us his beautiful plants and serving refreshments while we chatted. A Zen Buddhist, he had one of the loveliest faces I've ever seen. It looked as if it had been carved out of ivory, without a single line—despite his advanced years. Peace and serenity just shone from his face.

Another delightful experience was staying in an unusual hotel built on the rocks in Toba, overlooking the bay where cultured pearls are grown. (The oysters are suspended from large rafts floating in the shallow water.) We watched the young women divers collecting wild pearl oysters from the bottom. They were dressed from head to toe in tight white suits, with white caps resembling baby bonnets. We learned that they start training at age six so they can hold their breath for an incredible two minutes as they search the bottom on each dive.

When we arrived in the beautiful old city of Kyoto, I was thrilled to find Missy's friend Yoko waiting at our hotel. She showed me around a group of fascinating temples and gardens, then took me home to meet her husband (a physician), her two children and her mother. It was a joy and a privilege to be entertained in her charming Japanese house. We were served thick green tea and cookies while sitting on cushions around a low lacquer table. Yoko seemed truly happy to be able to return my hospitality of 25 years earlier.

As the trip continued, we visited a number of temples, gardens, museums and craft shops in various parts of Japan. During one stay in a typical Japanese inn, we bathed in a communal bath and slept on futons. Sharing a hot bath with a collection of other naked people was an interesting experience, but I must admit that I prefer the privacy of our tubs. I found it hard to sleep on the futon, too, but I guess you could get used to that.

Another stop was in the mountains at Nikko where we visited a beautiful garden carpeted in moss. I was interested to see how they tie up the trees to keep the branches from breaking under the weight of the heavy winter snow.

Overall, it turned out to be a fascinating trip, with good companions, glorious weather and the beauty of fall foliage and colorful chrysanthemums everywhere. It was exactly what I needed to boost my spirits at a difficult time. Although I had sad moments when I longed for Ben's company, I was too caught up in new experiences to dwell on my loss or worry about the future.

When I returned home, I didn't have to face the loneliness of an empty apartment because my oldest grandson, Benny, was living in our guest room. He'd moved in a year earlier after finishing college and starting work at his grandfather's old firm. He'd been a great help during the difficult last year of Ben's life—and was wonderful company during my first year on my own.

Ben had always advised me to postpone major decisions until at least a year after a death or traumatic experience. "It's too easy to make mistakes when you're emotionally distraught," he said. I didn't want to do anything I'd regret later, so I decided to remain in Brooklyn a while, even though Ben and I had long considered moving into Manhattan.

It had become increasingly difficult to park our car in Brooklyn and I didn't feel safe riding the subway at night. Taxis were not only expensive, but some drivers refused to drive to Brooklyn at all. I knew it would be much easier to get to Ben's medical appointments, participate in Snarks productions, go to the opera and pursue other interests if we were living in Manhattan, so I put our name on the waiting list of a modern building on East 66th Street in 1977.

We were on that list almost eight years before they called about a vacancy. When Ben and I looked at the apartment, he said, "It's a nice place; let's take it." It was significantly smaller than our Brooklyn apartment, though, and I was reluctant to make Ben move when he was suffering with Parkinson's. It was considerably easier for him to get around in a familiar place where he could quickly locate anything he needed. We stayed in Brooklyn.

A year after Ben's death, however, I contacted the agent at the 66th Street building again. The only vacancy was a one-bedroom apartment, but Benny—the grandson who'd been living with me—had just been transferred to Chicago, so I took it. I also added my name to the waiting list for a larger unit.

I lived in the small apartment for four years before I was able to move to one with two bedrooms and two baths. I love having the extra space because it allows me to invite friends and relatives to stay overnight—or even to live with me a while when they're working in New York. So far, my son-in-law, two grandsons and my granddaughter, Honor, have shared my apartment at various times. It's been wonderful to have the pleasure of their company.

I also love the convenience of my neighborhood. I can walk to everything—Central Park, several museums, the movies, the grocer, even the hospital. The Cosmopolitan Club, where I enjoy going for lunch and special events, is only two blocks away. I have good friends in my building, plus the security of doormen twenty-four hours a day, so it's really perfect. Being able to go out whenever I choose without depending on anyone else is very liberating. It enables me to stay active, which I consider very important at my age.

A Renewed Interest in Travel

Much as I enjoy my home, I still love to travel, so I continue to make interesting trips with friends and relatives. In 1988, I decided to join the Brooklyn Botanic Garden's trip to Australia and New Zealand. Instead of flying straight to Sydney with the group, I left early so I could visit my grandson, Tommy, who was teaching English to graduate students in Yogyakarta, Indonesia.

My first stop was Singapore, Malaysia, a city I'd wanted to visit since reading about it in a Somerset Maugham novel. I took a boat ride around the harbor, but was disappointed to find it so pristine. (I'd expected to see a jumble of small boats, with people living and working on them.) After visiting the Botanical Gardens, I paid homage to Maugham by drinking a gin sling at the bar of his favorite Singapore hotel, Raffles. Then I hired a bicycle rickshaw to take me back to my hotel. That was a little scary, but it was a new experience that I found exciting.

The next morning, I went out for a walk and noticed a bunch of Indonesians doing Tai Chi exercises in a park, so I joined them. Most of the participants paid no attention to me, but I did receive a few encouraging smiles as I did the Salute to the Sun and other Tai Chi moves that I'd learned at my classes in New York. It was a very peaceful experience—one that often comes to mind when I practice Tai Chi at home.

My next stop was Jakarta, where Tommy met me at the airport. The boat ride we took around that harbor was much more colorful than the one in Singapore. The waterfront was lined with miserable shacks and crammed full of wooden boats of every size and description. Once I saw all those poor families crowded into flimsy hovels and houseboats, I understood why Singapore was so proud of having "cleaned up" its harbor.

"Where can I take you to dinner?" I asked Tommy, expecting him to choose some glamorous restaurant where I could sample Indonesian cuisine. His answer surprised me.

"If you don't mind, Granny," he said, "I'd like to go to Pizza Hut. I can't get pizza in Yogyakarta, and I've been longing for it." That was the last place I wanted to go, but pizza it was. Afterwards, Tommy took me to the garden terrace of an elegant hotel where he knew members of the band providing the music. We both had a good time listening to them play, so it turned out to be a pleasant evening, after all.

The next day, I visited the beautiful Bogar Botanical Garden near Jakarta, which dates back to the 17th century. But my most memorable experience in Indonesia was riding around the bustling city of Yogyakarta on the back of Tommy's motorbike. "It's really the best way to get around in this traffic," he said as he handed me a helmet to wear. Once I got used to all the noise and confusion, it was great fun. But I must confess that I did feel a bit foolish hanging onto the back of a motorbike at the age of 77.

After sharing Tom's little house for a few days, we celebrated his 22nd birthday by flying to the island of Bali, one of his favorite places. We rented a jeep for four days so we could drive into the mountains. As Tom drove, I enjoyed seeing the serene countryside, especially the terraced rice paddies that climb up many hillsides. Our passage through one small village was delayed by a young girl sauntering down the middle of the road, guiding a flock of geese ahead of her. She was driving them into a rice paddy so they could feast on stray grains remaining from the harvest—and on insects that might damage the next crop.

We stayed in the delightful mountain village of Ubud, an artists' colony where we swam in a refreshingly cool, clean pool fed by a rushing stream. When we wanted something to eat or drink, we just banged on a gourd hanging on our porch. That was all it took to get our needs met by a charming young person who strolled down from the main house, wearing a colorful sarong and a flower over one ear.

Everywhere we went, I was struck by the grace and beauty of the Indonesian people, especially their hands. One young waitress told me that around age 12 all Indonesian girls are apprenticed to temples where they're trained to do the traditional Balinese dances that are integral to their worship service. It must be great training, for the women continue to move with the grace and style of dancers in whatever they do.

Life on Bali moves at a slow, relaxed pace that I found very restful and refreshing. From there, it took only about an hour to fly over to Sydney, Australia, where I met Betty Scholtz and the Brooklyn Botanic Garden group. My favorite part of our stay in that delightful city was seeing a play at the dramatic Opera House, which dominates Sydney's harbor. (We couldn't see an opera because that season had ended.)

The next day we boarded a large, comfortable bus. We didn't have enough time to visit the Great Barrier Reef, so we traveled south through the Blue Mountains, named for the haze produced by the many eucalyptus trees. We rode up and down mountains, around torturous curves and over small bridges that crossed spectacular ravines. Our destination for the night was the guest house at a picturesque old cattle ranch on the side of a mountain.

As we approached the steep, narrow driveway leading up to the ranch house, our driver—a rather hefty, jolly man—announced, "I'm going to walk up to make sure there's space to turn the bus around before I drive up there." Our guide, Margie, joined him for the short (about one quarter of a mile) climb. As they reached the reception desk, the driver slumped to the floor—dead of a heart attack.

Margie returned to the bus to give us the tragic news. We'd already grown fond of our friendly driver, so we felt terrible. To alleviate our helpless feelings, we decided to take up a collection to send with condolences to his family. But first we had to deal with the motor of our huge diesel bus, which the driver had left running. It took a while, but one of the men finally figured out how to turn it off. The next morning, a new driver arrived to take us on our way.

After a brief stop in Canberra, the capital city, we drove on to Melbourne, where we stayed in a very posh hotel. Ladies from the Friends of the Royal Botanical Garden gave us a guided tour of their beautiful garden. Betty and I both gave talks about the Brooklyn Botanic Garden—she spoke from the staff's point of view, and I talked about volunteers. Then the RBG's charming president, Lady Allison Hughes, hosted a delicious lunch at her home and garden.

On the following day, we drove to a sheep ranch where two men on horseback gave us an expert demonstration of how flocks of sheep are herded with border collies. Some of the dogs used barks, but others seemed to work the sheep just by using their eyes. It was fascinating to watch.

Melbourne is a beautiful city which we hated to leave—especially on the day of the Melbourne Cup, a horse race that's equivalent to our Kentucky Derby. As we gathered in the hotel lobby that morning, we were surprised to see waiters dressed in jockey silks pouring champagne. Models wearing the latest Paris fashions and enormous hats were being picked up by well-dressed men in Rolls Royces. I've always found it exciting to watch the crowds at major horse races, so I was disappointed to be leaving on such a big day.

"Why isn't the race included on our tour?" I asked. "Because," Betty replied, "it was included on a previous tour and no one was interested in going." Apparently, most of the people who enjoy touring gardens don't share my love of horses.

At the airport, we learned that our flight to Christchurch on the South Island of New Zealand was delayed. We decided to watch the Melbourne Cup on TV while waiting, so we organized a betting pool to make it more exciting. As the afternoon wore on and our plane still wasn't ready, the airline treated us to dinner at a nearby inn. We finally boarded around 9 pm, along with two jockeys carrying their saddles.

Christchurch in mid-November—their spring—was lovely. The city was settled mostly by people from England who brought their love of gardens with them, so colorful flowers were everywhere. On our first night we were entertained for dinner by local couples in their homes. Betty arranges such visits for all her tours, and they're usually the highlight for me. These generous couples, who made us feel like honored guests, gave us wonderful insights into their way of life as they showed us around their homes and gardens. I've learned so much about our cultural differences—and our surprising similarities—from the hospitable people who've entertained us on various BBG tours.

Our next stop was at the base of Mt. Cook in the Southern Alps, where we spent the night in a Swiss-type inn with balconies on every room. When the clouds lifted, we had a fantastic view of the mountain (12,349 feet high) covered by a glacier.

Next, we flew to the capital city of Wellington on the North Island. We visited a magnificent rose garden, then traveled by bus to the hot springs district. I took a day off to go fishing in memory of Ben, who'd always wanted to try fly fishing in the famous streams of New Zealand. That was too difficult to arrange, but my friend Mary Plowden-Wardlaw and I hired a guide with a boat to take us out on Lake Rotorua. We had a marvelous time fishing for rainbow trout with relatively light tackle. Mary won the pool for catching the most trout, while I won for landing the biggest—nearly five pounds. We had our fish smoked and frozen at the hotel so we could take them home. (I served mine the next week at a Hunt Club event at Norwig and Michele's house.)

As our tour continued, we visited the reconstruction of a primitive Maori village in Rotorua. I was most fascinated by the outrigger canoes that the early Polynesian settlers had used to travel thousands of miles to New Zealand. I learned that active volcanoes had wiped out all the animals native to New Zealand, so the settlers lived entirely on fish and birds. The lack of natural predators has also contributed to the island's great success in raising sheep and deer.

We had a glorious drive from Rotorua to Auckland, passing many sheep farms, backed by hills covered with tree ferns and Norfolk Island pines. Auckland is a magnificent city built around a large, beautiful bay. Houses built on a series of terraces surround the bay. I loved that city so much that I think I'd like to live there.

We flew home via Hawaii and Los Angeles, where I stopped over to see my old friend Edna Julian. All in all, it was a great trip to the other side of the world. Traveling in the Southern Hemisphere, where the seasons are the reverse of ours, really changes your perspective.

Another Health Crisis

About a year after my trip "down under," I received a setback. A routine mammogram revealed a lump in my breast. A biopsy indicated breast cancer, the same disease that had killed my grandmother Howard. In October 1989, I had a mastectomy to remove one breast. Since the disease was caught early, I did not have to suffer through chemotherapy or radiation treatments, so I recovered pretty quickly. To my mind, abdominal surgery is much worse. I get checked out regularly, of course, but with no recurrence in more than 14 years, I feel confident about my full recovery. I don't believe in worrying about my health anyway.

Shortly after my breast surgery, Betty Scholtz invited me to join her on a preview trip to India early in 1990. She always makes a personal visit (which she calls a "dry run") to check the gardens, accommodations and other details of each destination before leading a Botanic Garden tour there. This is great for me because we usually share a room and a rental car, which she pays for and I drive.

I was brought up on the stories of Rudyard Kipling, so India always seemed romantic and appealing to me. Ben refused to go there because he didn't want to witness the poverty or deal with the beggars. My daughter-in-law, Nora, shares my interest in India, though, so she joined me on Betty's preview trip. We had to skip a planned visit to Kashmir (due to political unrest), but we still saw a great deal of India.

One of the peak experiences, of course, was touring the Taj Mahal. We had close views of all the semi-precious stones inlaid in the marble walls. The stone work is very intricate—and in wonderful condition after more than 400 years. Back at the hotel, we discovered that Betty's room looked out on the Taj Mahal, so we had a spectacular view of it glistening in the light of a full moon. It was as magical as I'd always heard. It seemed to glow with the love (of Shah Jehan for his wife Mumtaz Mahal) that had inspired its creation.

In Jaipur, we climbed into a howdah on top of an elephant, which took us on a slow, bumpy ride uphill to the famous Amber Palace. Situated inside a walled city dating back to the 10th century, it's a jewel of a palace, full of mosaics and carved marble. I was especially impressed with the views of colorful gardens below. One formal garden was designed to look like a Persian carpet from above.

After spending the night at a hunting lodge that's been turned into a game sanctuary outside Jaipur, we visited a beautiful bird sanctuary. Many storks and water fowl had migrated there from Europe for the winter. When India was still part of the British Empire, British royalty (including Queen Elizabeth and Prince Philip) came to that park to shoot wild birds. Near a peaceful lake, we saw a bulletin board listing the names, dates and other details of numerous royal visits. The most surprising fact: more than 2,000 birds were shot in one day! Such wholesale destruction of beautiful fowl was appalling to me, so I was relieved to learn that shooting is no longer allowed. The park has been turned into a public preserve that welcomes all classes of Indians as well as foreign tourists.

Perhaps the most memorable part of our journey was the visit to Calcutta. We stayed in a large, lavish suite in a marble palace, which—like many other maharajas' palaces in India—has been converted into a hotel. Room service was provided by lovely young women wearing beautiful saris. Our rooms looked out on serene fountains and gardens. When we left the hotel grounds, however, we received a rude surprise. From quiet luxury, we were suddenly plunged into teeming masses of poor people.

My friend Betty Scholtz and I enjoy dining together during a preview
of a Brooklyn Botanic Garden tour.

It took us about two hours to drive to the Botanic Garden because the streets were so crowded the taxi could hardly move. We had to weave among pedestrians, donkeys hauling huge loads on their backs, bicycle rickshaws carrying several passengers, and sacred cows wandering freely. The driver had to watch out for women running into the streets to collect the cow dung, which they shaped into patties to be dried and used as fuel. It was really disturbing to see all those unfortunate people huddled together, living and even sleeping on the streets. I began to understand Ben's reluctance to visit India.

The director of Calcutta's Botanical Garden, the world's second oldest (after the one outside Jakarta) showed us around. The garden began as a research facility for the British who wanted to learn how to propagate medicinal plants, herbs, spices and rubber trees, among others. Today, it also features many beautiful flowers and the world's largest ficus tree whose branches cover four acres. After a lovely garden tour, we had another hot, tedious drive back to our air conditioned hotel. The dramatic contrast between the people in the hotel and those on the streets was very unsettling. But I believe such experiences are important in helping us understand what life is like in the rest of the world. They also make us appreciate just how lucky we are.

One of Betty's good friends now living in Brooklyn is the former Hope Cooke, the American wife of the King of Sikkim. Hope wanted us to visit Sikkim, a tiny country in the Himalayas that adjoins India, but Betty told her that was not possible. Hope then arranged for one of the king's relatives, also his Treasury Secretary, to meet us in Darjeeling instead.

He turned out to be an avid gardener who was so eager to meet Betty that he brought his lovely wife and daughter to join us for tea. Before we parted, he managed to persuade Betty to bring her tour group to Sikkim after all. We spent several days in the charming Windemere Hotel, the same place Hope Cooke had stayed when she first met the king. The sitting room featured a photo album of the royal wedding and the royal family, which we enjoyed seeing.

Our next stop was Nepal. My favorite part of that visit was driving to a small town, about an hour from Katmandu, to have tea with the head of the Botanical Garden. It was an interesting garden, with well-kept greenhouses and many plants that were new to us. As we sipped our tea, we had a beautiful view of Mt. Everest and the snow-capped Himalayas surrounding us.

We were fascinated by the numerous temples in Katmandu, many of which were decorated with strings of colorful prayer flags flapping in the breeze. I especially remember the Temple of the Living Goddess, with the little girl who'd been selected as Goddess (until she reaches puberty) looking somewhat wistfully out the window. To our surprise, she was wearing heavy makeup, even though she was only 8 or 9 years old.

We flew home from New Delhi, where Nora and I had an unusual experience on a morning walk. In the distance, we saw a big tree covered with bright red flowers, so we walked toward it. When we got closer, though, the "blossoms" flew away. They were actually red and yellow parrots who liked to perch there. It struck me as typical of a colorful country that is full of surprises.

Going to India with Betty was so much fun that I've accompanied her on several other preview trips for the Garden. We made two visits to different parts of France, where my knowledge of the language came in handy. I was pleased to be able to converse with our hosts in their language. I also went on preview trips to Spain and to Tucson, Arizona. I've joined Betty on several of the BBG's regular tours, too, including one to Ecuador and the Galapagos.

In 1999, Nora, Dawn and I joined about 15 other members of the BBG for a journey to Morocco. One day we drove to the edge of the Sahara Desert. We rode camels across the sand dunes so we could watch the sun setting in the desert. I loved riding the camel, despite an awkward gait that wasn't very comfortable, but the sunset didn't hold a candle to those we used to see from our Brooklyn apartment. The air in Morocco was apparently too clear. It takes clouds or smog or other particles in the air to make a sunset truly beautiful.

Our guide told us that we'd just missed Hillary Clinton, who was First Lady at the time. She'd stayed overnight in a tent so she could see the sun rise as well as set in the desert. I asked how far it was to Timbuktu, a place I'd heard so much about. "It's in Mali, about 68 camel days south of here," the guide replied. I decided to skip that journey.

On a trip to Morocco, I rode a camel into the Sahara Desert.

Ironically, one of my favorite experiences in Morocco occurred because our bus had a flat tire in the Atlas Mountains. The driver suggested we get off to stretch our legs while he fixed the tire. Since we were heading downhill, six or eight of us decided to walk down until the driver caught up with us. The views were spectacular—and much easier to see on foot than from the bus. We walked for about an hour before the bus came along, but I really enjoyed that.

The driver's assistant was a college student who helped us with luggage and other details. Near the end of the trip, he invited us for tea at his family's home in a quaint stone village. We could see his mother and aunts peering out the windows as we walked up to the house, but it was his party and they remained hidden. We sat on benches around a big open room and enjoyed mint tea and delicious almond cookies, but we never met the ladies who prepared everything. Still, it was a very special event.

I still make other trips with family and friends, too. When my grandson, Christopher, was in the Air Force, he was unable to get home one Christmas. He was stationed in Egypt at the time, so his mother (Nora) and I decided to fly over to see him. It was easy to get reservations on short notice because many people canceled trips to Egypt after terrorists attacked a tourist bus in 1992.

My interest in Egypt and its history dates back to my high school days, when archeologists first discovered all the gold and other artifacts in King Tutankhamen's tomb. I'd always wanted to see it for myself, so I really enjoyed visiting his tomb and others in the Valley of the Kings—especially without the hassle of the usual crowds of tourists.

Thanks to all the cancellations, only 36 of us were on board the Nile River cruise ship designed for 250 passengers. We visited a number of fascinating old temples along the Nile and saw the magnificent statues at Abu Simbel. (Those had been saved and moved to higher ground when the new Aswan Dam was built.) An unforgettable moment for me was driving the horse carriage to the magnificent Temple of Karnak in Luxor. I told the driver that I'd pay his price for the ride only if he'd let me drive—so he did.

Christopher was stationed near Giza, so he took us there and arranged for camel drivers to take us to the Sphinx and the great Pyramids. I enjoyed that, but the interior of the great pyramid was disappointing in comparison to the other temples we'd visited. One evening Chris and a buddy of his joined us for a dinner cruise on the Nile. The belly dancer who provided the evening's entertainment chose Chris's clean-cut, boyish friend as her partner. He was so embarrassed that it made everyone laugh. All in all, it was a great trip.

*I still enjoy dressing up, so I was delighted when Robert Lone and I won first prize for our **Merry Widow** costumes in 1997.*

I hope to continue traveling as long as I'm able to without being a burden to my companions. I find it very exciting to meet new people and to see strange and beautiful sights. I realize that I'm fortunate because I can afford to fly off to exotic places like Egypt and India, but I don't think you have to go very far to enjoy the benefits of travel. A change of scene, with different routines and new faces, is very stimulating—even if you just explore an unfamiliar neighborhood or another town a few miles away. I learn something new from every place I visit, and that helps me focus on areas outside of myself.

If the day should come when I can no longer travel, I'll continue to seek other ways to have fun—whether it's going to parties with relatives and friends or just puttering in my garden.

14

A New Career at 78

Around 1984, I happened to meet a professional designer of stage sets. "You should go into modeling," he told me. "Your white hair is beautiful—and casting directors are always looking for older women who are still decent looking. I could introduce you to a few people who'd probably give you modeling jobs."

The idea appealed to me because it sounded like another type of performing, which I still enjoy immensely. I went home and told Ben about it. "Oh, you don't want your face plastered all over everything," he said. His distinct lack of enthusiasm was enough to deter me from pursuing it. A seed had been planted deep inside my brain, though.

A few months after I'd moved into Manhattan at the end of 1988, the subject came up again. While working on sets for a Snarks production, I started chatting with my friend, Jean Atherton. A good-looking woman around my age, she talked enthusiastically about her work as a "granny model."

"Why don't you try it?" she asked. "You have a good strong face, and that's what they're looking for. Casting directors like people who've had professional acting experience—especially when they're casting television commercials. If you're interested, I could help you get started."

I hesitated at first, because I knew what Ben would have said: "Fool's names and fool's faces are often found in public places." *But,* I told myself, *times have changed and I'm on my own now.* I was also ready for a stimulating new challenge, so I decided to give it a try. Following Jean's advice, I arranged an interview at a place called "Actors in Advertising." I signed up for a series of lessons in "acting before the camera," taught by Joan See. According to Jean, "Joan See is an excellent teacher who knows what she's doing." I soon learned how accurate that was.

Acting before a camera was a new experience for me, but Joan was extremely helpful. She kept telling me, "Make it small." I'd always tried to reach the back row of a large theater with my voice and gestures, so I had to learn to tone everything down for the camera. We had about eight students in our class, and I was

clearly the oldest. Most of the others were either college students or recent graduates, but that made it more fun for me. We didn't have to worry about competing
for the same jobs, so I enjoyed learning about their very different lives during
breaks.

The instructor asked us to perform various skits and story-boards for commercials while she videotaped our performances. Seeing ourselves on screen for the
first time was demoralizing, but it turned out to be the best lesson of all. It gave
us a real understanding of what we were doing wrong. I felt a little foolish as I
watched those early play-backs, but I gradually improved. When I managed to do
a scene well enough to earn Joan's praise, I felt a real thrill. *Perhaps this old dog
can still learn a few new tricks*, I thought.

After I completed the first three-month course, Joan encouraged me to continue. Her most promising students are invited to take a shorter course that
includes performing for casting directors. That was terrific because we received
very helpful feedback. Next, Joan gave me excellent advice about getting a "composite" of pictures and head shots taken, then attaching a resume. Later on, she
introduced me to a top modeling agency, Cunningham, Escott and Depine,
which sent me out on quite a few casting calls.

When my composite was finished and I was ready to look for work in the
field, Jean Atherton introduced me to another top agent, David Roos of Gilla
Roos. He sent me out on a casting call the very next day. Much to my surprise, I
got the job. I was photographed for a magazine advertisement, which is known as
"print work." Performing for commercials shown on television is called "on-camera work." We're asked to audition for on-camera work, but applying for a modeling job in print is known as a "go see." Payment varies with the type of work.

My rate for print advertising is $250 an hour. Most photography sessions (or
"shoots") are scheduled for at least two hours, though we seldom work the entire
time. Sometimes I'm hired for a whole day for a flat fee of $1,500 to $2,000, but
the shoot may take only three or four hours.

On-camera work doesn't pay as much as print initially, but it has more poten-
tial for future earnings. We receive the Screen Actors Guild (SAG) minimum of
$285 per day. If the commercial airs only once, that's it. But if it's repeated (as
most are), we receive additional payment or "residuals" each time it appears. Last
month, for example, I received a check for $1,750 in residuals for a commercial I
shot more than a year ago. My total for that one job is more than $20,000 so far.
My grandchildren and various friends have seen the same commercial airing
recently, too, so it's continuing to pay off.

*One of my first modeling jobs produced this picture for Hallmark cards. I love
the quote from Mark Twain: "Wrinkles should merely indicate
where smiles have been."*

That may sound like easy money, but it's not. I spend many hours on go-sees
and auditions that lead nowhere. I may get five or six calls from agents in a week,

but I usually go out about ten times before I'm actually hired. I also have to keep visiting agents' offices to meet new employees and remind them that I'm still alive. One agent even told me, "We thought you'd passed on," when he hadn't seen me around for a few months.

I always ride the subway when I'm going to an audition. I don't treat myself to a taxi until I get hired. I began that practice when I was a young woman seeking theater jobs, and it's hard to change without feeling guilty. (Although my grand-children sometimes tease me about my thrifty habits, I believe they've served me well over the years. A little inconvenience when you're young can make life far more comfortable when you get older.)

After every audition, I still wait anxiously to hear if I got the job. I'm always hopeful—even though I have a lot of competition from other older women who've taken up modeling for retirement income. I believe that being optimis-tic—and having something to look forward to—are very important ingredients in aging successfully. I'm realistic enough to know that I won't get every part, but I'm always thrilled when I do get hired. I feel a real sense of accomplishment when I've succeeded in becoming another person for a short time.

Most of my calls are for print work, but those can be a lot of fun. In one shoot for an April Fool issue of *Advertising Age*, for example, I was photographed with my white hair up in a bun, sitting in a wheelchair—and rolling a marijuana ciga-rette. I enjoy portraying unusual characters in ads because it's like being a charac-ter actor in the theater. I keep a closet full of funny-looking clothes so I'll be able to go to any audition dressed for the part—whether it's a rag picker or a society matron. Putting together a costume for a meeting with a casting director reminds me of the good times I had playing "dress-up" as a child. Modeling still seems more like play than work to me, but I believe playing helps keep you young.

One day an agent told me that an advertising agency was looking for a "typical grandma," so I put on my favorite granny outfit: a full skirt and a lace-collared white blouse with a cameo at the neck. I pinned up my hair and added a hairpiece twisted into an old-fashioned bun on top. When I walked into the casting direc-tor's studio with a pair of "granny" glasses sliding down my nose, someone said, "She's it. That's exactly the look we want!" I felt pleased because I was really play-ing a role—that of the sweet old grandma. It turned out to be a commercial for a new email machine, which I was supposed to be using to send an email message to my grandson.

My "typical granny" persona has become very profitable for me. I've been hired for several other jobs requiring the same look—even though one of my grandsons told me I'd never get such a job because, he said, "You're not a typical granny; no way." He's probably right, but it's the look that counts. Just last week I did a shoot for *Scholastic Magazine's* series, "The Box Car Gang." Once again, I was Granny—the only adult photographed with four lively children.

I've landed several modeling jobs by appearing at auditions with this "typical granny" hairdo and clothing.

Each modeling job teaches me something new, so I've become a much better model over the years. One thing I learned the hard way was to stop wasting time and money sending my photos to everyone in the business. I now send new pictures and resumes only to the five or six agents who send me on the most casting calls. Sometimes, three different agents will call about the same shoot because they know the advertising agency is seeking someone about my age or looks.

One day a casting director asked if I could twirl a hoola hoop. "I don't know," I said. "I haven't been near a hoola hoop in decades, but I could try."

"Well, you have a week before casting begins," he said. I bought a hoola hoop the next day and asked my teen-aged granddaughter, Maria, to teach me how to spin it around. We both laughed a lot that day as I struggled to get the hang of it. I never became very good, but I still got the job—perhaps because I was the only white-haired woman in New York City who could manage to get a hoola hoop to stay up at all.

The client was a hospital that wanted "before and after" pictures for a print ad. In the "before" scene, I looked very bedraggled, wearing sweat clothes and no makeup. I was trying desperately to climb up one step, with an attendant standing nearby, encouraging me. In the second photo, supposedly taken after I'd had therapy at the hospital, I was wearing a party dress, with earrings and makeup—and feeling so energetic that I was swinging a hoola hoop around my hips. Thanks to Maria's helpful instruction, I managed to keep the hoop up long enough for the photographer to get a satisfactory picture.

I've been photographed many times for the health care industry, which seems to like older people in their ads. I'm usually the healthy one comforting another elderly person. In one ad for the Visiting Nurse Service, though, I was wearing a white robe and looking very dejected. A young African-American girl in a Visiting Nurse's uniform patted my hand solicitously. The caption says, *We still make house calls.* That ad was so successful that it appeared on the back of New York City buses for about six months. My grandchildren got a big kick out of seeing my face sailing down Manhattan streets.

About a year later, the doorman of my building stopped me. "Mrs. Tuttle" he said, "you know that picture of you that was on the back of the buses? Well, it's now on a huge billboard up in the Bronx." I found that hard to believe, so I drove up to the Bronx with a friend. Sure enough, the picture was stretched over the railroad tracks along Tremont Avenue. That's the only time I've seen myself on a billboard, but a friend saw my picture on a billboard in Moscow. He can't read Russian, so he didn't know what my face was advertising. My nephew Reiner saw me on another billboard in Union Station in Washington, D.C. That one was advertising a beach robe. Since photographers are often allowed to sell the unused photographs they've taken on an assignment, I never know where my face might turn up.

One memorable modeling job was for Breitling, a Swiss company that makes expensive watches. They booked me for the whole day at a fee of $2,000. When I arrived at the studio, they told me I didn't need any makeup; I just had to change into a nun's habit. I was supposed to be the Mother Superior of a convent, clutching my rosary and glaring at the camera. The focal point of the picture, of course, was the Breitling watch on my wrist. The caption was in French, but roughly translates as: *a professional from heaven doesn't dwell on material things.*

Over lunch that day, I chatted with the young man who'd come from Paris to supervise the photography session. I asked him why they hadn't shot the ad in

France. "After all," I said, "you live in a Catholic country. There must be thousands of French nuns you could photograph."

I had a good time playing Mother Superior for a Swiss watch company, even though the picture is not exactly flattering.

"Yes," he agreed, "but I like the strength in your face." The ad appeared only in glossy French magazines, but he sent me a copy. It's not a very flattering photograph, but it's still one of my favorites. I've shown it to a number of friends who went to convent schools. Most say the same thing: "We had a Mother Superior just like that in my convent—and she scared me to death!'

Now that I belong to Actor's Equity and the Screen Actor's Guild, I get calls to do other work as well. Quite a few movies and television shows are filmed in and around New York City, so I sometimes appear as an "extra" in one of those. The flat fee for a day's work is only about $200, but we get paid time and a half when they run overtime. Extras spend many hours sitting around waiting to be called for a scene, but I meet many interesting people that way. And I still get a kick out of seeing my face pop up on a TV screen or in a movie theater.

I've been an extra on the TV series *Law and Order* several times. In March 2003, the show *Criminal Intent* hired me to play an old lady in a nursing home being visited by her son. On the NBC comedy, *Ed*, I appeared in a scene at the hairdresser's. I just sat there quietly having my hair styled while all the action took place over my head. I've also appeared in four different skits on the Conan O'Brien show and in another on *Late Night with David Letterman*. Recently, I played the role of a librarian at Yale University in a forthcoming Julia Roberts movie called *Mona Lisa Smile*. A number of Yale students were also working as extras on the set that day, so I enjoyed talking to them while we waited for our scenes. I was amused to learn that some of them thought I really was the librarian.

One day I reported to a Manhattan location at five o'clock in the morning because filming had to be completed before the street became busy with traffic. All I had to do was walk down the sidewalk with other extras, carrying an umbrella. The script called for a rainy day, so a van sprayed water on us as we walked, while huge trucks with enormous lamps lit up the still-dark street. It was fascinating to see how they created the desired effect.

Playing a role for an advertisement or a TV scene that may end up on the cutting room floor is not as exciting as acting before an audience, but it's still creative and fun for me. At my age, it's very gratifying to get paid for doing something I enjoy so much. And, of course, I never know where a minor role might lead. I don't expect Hollywood to come looking for me, but some of the things that do happen are almost as much fun.

About ten years ago, for instance, a man I had worked with on a TV movie invited me to play the part of Lady Bracknell in *The Importance of Being Ernest* at an off-off Broadway playhouse on the Upper East Side of Manhattan. It was a low-budget production so I was paid very little for my performance. I didn't mind because I had such fun—and sitting in the audience one day was my old friend Betty Parsons. We had traveled to Europe together back in 1930, but we'd lost touch when she moved abroad with her husband many years ago. I was really delighted to see her again. She's now a widow living only a few blocks from my apartment in New York, so we've been getting together regularly every since. All my other childhood friends are gone now, so Betty is truly special.

*Betty Parsons, my oldest friend, and I reminisce about our childhood and a
memorable trip to Europe in 1930.*

Every acting job or modeling assignment does not have a happy ending, but I
can remember only one in the past 13 years that I did not enjoy. I was supposed
to be celebrating my 50th wedding anniversary at a romantic hotel in the Poconos
in Pennsylvania. Unfortunately, I didn't like the man who'd been hired to play
my husband. The script called for us to take a "champagne bath" together in a
giant stemmed glass—about four feet across—that was filled with bubble bath.
We wore bathing suits, of course, but it still made me uncomfortable.

I've learned, however, that even unpleasant experiences usually have a positive
side. Being photographed bathing in a giant champagne glass gave me another
amusing story to tell my grandchildren. I even have the ridiculous pictures to go
with it. I think my family enjoys hearing about something other than "the good
old days." And I'm convinced that it's healthy for people my age to have interesting new things to talk about instead of always living in the past.

15

Family Legacies

I've been interested in family history most of my life. It all began, perhaps, with a desire to know more about my own parents, who died when I was a child. Living with Great Aunt Mamie Kelsey, Grandma Howard's younger sister, undoubtedly stimulated my interest. Aunt Mamie never revealed her age, but must have been born in the 1850's. Like most unmarried women of her day, she never had a career (though she once confessed to me that she'd wanted to be a concert violinist). Despite her obvious talents in music and art, she was a selfless person who devoted her life to helping others.

Aunt Mamie kept house and looked after her elderly mother for many years after her father died. She was so close to my grandparents, Edward and Clara Howard, that they asked her to serve as godmother when my mother was born in 1877. Mamie watched little Esther grow up, and loved to tell us stories about our mother's childhood.

One of her favorites involved Mother's love of butter. In those days, it was customary to have a formal family dinner after church on Sunday. Henry Ward Beecher, pastor of Brooklyn's Plymouth Church that the family attended, was a frequent guest. One Sunday, Grandma asked Mr. Beecher to say grace. Always eager to preach, he was quite long winded. Little Esther, about six at the time, soon grew restless. Glancing around, she noticed that all the others had their heads bowed and eyes closed, so she decided to pop a butter ball into her mouth while no-one was looking. When the "Amen" finally came, however, all eyes turned to Esther, whose puffed-out cheeks (and empty butter plate) gave her away.

The history of family heirlooms was another favorite topic for Aunt Mamie. Mother was very proud of a lovely glazed pottery vase that Henry Ward Beecher had given her, but it was Aunt Mamie who told us what prompted the gift. "Your mother was sitting on Mr. Beecher's knee one Sunday after church," she began. "A restless child, she suddenly jumped up, yelping in pain when her long hair got caught in the buttons of his waistcoat. Mr. Beecher told her to be very quiet while he gently untangled her hair. She didn't cry, so he gave her the vase as a reward."

Aunt Mamie's favorite story-telling "prop" was a special cane with a sword concealed inside. "This belonged to my father, Theron Kelsey," she told us. "After the Civil War ended in 1865, he moved the family to New Orleans where his coal business was flourishing. Yankees weren't exactly popular in the South in those days, though, so Father got special permission to carry this cane in case anyone ever accosted him on the street."

Aunt Mamie left her father's cane to my brother Howard, who later left it to his oldest son, Ned. Throughout her life, though, Aunt Mamie loved to demonstrate that cane, which triggered my imagination. I asked her numerous questions about family history. Her answers prompted me to begin reading some of the books we had around the house. One, privately printed in 1909, is based on letters and journals kept by my great-grandparents, John Tasker Howard (1808–1888) and Susan Taylor Raymond (1812–1906). The little volume begins with a brief history of the Howards in America. Abraham Howard, a ship merchant who settled in Marblehead, Massachusetts in 1721, came first. Abraham had eight children; his son John, born in 1755, had nine children. John's oldest son, Joseph, was the father of eleven, all born in Salem.

My great-grandfather, John Tasker Howard, was Joseph's second child. He attended a one-room school in Salem where he sat next to an older boy named Nathaniel Hawthorne. (About thirty years later, Hawthorne became famous for his novels, including *The Scarlet Letter* and *The House of Seven Gables*. In 1853, Hawthorne published *Tanglewood Tales*, a children's book named for the estate near Lenox, Massachusetts, in the Berkshires where he lived.)

In October 1827, Joseph Howard moved his family to Brooklyn, a town of only about 15,000 people at the time. He and other family members who soon followed believed that New York provided better opportunities for their shipping business than Massachusetts. (I still have the folding sea captain's desk which Joseph used when he crossed the ocean in one of his ships.) Joseph's son, John Tasker, was 18 when the family moved to Brooklyn. He also went into the family shipping business, J. Howard and Son, located on South Street in Manhattan.

On November 1, 1831, Tasker, as he was called, married Susan Taylor Raymond, daughter of a prominent Brooklyn family who traced their American ancestors back to 1630. Susan's Great Aunt Polly Raymond married Charles Sherman and gave birth to two sons who had outstanding careers. William Tecumseh Sherman, a Union General during the Civil War, was famous for the march through Georgia. His brother John, a U.S. Senator, Secretary of the Treasury and Secretary of State, lent his name to the Sherman Anti-Trust Act.

The Shermans never lived in Brooklyn, but many of Susan's other relatives did. Her oldest brother, Israel Ward Raymond, married Tasker's sister, Frances (Fanny) Howard. They lived in Brooklyn for about ten years before moving to San Francisco, where he represented the Pacific Mail Steamship Company. Susan's other two brothers were educators who spent many years in Brooklyn. John Howard Raymond, was the first President of the Brooklyn Polytechnic Institute—a job he left to become the first president of Vassar College in 1864. He remained at Vassar until his death in 1878. Robert Raikes Raymond, another brother of Susan's, was a Baptist minister who later became Professor of English at Brooklyn Polytech.

John Tasker Howard was successful in several business ventures and is said to have crossed the Atlantic Ocean 52 times for various negotiations and meetings. He is best known, however, for his role in starting Plymouth Church in Brooklyn Heights—and for persuading Henry Ward Beecher, only 34 at the time, to be the first pastor. Some residents didn't think Brooklyn needed a second Congregational Church (the Church of the Pilgrims was only two years old), but Tasker was so impressed by Beecher's oratorical skills that he was determined to bring him to Brooklyn. He put up money to buy a church that had been vacated by the Presbyterians. He then persuaded other investors to participate.

Plymouth Church opened on June 13, 1847, with 21 members. Henry Ward Beecher began his ministry on October 10, 1847, and stayed until he died, 40 years later. By 1867, Beecher was "possibly the most celebrated man in the United States," according to *Mr. Clemens and Mark Twain,* a biography by Justin Kaplan. Plymouth Church was not only full every Sunday, but, adds Kaplan, "the pavement was crowded with people trying to get in. Beecher knew how to dominate and mesmerize an audience." (It seems that Beecher had also played an important role in Mark Twain's life at one point.)

Reverend Beecher was also very influential as he crusaded from the pulpit in favor of temperance and against slavery. After the Brooklyn Bridge finally opened in 1883, New Yorkers had a popular saying. When anyone asked, "How do you find Plymouth Church?" they'd answer, "Just follow the crowd going over the Bridge on Sunday morning."

Over the years, the Howards and the Beechers became close friends. They were frequent guests for dinner at each other's homes—occasions that Aunt Mamie and other relatives remembered fondly. Aunt Mamie also told us, with obvious pride, that Henry Ward Beecher had baptized my mother. But the clearest indication of the friendship between the two families may be the bronze plaque in the vestibule of Plymouth Church. It is dedicated to the memory of John Tasker Howard, *"founder of Plymouth Church...The earliest, and latest, and life-long friend of Henry Ward Beecher. HWB."*

Great-Grandmother Susan also developed a close friendship with Reverend Beecher's sister, Harriet Beecher Stowe, who wrote the famous novel, *Uncle Tom's Cabin.* In fact, they spent several months together in Italy in 1860. Both women were traveling abroad with two of their grown children, but Susan's daughter, Annie, died tragically in Milan on June 6, 1860. She was only twenty-one. Mrs. Stowe dedicated her book, *Agnes in Sorrento,* to the memory of Annie Howard and wrote a touching poem called, "Lines to the Memory of Annie."

The family's friendship with Reverend Beecher was tested in 1875 when he was put on trial for adultery (or "alienation of affection"), but they remained loyal. It was a long, sensational trial because the parishioner he was accused of seducing was the wife of Theodore Tilton, the editor of the *Brooklyn Daily Union* and of a weekly religious paper. The Howards believed Mrs. Tilton was the one at fault, but the trial ended in a hung jury.

Tasker and Susan Howard had nine children, two of whom died in infancy. Two others died in their twenties—Annie at 21 and Frank at 22. Sadly, Susan even outlived her youngest son, Henry, who died in 1906 at the age of 56. The oldest son, Joseph, was a journalist for fifty years. He wrote for *The New York Times, The World* and a number of other newspapers. He was also editor of the New York *Star* and president of the New York Press Club. Joseph died in 1908, several years before I was born.

John, the second son, also wrote for newspapers after leaving the Union Army in 1865. Later on, he became a book publisher. In 1871, he married Susan Raymond Merriam, the daughter of his mother's good friend. I knew some of his grandchildren, but the only time I actually met Great Uncle John was at a family wedding in Montclair, New Jersey, in the thirties. He and his wife were both in their nineties at the time. (He was born in 1837, but I'm not sure when he died.)

Edward Tasker (Ned) Howard, my grandfather, was born in his parents' home at 174 Hicks Street on Brooklyn Heights in 1843. He was the third son and the only one who didn't go to college. The Civil War began the same year he finished high school and I believe he was too ill to leave home at the time. Unlike the rest of the family, he went into the advertising business and started his own firm, E.T. Howard and Company. He refused to advertise liquor or cigarettes, but became very successful nonetheless. He was known as "the dean of advertising" in New York City in the early 1900s.

In 1873, Gramp married Clara Kelsey, the daughter of Theron and Lydia Maule Kelsey. Theron's family came from Kelso, Scotland, while Lydia's family had settled in Evans Mills, a town near Poughkeepsie, New York, in the early 1800's. Clara had only two siblings—a younger brother who drowned in the Mississippi River as a young man, and a younger sister, Mary Louise, known as Aunt Mamie.

The only one of Gramp's siblings that I really knew was my namesake, Esther Howard, who made frequent visits to our summer home, Howarden. Aunt Essie was married in 1866 to General Horatio C. King, a lawyer who had received the Congressional Medal of Honor for "conspicuous gallantry" during the Civil War. (He served for a time with Uncle John, who became a good friend and introduced him to Essie.) Uncle Rach, as we called him, was a fine musician who wrote numerous songs and served as organist at the Plymouth Church for many years. He had a talent for repairing and tuning pianos—a skill he used to provide music for the troops when they were stuck in camp for long periods.

Unlike Uncle Rach, who was rotund and rather jolly, Aunt Essie was slight and straight as a ramrod. She wore toque hats and a lace guimpe around her neck, making her look a bit like old Queen Mary. Aunt Essie lived until 1925, but was in mourning for the last seven years, wearing nothing but black after her husband's death on November 15, 1918.

The Kings had nine children, eight of them girls. Their son and two daughters died in infancy; a third daughter died at age 19 in 1897. The other five girls grew up in Brooklyn Heights, along with our mother and her younger sister, Ruth. Fortunately, Gramp's brother John had eight sons, so there were plenty of boy cousins around to keep things lively at the Plymouth Church youth group.

Mother's sister, Ruth, married twice but never had any children. She divorced her first husband, Henri Hoguet, around 1920 and married Wells Hamilton about two years later. Uncle Wells was a clever man who converted an old bus into a mobile home which they used to travel all over the country. I remember Aunt Ruth as a very pretty woman who wore beautiful clothes. She was a talented singer and a great flirt, but not very good at anything else. She depended so heavily on my mother that Grandma Clara used to say, "If Ruth ever gets to heaven, it will have to be on Esther's apron strings."

My mother was 22 when she married my father in 1899. Daddy was nearly seven years older than his bride. By all reports, they had a very happy marriage for more than twenty years. Unfortunately, it was cut short by the death of my father in November 1919. My mother was an extraordinary single parent until her own death in June 1923.

These formal portraits are the only pictures I have of my parents,
Esther and Woodruff Leeming.

The Leemings

Since I was only eight when my father died, I didn't know much about his family. When Ben and I moved back to Brooklyn in the 1940s, however, I found many Leeming cousins still living there. I developed a close friendship with my first cousin, Helen Leeming Thirkield, who lived nearby. Together we researched that branch of the family.

I never knew my Leeming grandparents, but I learned that my grandfather, Thomas Lonsdale Leeming, was born in Burnley, England, in 1837. He moved with his parents to Montreal, Canada, in 1840. About 40 years later, Grandfather started a drug import business with exclusive rights to Ben Gay, Pacquins, Visine and other products. After 80 years, Thomas L. Leeming Company was sold to Pfizer in 1961 for a reputed forty million dollars. (The money went to the brothers who worked for the firm, and my father was not one of them.) Grandfather, who settled in Brooklyn in 1888, was an amateur sailor and one of the founding members of the Siwanica Yacht Club in Oyster Bay, Long Island.

My grandmother Leeming was born Helena Arethusa Woodruff. She was the daughter of Isaac Ogden Woodruff and Arethusa Helena Dewey. Her parents were married in Albany, New York, later traveling by canal boat to Quincy, Illinois. As his family grew and his business prospered, Great-grandfather Woodruff built an elegant Victorian house in 1868. One of the finest homes in Quincy, it was selected to house the local history museum after the death of his last surviving child, Theresa Dewey, in the 1920s.

Years later, when the city's business district surrounded the house, the local Historical Society decided to move to a less congested location. Before the Woodruff house was demolished, however, various doors, windows and fireplaces were saved and moved to the new museum. To this day, docents dressed in period costumes tell visitors about Arethusa and Isaac Woodruff, and how they became one of the founders of Quincy.

Thomas and Helena Leeming had five children. My father was the middle child, with two sisters and two brothers. His older sister, Helena Woodruff Leeming, a graduate of Barnard College, married Dr. Smith Ely Jelliffe, a psychiatrist described in Chapter 6. (After Aunt Helena died of a brain tumor in 1916, Ely married the colorful Belinda.) The Jelliffes had five children: Sylvia Canfield, Winifred Helena, Smith Ely Jr., William Leeming and Helena Woodruff.

Ely and Helena's oldest child, Sylvia Jelliffe, married Dr. Gregory Stragnell and had two children, Barbara and Robert. Winifred married Dr. Alfred Emerson, an etymologist, and had two children, Helena and William. Ely married

Yvonne Reilly and had three sons: David, Donald and Gordon. The youngest son, William Leeming, married Mila while he was in medical school, but died in a tragic accident soon afterwards. Their son, John, who's now an architect, was born after he died. Helena married Carel Goldsmith and had two sons, Adolph and Ely.

Daddy's older brother, Joseph, joined the family firm at age 17 and became a partner at 21. In 1893, he married Emily Howland. They had four children: Katherine Avery (who later married Eric Douglas), John Howland, Joseph Lonsdale and Elizabeth Lonsdale (who married H. Wickliffe Rose). In 1906, when the children ranged in age from two to twelve, Uncle Joseph died of tuberculosis. His widow and children moved back to her parents' home in Buffalo, so I didn't see much of those cousins while we were growing up.

In 1924, Aunt Emily was remarried to Theodore Lyman and continued spending summers at Meadowood Farm, near Great Barrington, Massachusetts. Their lovely house, which was redesigned and updated by my father, is only about 45 minutes from our farm in Kinderhook. The children and grandchildren vacationed there also, so we became reacquainted during the summers.

Daddy's younger brother, Thomas Lonsdale Leeming, graduated from Columbia College in 1894 and married Gertrude Busby in 1898. He joined his brother Joseph in the family importing business, which they took over when their father died in 1902. Uncle Tom and Aunt Gertrude had three children: Helen Schuyler (who later married Gilbert Thirkield) Leonard Busby and Thomas Lonsdale, Jr. All three were raised in Brooklyn and in Grandfather Busby's mansion in Glen Cove, Long Island.

The Thirkields had three children: Pamela, Gilbert and Robert. Leonard Leeming and his wife, Ruth Watt, had one child, Joan, born in 1930. Thomas Jr. and his wife, Jane Read, had two children. Their daughter Nancy died in a camping accident in 1942. Their son, also named Thomas Leeming, went on to have five children.

Through my cousin Helen, I learned a lot about her father, Uncle Tom, who'd been president of the Riding and Driving Club in Brooklyn, as well as President of the Brooklyn Academy of Music. Uncle Tom was influential in arranging for the Boston Symphony and the Metropolitan Opera to perform in Brooklyn. The opera company appeared at the Academy six or eight times a season for many years. That was how Uncle Tom became friends with Enrico Caruso, the Metropolitan's most famous tenor from 1903 to 1920. Caruso was singing at the Brooklyn Academy of Music when he first experienced the throat hemorrhage that ultimately led to his death in Naples in 1921.

Daddy's younger sister, Winifred, was one of the first students at Smith College. She was married in 1903 to Dr. Karl Vogel, a surgeon who taught at the College of Physicians and Surgeons. Five years later, at age 30, Aunt Winifred died of tuberculosis, like her two brothers. She had no children and was buried in her wedding dress.

Uncle Karl never remarried. I remember him as a man with many hobbies. His great interest in ships led to building models of sailing vessels. His model of the *USS Constitution* is on display at the Mystic Seaport Museum in Mystic, Connecticut. Uncle Karl used jeweler's tools to make his models, so he also became very skillful at repairing old watches. During my single days in Manhattan, I had tea with Uncle Karl regularly. He also came to the opening of my first play on Broadway.

In the course of my family research, I learned about The Rembrandt Club, which is well-known in Brooklyn. It's a small private club for gentlemen who have a special interest in the arts. Most members are collectors and/or sponsors of museums, theater, concerts and other arts. When the Club celebrated its centennial in 1985, I discovered that Gramp Howard had been one of the original members—and that my father and Uncle Tom had also belonged.

The Rembrandt Club has never had a club house; members meet monthly for dinner in each other's homes. Once a year their wives or other female guests are invited to join them. According the 100th Anniversary book, my father hosted a dinner at our house on Brooklyn Heights in October 1911, when I was only three months old.

My father received his architecture degree from Massachusetts Institute of Technology (MIT). Afterwards, he attended *L'Ecole des Beaux Artes* in Paris for a year. One of his first jobs as an architect was working with the firm of Heins and La Farge on the famous Cathedral of St. John the Divine in New York City.

Daddy was a good friend of Dan Beard, the illustrator who helped start the Boy Scouts of America in 1910. When I was quite young, Daddy drove us all up to Redding Ridge, Connecticut to see Dan Beard. What I remember most about that visit was the enchanting pet fawn that Beard kept in a cage behind his house.

One of the first Boy Scout leaders in Brooklyn, Daddy designed and helped build a scout camp named Camp Leeming at Bear Mountain State Park in New York. Years later, I asked a Boy Scout executive if he'd ever heard of Camp Leeming. "Of course; I was a Camp Leeming boy," he said. It has now been incorporated into a larger camp, but the executive told me he attends a Camp Leeming reunion lunch every year at Rockefeller Center.

My grandmother Leeming died in 1898, my grandfather in 1902. Daddy, who outlived three of his siblings, died of tuberculosis in 1919. Uncle Tom, the last survivor, died in 1925 at the age of 52. Aunt Gertrude lived another sixteen years, dying in Palm Beach, Florida in 1941.

The Tuttles

My husband, Franklin Benjamin Tuttle, was born in Naugatuck, Connecticut. He traced his family back to William Tuttle, who arrived in this country in 1635. His father, Frank James Tuttle, was a physician as was his grandfather, the first Franklin Benjamin Tuttle. Both were general practitioners associated with the hospital in Waterbury, Connecticut. Ben's grandfather worked his way through Yale Medical School, graduating in 1862. Ben's father, also a graduate of Yale, died in 1933, so I never met him. But his mother, Mary Worrall Tuttle, lived with us for nearly 20 years before she died in 1963 at 92.

Naugatuck has many buildings designed by the famous architect, Stanford White, including the high school that Ben graduated from at age 15. His parents sent him to Kent School for a year after his graduation because they thought he was too young for college. He entered Yale a year later, graduating in 1922.

Ben had only one sibling, his younger brother Tom who married Laura Carr in 1933. After graduation, Laura (who'd been president of her Smith College class) started a bookstore in Montclair, New Jersey with her sister, Lucy. They sold it when they married, but the Montclair Book Store is still in business. Tom worked as an engineer for International Telephone and Telegraph, so the family lived all over the world, including Bermuda, Brussels, Rio de Janeiro, Havana and Monterey, Mexico.

Tom and Laura Tuttle had three sons: Thomas, David and Allan. Tom was killed in a tragic plane crash two weeks before his graduation from the University of Michigan. Allan is a brilliant graduate of Yale Law School who now works as head attorney for Gucci in London. He has one daughter, Katherine, by his first wife. He's now married to Ellen, who has three children (Mario, Gina and Reiner) from a prior marriage. David attended MIT, then graduated from Miami University in Ohio and went into the computer business. He has a lovely wife, Mary, but they have no children.

Tom, Laura and the boys spent several weeks with us (and their Grandmother Tuttle) at the farm every summer. Since they moved frequently and lived all over the world, our farm was the one constant in their lives. We all became very fond of those adventurous and entrepreneurial boys. When they were in grade school,

Laura told us, she left them playing in the garden of their hotel in Rio while she ran a quick errand. On her return, she found her sons sitting barefooted in the lobby selling flowers (which they'd picked in the hotel's garden) to tourists. She was so horrified that she made them give all the cash they'd received to charity.

One summer while Allan was still at Yale, he and David decided to hitch-hike from New York to Mexico. Finding it difficult to hitch rides together, they split up, agreeing to meet at a friend's place in New Orleans. They had a $5 bet on who'd get there first, so they often waved to each other from trucks along the way. After three days of travel, they arrived in New Orleans only five minutes apart. From there, they went on to Acapulco. Their mother was quite worried until a friend, who'd just returned from Mexico, called her. "Don't worry," she said. "I saw your boys on the beach. They have a flourishing little business doing translations for tourists."

My Own Generation

I was the youngest of my generation—younger than all twelve of my first cousins, as well as my three siblings. Thus, it's not surprising that I'm the only one still alive. My last surviving cousin, Elizabeth Leeming Rose, who turned 98 on July 25, 2002, died two months later. Some of the others also enjoyed long lives.

My older sister, Honor, lived until 1997, when she was 96 years old. Her third marriage—to Savington Crampton in 1970—was the longest and perhaps the happiest of all. Her first husband, Mortimer Banks, was the father of her only child, Honor, born in 1930. After divorcing Mort, Honor married Roderick Luttgen, in 1937.

A talented artist who studied at Parson's School of Art in New York and in Paris, Honor began her career doing set design work for Norman Bel-Geddes. She later worked as an interior decorator. Her daughter, Honor Banks, married Malcomb O. MacLean in 1950. Their five children—Putnam, Honor, Malcomb, Katherine and Sarah—were born in quick succession from 1951 to 1958.

My only brother, Howard (also known as Monk), married Helen Stover in 1936. They had two sons who were named after their father and grandfather. Edward Howard (Ned) Leeming was born in 1937, and Woodruff Leeming in 1938. Their sister, Holly, a surprise addition to the family, was born in 1957, the same year her father turned 50. My brother died of stomach cancer in 1981 at the age of 74.

My nephew, Edward Howard Leeming, Jr. married Susan Bacon in 1965. They have two sons, Benjamin and Nicholas. His brother, Woodruff, married

Gail Ann Collette in 1976. After giving birth to two daughters, Katherine and Emily, Gail died in December 1982. A few years later, Woody married Barbara Johnson. Holly is married to Lawrence Frost and has two lovely daughters, Jennifer and Julia.

My younger sister, Lee (born Elizabeth Lonsdale) married her childhood sweetheart, Charles Minor, in 1932. They had a very happy but somewhat stressful marriage that was cut short when Lee died of a stroke in January 1962. She was only 51. Lee and Charlie had two children: Elizabeth Lonsdale (Lonnie) born in 1939 and Allan Hadley, born in 1947. Allen, who has never married, has an associate's degree in architecture and works as a draftsman and framer.

Lonnie eloped with Derwood Crocker when they were both students at Cornell. They had one son, David, born in 1959, who became a successful lighting engineer and a teacher at Bard College. In 1972, Lonnie married Donald Webster, a curator at the Royal Ontario Museum in Toronto. They had two children: Nathaniel, born in 1974, and Sarah, 1976. When they were little, Lonnie and Donald brought them to our farm for visits. As a result, Sarah and my granddaughter, Honor, are still good friends. Lonnie was a heavy smoker who died of emphysema at age 57. Even sadder, Lonnie's older son, David Crocker, died in 1992 at 33—also of emphysema. (Lonnie's father, Charlie, suffered from the same disease, but it was not fatal in his case.)

Looking to the Future

One of the most enjoyable aspects of living into my nineties is watching my eleven grandchildren grow up—and getting to know many of my great-grandchildren, as well. Although I've never been one of those grannies who likes to baby-sit, I really enjoy being with the grandchildren when they're old enough to take care of themselves. I especially like to teach them things—about horses, or flowers or other subjects I'm interested in.

I feel very privileged to have attended the weddings of seven grandchildren so far. The oldest—Jim and Nora's son, Ben—went to Denison like his father. He and his wife, Sally (Carper) have two children—Cassie, Sally's daughter by a prior marriage, born in 1980, and Frank James (called Rex), born May 23, 1997.

Nine of my grandchildren helped me celebrate my Forsythia Award in 1988.
From left to right: Gerhard, Christopher, Ben, Elizabeth, Honor, me, Peter,
Tommy and Tammy holding Maria. Jeff couldn't make it and
Tristan was born a year later.

Tommy is the grandson I've spent the most time with. After graduating from Princeton, he spent a year in Indonesia. When he returned, he got a job in New York City with Morgan Stanley, so he shared my apartment. After about two years, they sent him to Hong Kong. His knowledge of the Indonesian language led to frequent business trips to Jakarta. (Nora, Jim and I had a great visit with Tommy in Hong Kong about 1992. From there, we took a tour of China, visiting Beijing, the old city of Xian, the Great Wall and the fascinating site of the buried terra cotta warriors.)

When Tommy returned to New York, he lived with me again before going to Harvard Business School for his MBA. After graduating third in his class, he and a friend started their own business, the GEM Corp. (or Global Emerging Markets), which has been very successful. Tommy is married to a lovely Indonesian girl known as Mila (born Sharmila Hainum Atmosudidrjo). She's a graduate of Columbia and they met in New York City, not in Indonesia. Their first child, Kieran, was born on January 22, 2004.

Christopher, Jim and Nora's youngest son, spent four years in the Air Force, then returned to Paul Smith College. He married Heather Burnak, who he met while studying for his degree in hotel management, in a lovely wedding on our farm. Their three children are Joey Burnak, her son by a prior marriage, born in 1989, Brooke Anne, born in April 2001, and Garrett Edward, October 2002.

Tammy, the beautiful oldest daughter of Ted and Dawn, married Steve Noxon. They have two darling children: Alexandria, born July 8, 1994, and Jonathan, born June 13, 1997. They are now living in Connecticut.

I feel particularly close to her sister Elizabeth, who spent several summers with me when she was a teenager. She learned to care for horses and became a fine horse woman, competing in the National Pony Club Rally in Lexington, Kentucky. She went on to become Captain of the Equestrian team at Alfred University and a licensed farrier. (For those who don't know the term, she shoes horses.) In 1996, Elizabeth married Robert Carroll. Their three sons are William Robert, born January 31, 1999, Thomas Edward, born August 28, 2001, and Filip Leeming Carroll, born in February 2003.

I'm surrounded by great-grandchildren—Jonathon and Alexandria Noxon and Allison Tuttle—at the christening of their first cousin, William Carroll, in 1999.

Jefferson, Ted and Dawn's youngest, received degrees in both Electrical Engineering and Computer Engineering from Purdue University. A year later he married Jennifer Foust, a beautiful young lady he met at Purdue. Their darling daughter Allison was born on Dec. 13, 1997 and their son Benjamin on October 26, 2000. He is the first of the great-grandchildren to be named after my husband. Jeff and Jenny now live in Rochester, New York, where Jeff has just received his master's degree in computer engineering and works for Xerox.

Gerhard, the oldest child of Norwig and Missy, is the only one of that family to get married so far. He now lives in New Jersey with his beautiful wife Amy Stohner, who grew up in Cherry Hill, a suburb of Philadelphia.

Gerhard's sister Honor is still single at age 26. She received her master's degree in education and is now teaching math in a private school in Virginia. (In an interesting coincidence, Honor's stepmother, Michele, also received her master's degree in education in the summer of 2002 and is now teaching in Chatham, New York.)

The three youngest members of the Debye-Saxinger family—Peter, Maria, and Tristan—are still living with their parents on the family farm in Kinderhook.

In 1993, I began a tradition of taking the entire family on a Christmas trip. The first year we visited a ski resort at Klosters, Switzerland, so we left young Maria and Tristan at home. Eighteen of us stayed in a beautiful inn near the ski lifts. The expert skiers in the family went up the mountain, while others skied on cross country trails, hiked, shopped or swam in the hotel's heated pool. The food was delicious, so we all enjoyed gathering in the dining room to relax over a good dinner and talk about the day's adventures.

One evening, I described my experience in the hotel's hot tub, which I'd shared with two young English girls. I had no idea who the girls were until their mother came to pick them up. I recognized her instantly: Sarah Ferguson, the Duchess of York and wife of England's Prince Andrew. "While you were skiing," I told my family that night, "I was soaking in the hot tub with British royalty."

In 1994, we spent Christmas week sailing around the Caribbean on *The Star Clipper*, a four-masted schooner. We boarded at Antigua and sailed to various islands in the Windward chain at night, anchoring during the day at resorts where everyone had fun swimming, snorkeling, scuba diving or shopping.

Another year we went to a Club Med on the island of St. Lucia. That was fun because the resort provided a variety of sports, games and other activities for all ages. In addition to swimming in pools and the sea, some of us played golf or rode horses on the beach.

One Christmas our destination was the Wickenberg Dude Ranch near Phoenix, Arizona. Almost everyone—including me—went horseback riding every day. The kids loved participating in the roundup and various rodeo games. The young ones usually swam in the pool after their trail rides with resident cowboys. In the evenings, we often sat around a crackling fire where the entertainment included Native Americans performing traditional dances.

I don't usually ride a Western saddle, but this picture was taken during a family visit to a dude ranch in 1998.

We start planning our Christmas trips in May so we'll be able to get reservations at a special place. The only locale we've visited more than once is the Caribbean coast of Mexico. In 2001, we rented a group of four *casas* (or villas) at Playa del Carmen, a beach resort south of Cancun that's close to several Mayan ruins. It offered superb swimming, snorkeling and scuba diving, as well as interesting sightseeing for our growing group of thirty-five people. (We liked it so much that we are planning to return in December 2003.)

In 1999, we decided to gather at the family farm because both Jim and Ted had just retired to the area. The older generation stayed in their own homes, while younger ones bunked with parents or grandparents. Mother Nature provided a lot of snow that winter so our farm looked like a Currier & Ives print. The little children were able to sled down the hill in front of my house or ice skate on the pond. An older group of grandchildren, spearheaded by Tom and Tristan, cleared the snow off the ice and put up a hockey net on the pond in front of my house. Others explored woodland trails on cross country skis or skied downhill at one of the nearby resorts.

I had a delightful time making cookies and hot chocolate in my kitchen, while watching all the fun and games out the window. When the children grew cold playing in the snow, they'd come into my kitchen to warm up and chat happily. Most nights, I took everyone out to dinner so no one had to be bothered with doing much cooking.

On the night of December 31, we had a delicious dinner at Norwig and Michele's, then sat on bales of hay around an enormous campfire beside frozen Merwin Lake. We celebrated the occasion with prayers, songs, champagne and glorious fireworks. It was a joyous welcome to the new millennium, and I felt very privileged to be part of it.

Our Christmas reunions have become such a treasured tradition for my children, grandchildren and great grandchildren that we plan to continue them as long as possible. It seems to me that these happy gatherings strengthen family connections in ways that benefit us all.

Over the years I've spent a great deal of time and effort developing and maintaining ties with members of my extended family—including aunts, uncles, cousins, nieces and nephews. I began seeking out older cousins many years ago in hopes of finding a connection with the parents I lost so early. Later on, I continued reaching out to relatives of all ages because I enjoyed their company. I now realize, however, that it has been a terrific investment. The love and support I've received in return has enriched my life in many ways. If the experts are right about the effect of social support systems on health and longevity, family ties have helped to prolong my life as well.

16

Living Longer—and Better, Too

"How do you manage to be so active at your age?" is a question I hear, in one form or another, regularly. Many people seem surprised to meet a woman in her 90s who still enjoys a full life. I guess I've always believed, as some sage once put it, that "It's much better to wear out than to rust out."

I'm also asked, *"What's your secret?"* I didn't think I had a secret until my grandson, Tommy, suggested writing a how-to-book. According to him, "Many women act as if their lives are over when they reach 60 or 65." That comment made me realize that I probably have learned a few things that others don't seem to know.

As I look back on more than 90 busy years, my life seems like a colorful pageant of loving, learning, losing—and experiencing great joy. I'm not an expert on longevity, but I do believe that certain qualities are important if you want to have a long life—and enjoy it, too. Here's my list:

Good health. I'm fortunate to have a strong, healthy body, but I don't take it for granted. My parents taught us to take care of our bodies without dwelling on minor illnesses, so I've tried to do that. I must confess, though, that I haven't always been as careful of my health as I am now. In my youth, I smoked cigarettes, drank too much and overate, too. I learned from painful experience, however, that the fun of the moment wasn't worth all the discomfort I suffered later. I gave up smoking and started practicing moderation in eating and drinking. I found that I enjoy life much more when I'm feeling fit.

I do have one healthy habit that I've managed to stick with, though. Exercise has been an essential part of my daily routine since my school days. It's so crucial to my sense of well-being, in fact, that I was delighted to read, in the book *Successful Aging* (by John W. Rowe, MD, and Robert L. Kahn, Ph.D.) that "Physical activity is at the crux of successful aging, regardless of other factors." I'm also pleased to see reports of all the new studies confirming the important role that exercise plays in preventing heart disease, cancer and a host of other life-threatening illnesses.

My husband also believed in exercise, which made it easier for me to keep it up. When we were first married, the doctor Ben was seeing for his allergies (Blake Donaldson, MD) told him it was important to be out of bed for at least an hour before eating or drinking anything but water. He prescribed a brisk 30-minute walk every morning, so Ben and I usually walked together before breakfast. Then, on Blake's advice, Ben ate half a grapefruit and half a pound of chopped meat, accompanied by one cup of black coffee. His lunch and dinner also included half a pound of meat, plus vegetables and fruit.

Dr. Donaldson's regime worked so well for Ben that I started eating a similar diet. Blake guided our health for thirty years, until he died in 1973. I'm convinced that our longevity is largely due to him. According to his book, *Strong Medicine* (published back in 1960), fat meat contains all ten of the essential amino acids which the body needs to repair damaged cells. (It is interesting to note that Dr. Robert Atkins, who became famous for advocating a low-carbohydrate diet, studied with Blake Donaldson and shared many of the same ideas.)

I no longer eat a lot of meat because my oncologist insists that my breast cancer was "induced by hormones." I've never taken any hormones, so I decided the culprit must be the hormones that cattle producers feed their animals. I still follow Blake's advice in other areas, though. I try to get eight hours sleep every night and I usually do a series of stretching exercises prior to taking a 40-minute walk before breakfast every morning.

I'm also a firm believer in annual physicals. Most of my checkups just give me an excuse to brag about my good health, but the occasional exceptions are what matter. I might have shared the fate of my grandmother Howard (who died from breast cancer) if I hadn't had regular mammograms that led to the early detection and cure of my own disease. When a routine blood test revealed a thyroid deficiency, I began taking a daily thyroid pill. On my doctor's advice, I also take a baby aspirin every day, but that's all the medication I use.

A positive attitude. My parents told us, "Never feel sorry for yourself," but I didn't always appreciate the wisdom of that—especially when I received constant rejections from theatrical agents and producers. I remember struggling onto a crowded subway after a long, tiring day at Macy's. When I got home to the Jelliffes' house, I complained to Belinda and Uncle Ely. "I've had an exhausting day," I began. "And it was so irritating to face all those people on the subway pushing and shoving and getting in my way." To my surprise, I received no sympathy.

"Just think of all the energy those pushing, shoving people are giving off," Uncle Ely said. "It's yours to use if you just gather it all in." Dr. Jelliffe was a very wise psychiatrist and his words hit home. He made me realize that even if I couldn't alter the circumstances of my life, I could change the way I reacted. I began developing a totally different attitude after that.

Mental exercise. Ben's mother, who stayed physically and mentally active until she died suddenly at 92, taught me the value of mental stimulation. She kept her mind sharp by doing numerous crossword puzzles and playing a competitive game of bridge. When she thought her memory was slipping, she fought that decline by memorizing dozens of pages of Sir Walter Scott's long narrative poem, "The Lady of the Lake," when she was nearly 90.

Her success inspired me to learn parts in plays—such as those written by William Shakespeare—that I knew I'd never be able to perform. I've also exercised my brain by studying foreign languages. When we were planning a trip to Rio de Janeiro, for example, I took lessons in Portuguese. For years I tried to read one book in French for every six books I read in English. I continued taking advanced classes in conversational French because I didn't want to lose my ability to read and speak that beautiful language. I now believe that my effort to stay fluent in French has had other benefits as well.

Living with an intellectual husband for 47 years probably influenced me, too. Ben and I never watched much television; we preferred to play bridge, read books and do research on the foreign countries we wanted to visit—all of which are mentally stimulating. I've always loved to read, too, so I joined a book club. That introduces me to new books and provides the added pleasure of discussing those I've read with other members.

About ten years ago, I appeared in a skit with my childhood friend, Ethel Barrymore Colt. Although her part was much longer than mine, she learned her lines faster than I did. When I asked how she did it, she said: "My dear, the brain is a muscle. I decided long ago that I'm not going to let that muscle atrophy from lack of use."

Everything I've read about aging suggests that Ethel was right, so I've become even more determined to exercise my brain. When I'm asked to do a play reading with an open script, I try to memorize my part. I also memorize the various talks I give to garden clubs and other groups. Projects like writing these memoirs undoubtedly help, too. Now that this is finished, I'll seek other ways to stay mentally active.

Friends. My sister, Lee, was my best friend during my childhood and early years in New York City. We remained close all her life, but she died more than 40 years ago. Fortunately, I've always had other friends whose companionship I cherish. I enjoy people and tend to seek them out. One of the easiest ways to make lasting friends, I've learned, is to get involved with others on a play, a committee or a major project. My volunteer work has enabled me to make friends of all ages. In fact, some of my favorite companions are 10, 20, even 40 years younger than I am—which is very fortunate now that so many of my contemporaries are gone.

Like anything worthwhile, friendship requires time and effort. When I meet an appealing person who shares my interests, I follow up with an invitation to lunch, a play or another activity. If a good friend moves away or becomes ill or disabled, I continue to call, send postcards and visit regularly. I still have a good time with four women I've been close to for more than 50 years, even though they're mostly housebound now. Old friends with whom I've shared joys and sorrows for decades are truly special, but new friends are fun, too, so I continue to seek them wherever I go.

Laughter. In his book, *Anatomy of an Illness,* Norman Cousins claims to have cured a debilitating illness by laughing at comedy shows and funny books. I'd hate to rely on that when I'm sick, but I know laughter lifts our spirits. I love to laugh—and to make others laugh, too. I have a gift for mimicry, so I try to use the appropriate accent—Irish, French, Southern, Yiddish—when I'm telling a story. That seems to amuse people, and their pleasure makes me feel good, too.

There's usually a funny side to every situation, no matter how serious it seems at the time, so that's the side I seek out. Instead of dwelling on any pain or sorrow I may experience, I try to focus on the humorous aspects of life. Being gored by a pet pig wasn't much fun when it happened, but I tried to ignore the pain by focusing on how ridiculous it was to have such an injury in my 80s. I also had great fun telling the story—and laughing about it—afterwards.

Another experience that still makes me laugh was both terrifying and embarrassing at the time. About 20 years ago, I was hitching my horse, Tansy, to a cart in preparation for a formal carriage show I was scheduled to drive in. As a friend held the rope attached to the bridle, Tansy suddenly startled and broke free. The harness that I'd been putting on her flapped as she ran, which frightened the poor horse even more.

My niece, Holly, and I must have looked ridiculous as we chased Tansy down the main street of Kinderhook. I was chagrined that I'd let my horse get away—and fearful that she'd get hurt or cause a serious accident. A policeman finally helped us catch her after hearing a screech of brakes. "I was waiting for the crash of broken glass and metal that usually follows that sound," he said, "but all I heard was the clop clop clop of horse's hooves." Luckily, no one got hurt, so we were all laughing by the time we caught Tansy in a cornfield about a mile away.

Focus on the future. I've tried to spend my life looking forward, anticipating the pleasures of the next adventure instead of dwelling on the past. I like to keep a full calendar so I always have something to look forward to—whether it's an opera, a special party or my next trip. I don't wait for invitations, either. I'll gladly organize my own entertainment, if necessary.

According to reports I've read, studies show that elderly people—even those suffering from a terminal illness—often manage to stay alive long enough to participate in special occasions, such as a milestone birthday or the marriage of a loved one. I hope that works for everyone, because my wonderful grandchildren provide many opportunities for me to anticipate and share the joy of graduations, weddings and births. I'd hate to miss any of these events.

An adventurous spirit. I've always enjoyed new experiences, and age hasn't changed that. I refuse to waste my energy worrying about possible disasters. "Aren't you frightened?" friends asked when Nora and I booked a flight to Egypt in January 1993, just a few weeks after terrorists fired on a group of tourists. "You could get killed!" they said.

"Maybe," I replied. "But I could get killed crossing the street in Manhattan, too, and I'm not going to stop crossing streets." Life doesn't come with a money-back guarantee. I've lived a long time, but I'd hate to die without seeing King Tut's tomb. That trip turned out to be a grand—and perfectly safe—adventure that was enhanced by the scarcity of other tourists. I'm so glad that I didn't let a few terrorists keep me away.

Like most individuals, I don't consider my everyday life to be very remarkable, but my family tells me otherwise. "Just riding the New York subway is an adventure at your age," one granddaughter told me. My grandson Gerhard responded to that by describing his favorite image of me: "You were driving our ancient tractor," he said, "pulling a full load of hay behind you. Perched on top of the hay was a bunch of giggling grandchildren. You were at least 89 at the time—and I'll never forget that joyful look on your face."

I was pleased to learn that Gerhard likes to picture me doing something unconventional that others consider "too risky for an old lady." At my age, almost everything is risky, but I just accept that. I did have a serious accident at 91, but I wasn't driving a tractor, riding my horse, or doing anything dangerous at the time. I simply fell and broke my ankle while climbing into my own bed. I ended up spending six weeks in a wheel chair, but it didn't slow me down for long. Within five months, I had resumed all my usual activities, including dancing at parties.

Being useful. As the youngest child in my family, I was so eager to please that I was always running errands for anyone who needed help. That habit led Aunt Mamie to call me "Willing Little Legs." Later on, Ben dubbed me "Willing Little Wheels" because I was constantly driving my children and their friends all over the place. I actually enjoyed all that running around, though, because it made me feel useful and needed.

As my children grew up and needed less from me, I began putting more effort into volunteer work. My early successes gave me enough confidence to take chances with new situations and to attempt (not always successfully) jobs that others feared. I've never been afraid to make a commitment—or a mistake. I still receive great satisfaction from acting, modeling and volunteering because I feel that I'm making a contribution.

Recently, a friend told me that her elderly mother "wants to die because, she says, 'I'm no use to anyone any more.'" I understand how that mother feels, but I think we can always find ways to be useful. I plan to keep trying anyway.

Dealing with loss. I think faith in God is very important for peace of mind—especially during difficult times. It undoubtedly helped me cope with the series of losses that began with my father's death when I was eight. I was even more devastated, of course, when my mother died three years later. Looking back, I believe those experiences helped me to cope with other tragedies later in life. I somehow developed an intuitive understanding that I could survive and be happy again after suffering great losses.

Although I've had more than my share of tragedies, I've never become bitter or blamed God for that. On the contrary, I just thank the Lord for all the blessings I have had—for the beauty of nature and all the good times and happy moments I continue to enjoy.

Family. The people whose lives I've had the pleasures of sharing have always been important to me. I was blessed with loving parents and siblings as well as a darling husband and daughter—all of whom are gone now. But I still have my wonderful sons and daughters-in-law—and my dear grandchildren. I feel privileged to be a part of their lives and to count them as friends.

Although my family insisted that I give up riding my horse a couple of years ago, I still drive my car and ride the subway all over New York City. At 92, I continue to enjoy swimming, hiking in the woods, working in my garden and taking care of the horses at the family farm. Attending the opera and theater, going on auditions and working as a granny model still give me great pleasure, too. I know I'm not going to live forever, but I remain optimistic and determined to enjoy every day I'm allowed to spend on this earth.

About the Authors

<u>Esther Leeming ("Faity") Tuttle</u> has had four distinct careers. In the 1930s she was a professional actress who appeared on Broadway with Humphrey Bogart and in summer stock with Henry Fonda, among others. Her second career—as a devoted wife and mother—began when she married in 1940 and gave birth to three children in less than four years.

Eager to help her country during World War II, Faity started volunteer work—and has never stopped. Chairman of the Board of Trustees of the Brooklyn Botanic Garden for seven years, she received that organization's prestigious Forsythia Award for "outstanding service to organizations throughout the New York area" in 1988.

In 1990, she launched her fourth career as a "granny model." At the age of 92, she continues to appear in commercials, in bit parts on television shows (such as *Law and Order* and David Letterman) and in movies (including Julia Roberts latest, *Mona Lisa Smile.*) A life-long New Yorker, Faity splits her time between New York City and a farm upstate in Kinderhook.

Rebecca E. Greer left her position as senior articles editor of *Woman's Day* Magazine to pursue a freelance writing career. She is the author of four hardcover books reprinted in paperback. Two of those books—*Why Isn't a Nice Girl Like You Married?* (published by Macmillan) and *How to Live Rich When You're Not* (published by Grosset and Dunlap) were translated into German. She has also written more than 85 articles published in major consumer magazines.

0-595-30454-0